# Dyno Testing and Tuning

Harold Bettes AND Bill Hancock

*CarTech®*

Copyright © 2008 by Harold Bettes and Bill Hancock

All rights reserved. All text and photographs in this publication are the property of the authors, unless otherwise noted or credited. It is unlawful to reproduce – or copy in any way – resell, or redistribute this information without the express written permission of the publisher.

All text, photographs, drawings, and other artwork (hereafter referred to as information) contained in this publication is sold without any warranty as to its usability or performance. In all cases, original manufacturer's recommendations, procedures, and instructions supersede and take precedence over descriptions herein. Specific component design and mechanical procedures – and the qualifications of individual readers – are beyond the control of the publisher, therefore the publisher disclaims all liability, either expressed or implied, for use of the information in this publication. All risk for its use is entirely assumed by the purchaser/user. In no event will CarTech®, Inc., or the authors, be liable for any indirect, special, or consequential damages, including but not limited to personal injury or any other damages, arising out of the use or misuse of any information in this publication.

This book is an independent publication, and the author(s) and/or publisher thereof are not in any way associated with, and are not authorized to act on behalf of, any of the manufacturers included in this book. All registered trademarks are the property of their owners. The publisher reserves the right to revise this publication or change its content from time to time without obligation to notify any persons of such revisions or changes.

**CarTech®**

39966 Grand Avenue
North Branch, MN 55056
Telephone (651) 277-1200 • (800) 551-4754
Fax: (651) 277-1203
www.cartechbooks.com

OVERSEAS DISTRIBUTION BY:

Brooklands Books Ltd.
P.O. Box 146, Cobham, Surrey, KT11 1LG, England
Telephone 01932 865051 • Fax 01932 868803
www.brooklands-books.com

Brooklands Books Aus.
3/37-39 Green Street, Banksmeadow, NSW 2019, Australia
Telephone 2 9695 7055 • Fax 2 9695 7355

*Cover:*
*Photo courtesy Brian Reese*

*Title page:*
*Here is a glimpse of the engine dyno room at experienced engine builder and tuner Kenny Duttweiler's shop.*

*Disclaimer:*
*This book is for reference purposes only. It is up to each individual who participates in the process of dynamometer testing to ensure his or her own safety by following equipment manufacturers' instructions, common sense, and the directions, cautions, and rules of the dynamometer facility. Engines are inherently dangerous, producing lethal forces and gases, and making use of flammable fuels.*

*The authors accept no liability or responsibility for either poor or non-extant information from manufacturers, operators of facilities, or your safety. The ultimate responsibility for your safety rests with you, the reader. If you want to test on an engine dyno or a chassis dyno, it is necessary that you discuss the pertinent issues of safety and responsibilities, including liability, with the owner/operator of the test facility or the manufacturer of the test equipment. Everything from learning how to use fire extinguishers, using carbon monoxide (CO) sensors, and keeping your fingers out of whirling things, is also the responsibility of the facility where testing is done or the manufacturers of the individual equipment.*

*Most dynamometer facility operators will have you sign a release of liability to cover them in the event that your engine expires or your vehicle fails on the chassis dyno.*

*Racing engines and performance vehicles are dangerous, and racing on the street is illegal. No information in this book, individually or collectively, is intended to encourage violation of traffic laws and the authors expressly condemn such behavior. If you want to go fast, do it under proper, legal conditions at a racetrack.*

# CONTENTS

The Authors' First Experiences with Dynamometers ................................ 4
Foreword by Jim McFarland ................................................................ 4
Dedications and Acknowledgments ...................................................... 5
Chapter 1: Introduction to Dynamometers ............................................ 6
Chapter 2: Types of Power Absorbers .................................................. 16
Chapter 3: Numbers and Formulas ...................................................... 25
Chapter 4: Goals and Objectives .......................................................... 34
Chapter 5: Let's Test ............................................................................ 52
Chapter 6: Tuning ................................................................................ 65
Chapter 7: Testing Tips on How to Use a Dyno .................................... 78
Chapter 8: Accuracy and Repeatability ................................................ 85
Chapter 9: Correction Factors: Problems and Procedures .................. 102
Chapter 10: Troubleshooting .............................................................. 110
Chapter 11: What to Look For in a Dyno Facility ................................ 117
Chapter 12: How to Read a Dyno Sheet .............................................. 127
Chapter 13: Tuning with Dynamometer Data ...................................... 135
Appendix A .......................................................................................... 139
Appendix B .......................................................................................... 140
Glossary of Dynamometer Testing Terms ............................................ 141
Reading List and Resources ................................................................ 143
Resources ............................................................................................ 144

# THE AUTHORS' FIRST EXPERIENCES WITH DYNAMOMETERS

*"When you can measure what you are speaking about and express it in numbers, you know something about it."*

–Lord Kelvin, 1883 lecture

**Harold Bettes** had his first dynamometer experience in West Texas at the age of about 15. Harold's dad was an oil-field equipment engineer and designer, and they were testing a very big diesel engine connected to a huge water pump. The test was moving water from a large tank back to the same reservoir. By measuring the gallons per minute of fluid moved and measuring the pressure in the line, they gathered enough data to calculate the horsepower of the engine doing the work. As he recalls, the engine produced about 300 horsepower. They used slide rules because battery-powered calculators were not yet available. A few years later, Harold got to observe a high-performance dynamometer test of a small block Chevy at Jim Hall's and Hap Sharp's Chaparral Race Cars, also in West Texas. Ever since then, Harold has been hooked on testing and applying horsepower. Those experiences were primarily the ones that encouraged him to go to college and on to engineering schools, where his dyno experiences expanded. It has been a great time to be a gearhead.

**Bill Hancock** first encountered a dynamometer as an engineering student at Vanderbilt University in 1967, when he worked on a fuel injection project for a thesis. After enduring the frustrations and labors of manual data gathering, he could really appreciate automated data acquisition when it came along. Today, Bill marvels at the speed and accuracy of modern data gathering, though dyno testing's underlying fundamentals and principles have not changed. In 1967, simply correcting a run often took an inordinate amount of time, especially when time was in short supply. Today, all of the correction factors appear instantaneously, yet he insists on believing only barometric pressure values calibrated by using the mercury column barometer mounted in the dyno cell area. Bill always takes a hands-on approach based on common sense. He still views a dynamometer as one of the most valuable but least understood tools available to the racer.

## FOREWORD

Both Harold Bettes and Bill Hancock are mavericks. They have spent long, productive, and comparable careers characterized by independent thinking and experience that are now translated into the informative and helpful contents of this book. The material is long overdue. Their combined knowledge will enhance your dynamometer experience, whether as a casual observer, participant, or conversationalist. It's all here.

As a graduate mechanical engineer from Texas, Harold has spent his entire professional career as, according to him, "an inquisitive gearhead." For more than 45 years, he has immersed himself in virtually every aspect of dynamometer testing, from the grassroots racer level to the most sophisticated powerplants in motorsports. His inquisitive perspectives have even left their marks upon the Society of Automotive Engineers and within the OEM community.

Among his many accomplishments and recognitions, his leadership in founding and building the renowned Advanced Engineering Technology Conference (AETC) has helped perpetuate his desire to "give back" to the industry in which he built a career. In fact, in 2005 he received the Lifetime Achievement Award from the AETC for his dedication to the high-performance industry.

Further proof that he is not an armchair engineer, Harold has been the "go-to" person for countless manufacturers of high-performance and racing engine components, particularly at times when engine testing and data analysis issues were complex and required easy-to-understand explanations. You will find that same approach woven into the fabric of this book.

Bill Hancock is also a mechanical engineer who brings a strong background in racing onto these pages. As a native Virginian, Bill's motorsports experience grew from a start in drag racing before he joined the Chrysler Corporation as engineering liaison to selected NASCAR teams. In this capacity, he provided technical consultation and technical direction in a hands-on fashion typical of engineers who know their craft.

Following his career at Chrysler, Bill founded Arrow Racing Engines in 1979. Based on a business model of engine testing and development, more than 200 separate, private-label engine parts and packages have evolved, obviously accomplished with ongoing testing and data evaluation techniques that are shared on the ensuing pages.

Like Harold, Bill continues to compile technical papers and make presentations to audiences that range from motorsports enthusiasts to students within the academic community.

It is important to understand that engine testing and data analysis are closely linked topics. To approach the evaluation of either without the other reduces the probable success of virtually any test program. In fact, it has been said that engine testing programs are only as good as the ability to understand and use the results, not only at a project's conclusion but while on that path. You are holding information that will greatly enhance your chances of participating in successful engine testing and data evaluation. It culminates decades of hard-earned experience that Harold and Bill have elected to share. Contemplating and absorbing their collective knowledge will provide a clearer understanding of what can be an otherwise complex experience, and you will become better informed for the effort. In the end, you'll discover this book is an extremely valuable tool.

*Jim McFarland*

*High-performance writer, expert and consultant to Hot Rod, Car Craft, SEMA and four decades of racing enthusiasts.*

---

## DEDICATIONS AND ACKNOWLEDGMENTS

I dedicate this work to my wife, Paula. Thanks also to her for dealing with many issues while I was doing my part to bring this book to fruition.

Mere words cannot express the importance that I place on the friendship and tireless efforts of co-author, Bill Hancock. He is special and I am blessed to call him my friend. Thanks to Pam and Billy for sharing so much.

A special thanks to Jim McFarland and his friendship over many decades.

Thanks to Rick and Steve at Westech Performance Group. Thanks to Dan of Dynamic Test Systems. At the risk of forgetting to mention someone in a very long and distinguished list of folks that should be thanked, we offer our blanket thanks and appreciation.

Our combined acknowledgement is offered to the thousands of dedicated gearheads and engineers that work hard at doing things right even when others say it can't be. You are really what this is all about and this book is for you. Share your passion and knowledge with others and the return is ten fold.
*Harold Bettes*

It has been a privilege to work with and learn from the following engine experts with whom I have been associated over the past 45 years. Most notably, Dr. Tom Asmus, Keith Black, Paul Brothers, Todd Claucherty, Bruce Dennert, Dema Elgin, Ted Flack, Kevin Hoag, Tom Hoover, Alan Lockheed, Dale Matthews, Albert Nichols, Devin Pearce, Sven Pruett, Maurice Petty, Larry Shepard, Ted Spehar, Bill Weertman, and John Wehrly.

I would especially like to recognize my co-author Harold Bettes and thank him for his help and advice for the past 25 years.

I dedicate this work to, and thank, my wife Pam and son Bill for their enduring support over the years.
*Bill Hancock*

# CHAPTER 1

# INTRODUCTION TO DYNAMOMETERS

A dynamometer is a tool—a complex and useful tool. Like any other, it can help performance enthusiasts get more out of their vehicles, but only when they understand its capabilities and limitations, and how to use it properly. That is the adventure on which we will embark here.

The magazines and websites of the world are filled with performance parts and claims, modest to sweeping, as to their potential. What a different crankshaft, camshaft, set of valvesprings, intake manifold, new heads, different timing, different fuel map, etc., can do for you on the track is the subject of much speculation. Published parts tests are good, but your own dynamometer tests are a whole lot better.

The dynamometer is a force measurement tool. Set it up and use it properly and it will tell you exactly what those parts you're contemplating can and cannot do. Reading someone else's test results won't prove how your engine will perform. Renting a racetrack for a day and running laps with every combination is fine if you have unlimited cash to turn a racetrack into your testing lab. A dyno, properly used, is the best alternative and the one that race teams and serious performance buffs have relied on for as long as anyone can remember.

To run a dyno, you need to understand some basic math—the forces to be measured, calculated or estimated. Don't be put off by the math. We'll cover that in very simple language. Everyone who runs dynos knows and uses it, and they aren't all Albert Einstein's descendents. You can do it. This book will show you how.

### A Short History of Dynamometers

The dynamometer, which has hit the big time as an essential racer's tuning tool, has been in use for hundreds

*This 16-year-old is having a chance to start on his dream. He works hard at a dyno shop (after school), loves to learn, and is quickly becoming a gearhead. He has the fire in the belly called "passion."*

*These items should be constant companions if you are going to do anything around dynamometers or testing engines or vehicles. "Figures don't lie, but liars figure" is a given. As you learn where the numbers come from, you will be comfortable with how the numbers came to be and how to interpret them as well.*

DYNO TESTING AND TUNING

## INTRODUCTION TO DYNAMOMETERS

*Wherever people with an interest in vehicles gather, the talk eventually turns to horsepower. "How many horses does she make?" is a common point of discussion. Photos by Rob Kelly and Kathleen Henry*

of years for measuring force or mechanical power. The word comes from the Greek *dunamis* (force) plus *metron* (measurement) and may seem abstract until you learn a little something about them.

The first order of business is to refer to them properly. A dynamometer is not a dyno-meter. The latter is an entirely different type of force measurement equipment. "Dyno" is a convenient nickname, and there are others. Sometimes the "water brake," or "water brake absorber," types are called "pumps," while chassis dynos are sometimes called "rollers" or "rolling road." You may also hear people in the dyno world calling them "lie detectors" and "heartbreakers." Sometimes the electric dynos are referred to as "inductors," coming from the reference to inductive motors. So you can understand the meaning if you see a dyno room labeled "polygraph room."

Regardless of name, the dynamometer is a very useful and dependable tool and virtually essential in the development of a racing engine. It is also increasingly becoming a tool for any driver or car builder who wants to hit the racetrack. The testing part is not magic, and anyone can learn it.

Learning the language of dynamometer testing and racing-engine tuning at the same time can be a bit confusing, but it can be beneficial in the long run. Some of these terms may initially seem strange or complex. Hang in there. Once you know how to use them, they'll become as familiar as the more basic tools in your tool chest. Some of the language is technical and some is plain old slang, yet it is the language of the testing community. Testing proves more than guessing does, so learn the process that leads to the winner's circle.

You're learning a technology that goes back hundreds of years, and if they could use it back then, you can learn it in the 21st century. Here are some milestones in dyno development to put this important tool in perspective.

*1758:* John Smeaton (1724–1792), who was first to refer to himself as a civil engineer (British), used a rope-type dynamometer on windmills. When the ropes got hot, he cooled them with water (England).

*1780:* Scottish engineer James Watt (1736–1819), using the same rope-type dynamometer as Smeaton, made the first reference to "horsepower." His word would become a measuring stick to engineers, gearheads, and racers the world around. It just took some time (Scotland).

*1821:* Gaspard de Prony (1755–1839) invented the prony brake, which was a braking device around a shaft using blocks of wood for friction surfaces rubbing against the metal shaft or rotating hub (France).

*1822:* Plobert and Faraday made the first reference to brake horsepower when using a prony brake. As the rubbing material got hot, they poured water on it (England).

*1838:* The first instrumented dyno involved pulling a rail car on railroad tracks. The car weighed more than 54,000 pounds and had recording instruments and automatic graphing (on a rolled paper recorder) for locomotives. This was a forerunner of today's towing dynamometers. The idea is the same, but the instrumentation has improved (England and USA).

*1858:* William Thomson Lord Kelvin (1824–1907) used a prony brake dynamometer during his studies on heat energy (Scotland and England).

*1877:* William Froude (1810–1879) referenced the first use of a hydraulic dynamometer. This sluice gate dyno (Froude's design) was working at 1,997 brake horsepower and 90 rpm. That was a brake torque of 116,536

DYNO TESTING AND TUNING    7

# CHAPTER 1

*This old scale used to be the way that torque was measured on dynos a long time ago. Note the "honest weight" comment. This was installed on one of the most famous dynamometers on the west coast in the 1960s. Working on the beam balance principle, the scale had to have a steady needle before the operator took a reading of all the panel instruments.*

*This old Heenan-Froude dynamometer power absorber is a water brake type that helped to birth the engine legends from TRACO Engineering in the late 1950s and into the early 1970s. If this old soldier could talk he would whisper of the magic that was made under the gray paint in the days of Can Am racing and more.*

*Measuring and solidifying performance tweaks on the dynamometer provides more confidence for what will happen on the racetrack. Many details can be worked out on the dynamometer in order to make the efforts put in at the racetrack more effective.*

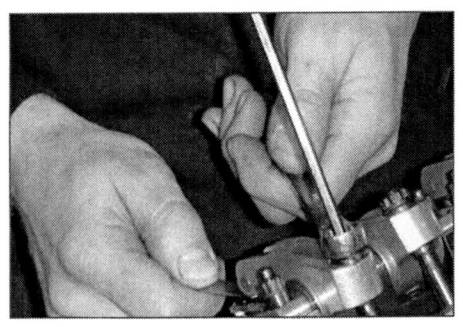

*Adjusting valves is such a common experience that you wouldn't think of it affecting performance until you measure the results on the dyno. All kinds of effort is put into making parts right and bringing everything within tolerance, yet we still set the valve lash with a feeler gage. In a fun test one time involving many name engine builders using a test rig, it was found that for a target clearance of .020", the actual clearances varied from .015" to .024."*

pounds-feet! It was big and was used with steamships (England).

*1906:* General Electric is credited with the first electric dynamometer. GE also marketed water brakes, but it was best known for its electric dynamometers (USA).

*1910:* Osborne Reynolds (1842–1912) did the first evaluation of the toroidal flow of water inside a water brake absorber dynamometer. (England)

*1911:* First Indianapolis 500 Mile Race winner. Dynamometers were part of the scene for Indy 500 racers and later became part of the winning teams' strategy and preparations (USA).

*1916:* The Society of Automotive Engineers (SAE) changed its name from the original Society of *Automobile* Engineers, which was originally founded in 1905. The first vice president was Henry Ford. Early on, the SAE began to concentrate on establishing standards, and one of them was for dynamometer testing. The SAE became the engineering society for all the mobility industries (USA).

*1928:* Carl Schenck was the first to use an automotive chassis dynamometer with brake testing (Germany).

*1930s:* Stationary chassis dynamometer introduced, using Froude water brake absorbers for testing steam locomotives. It was a very large unit (England and France).

*1931:* Martin and Anthony Winther invented the eddy current absorber dynamometer (USA).

*1938:* Clayton Industries provided an easy-to-use automotive chassis dynamometer to test complete automotive vehicles (USA).

*1940s: Hot Rod* Magazine and other pioneering automotive magazines published articles on and made references to dynamometer testing and auto racing. It has never been the same since; gearheads could then

## INTRODUCTION TO DYNAMOMETERS

*The U.S. was changed forever by the events of WWII, and afterwards the high speed of the dry lakes provided challenges for interested gearheads in a thriving economy. Hot Rod magazine was one of the first to publish results of these lakes meets and the aftermarket started trying to keep up with the interest in going fast.*

*The in-depth technical articles in Hot Rod magazine and others helped many to understand how things worked. Many of the readers had not had the opportunity to go to college because they were involved in helping win the worldwide struggle that was World War II. These technical articles also helped many decide to go to college or to trade schools in order to learn more.*

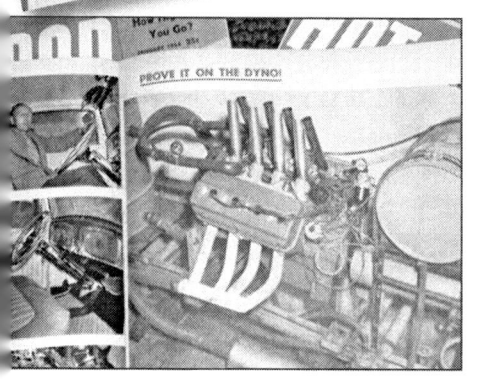

*Regular magazine articles about dyno testing began to appear and dynamometers were commonplace all over the country. Horsepower became a common language with a growing gearhead community. Even the OEM saw the importance of relating to the marketplace with power numbers.*

compare or attempt to compare numbers and try to equate them to performance. As WWII started, hundreds of dynamometer facilities were cranked up across the country and provided important assistance in engine development for military applications, which greatly improved engine programs. Also introduced in the pages of the above publications was the "Great White Dyno" at Bonneville, Utah. World land speed record attempts are still run there today. The first legal dragstrips launched the performance industry. NASCAR was started in about 1949 and grew rapidly in the post-WWII boom. Dynos were part of the scene then and continue to be an important facet today (USA).

*1950s:* All types of dynamometers became popular. The OEM car companies very rapidly became involved in NASCAR and drag racing to get their share of the "what wins on Sunday sells on Monday" market. Most of the more competitive teams sought dynamometer development time. In motorsports activities, the water brake types manufactured by Heenan-Froude or Clayton Industries were the common units (USA).

*1960s:* Stuska Dynamometers (Harvey Stuska) and Go-Power (Neal Williams) introduced inexpensive water brake engine dynamometers. The first dynamometer used for go-karts engines (USA).

*1968:* N.N. Rao wrote an SAE paper (680178 – "The Basic Theory of Hydraulic Dynamometers") on water brake absorbers that has become the standard of a short list for required reading about design and evaluations of water brake power absorbers (India).

*1969:* Go-Power Systems produced an engine dynamometer absorber that bolted right on the engine bellhousing, just like a transmission. The operator was "danger close," but it sped up engine development. Competitive NASCAR engines made about 450 horsepower at that time (USA).

*1980s:* Neal Williams introduced the first completely packaged, computerized engine dynamometer for racers, which provided data as good as or better than what was available from the automotive "Big 3" manufacturers at the time and provided automatic acceleration testing. Several enterprising companies applied computer data acquisition systems to older dynamometers. More development, outside the OEMs, was done as testing capability grew in the aftermarket (USA).

*Present day:* Every performance enthusiast on the Internet is talking

# CHAPTER 1

*These devices are called rotors and are an important part in water brake power absorbers. They have both been modified from the original forms. The water inside the absorber follows a torroidal pathway as the power is absorbed and passes through the unit. The size of the rotor and stator establishes the capability of the absorber.*

*What you see here are all tools. In order to use the tools more effectively, you must learn how. In racing or tuning or any endeavor, the faster you learn, the better. Luck has very little to do with anything. Learning quickly will give you an advantage over other competitors. Sort of sounds like the same things that your parents tried to tell you.*

about dynamometers and what the numbers mean.

With ample help from dynamometer testing, today's NASCAR cup engines are making dyno numbers right at 800 hp at 9000+ rpm from 16-valve pushrod V8s at 358 cubic inches! Competitive F1 engines regularly produce about 750 hp from DOHC 32-valve V-8s of about 146 cubic inches at 19,000 rpm! Both engine types are naturally aspirated. (USA and International)

## Dynamometer Principles

A sound understanding of how a dynamometer (engine or chassis) works is very valuable to the student, an operator, or someone who wants to have testing done. Understanding how the equipment functions, or should function, is important in order to make sure that the data gathered is worthwhile. Without an understanding of where the numbers come from, you just might as well write your very own fantasy dyno sheet on a paper napkin and pretend that it is true.

Engine or chassis dynamometers rotate when driven by either the vehicle tire or drive axle (chassis dynamometers) or directly by the engine crankshaft (engine dynamometer). In either chassis or engine dynamometer designs, eddy current absorbers, water brake absorbers, or other power absorbers allow precise measurement of the output power (Horsepower, or HP). Because the absorption of power is generally by a brake (absorber) of some type, the absorbed power is often referred to as Brake Horsepower (BHP).

One important principle in dyno operation is that when power is absorbed, it turns to heat. Heat energy is also power. So, the absorbed power (heat) must be dissipated to air, water, or some other liquid.

We will take an in-depth look at only two major types of power absorbers in this book: the water brake absorber is very common on engine dynamometers and on some chassis dynamometers; and, eddy current absorbers are used in both engine and chassis dynamometers, but are generally the most common in chassis dynamometers that can provide a load.

We will also briefly examine the inertia-only types for some clarification and general information. There are thousands of inertia-only chassis dynos around the country. Learning where the numbers come from and what they mean will expand your understanding.

*Eddy current* power absorbers are typically built with a ferrous (cast iron, cast steel, or cast nodular iron) rotor or rotors that rotate through a magnetic field, and electro-magnets that resist the rotation of the rotor(s). As the electrical current is increased to the multiple electro-magnets, the magnetic field gets stronger and provides more resistance to the turning rotors. Typically, the absorber is mounted on bearings on the main shaft so that the housing can be equipped with a strain gauge that provides a torque signal. Eddy current absorbers are manufactured in many different sizes and the larger they get, the slower the speed. Most eddy current absorbers used in chassis dynamometers rotate at speeds between 2000 and 5000 rpm. The torque capacity of the eddy current absorber is dependent upon its size and the capacity of its electro-magnets. Although the rotating element should not physically contact the electro-magnets (the nominal spacing is from .030 inch to .080 inch),

# INTRODUCTION TO DYNAMOMETERS

*The availability of comparatively inexpensive water brake dynamometers for first the go-kart market and then the automotive market caused engine development to grow exponentially. The small unit that you see here is a Go-Power DY-7 and is still in service today. It was built in the mid 1960s.*

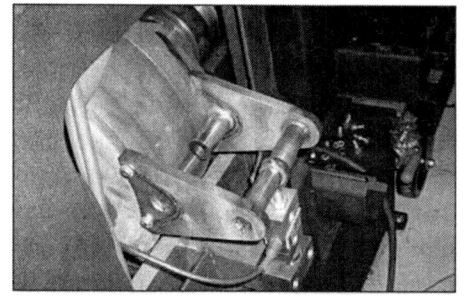

*This torque arm has been modified to provide more horsepower capability. The device directly below the torque arm is a strain gauge that sends an electrical signal to the data acquisition system when the load "stretches" the strain gauge. Photo courtesy of Dynamic Test Systems.*

the resistance of the magnets can be so severe that bending of the rotor(s) can occur and the pieces become damaged from contact. The resistance of the magnetic field can be so great that the rotors turn blue, indicating a temperature of at least 570 degrees F to 600 degrees F. The eddy current absorbers transfer their heat to air or liquid, depending on design.

*Water brake* power absorbers are made with a rotating element called the rotor (some use multiple rotors) attached to the mainshaft. The stationary element is called a stator. Both rotor and stator are equipped with cups or vanes, and the only coupling between the rotor and the stator is the water flowing through the absorber. Oddly enough, the "hydro-kinetic thermal exchange" occurs as a toroidal (donut-shaped) path where water transfers energy from the rotor to the stator in a constant exchange. Inside the water brake absorber are areas that actually don't see much water and are air vents to the ambient atmosphere. Without the air vent in operation, the transient response of the absorber is "sluggish" or "lazy" and placement of vents and water inlets is as much art as science.

Mathematically, the torque capacity of a hydraulic (water brake) absorber is a function of the fifth power of the rotor diameter. The power capacity of the water brake absorber is a function of the third power of the rotor diameter. The shape of the cups or vanes and the angles that are employed are quite often the result of empirical testing inputs into the final design. Some of the same techniques used to study water brake absorbers are used in the design of automatic transmission torque converters.

The early control systems on water brake absorbers were difficult to use with precision. Modern-day electronics and good integration of electromechanical control valves have greatly improved control. It is not uncommon to have control as tight as +/- (plus or minus) 5 rpm in a careful steady-state test.

The major problem with water brake dynamometers is their poten-

*These two rotors are modified to provide improvements in dynamometer operation. The holes drilled in the rotor on the left help to relieve pressure in the pockets on its reverse side, decreasing cavitations. The rotor on the right has been reduced in diameter, which reduces the torque capacity of the absorber. So that some people don't become alarmed, neither unit was in warranty and both were modified to solve particular problems experienced by operators in the field.*

tial for cavitation damage, which can cause surface pitting and erosion. The design and the materials selected by the manufacturer are critical in reducing the potential damage from corrosion and cavitation. The temperature of the water is also a crucial item to control within the suggested limits and ranges.

## Chassis Dynamometers

An "as-installed" engine power evaluation can be made by testing racecars or street-performance vehicles, including motorcycles, on a chassis dynamometer. In order to get meaningful results, good testing procedures must be followed. It is also necessary for the test equipment to be very accurate. Atmospheric correction methods must follow established (or well-defined) guidelines so that known standards can be used for data comparison.

# CHAPTER 1

*How Chassis Dynamometers Function*

The drive wheels are positioned in contact with a roll (roller) so that the power that is transferred through the tire contact patch can be measured. The roll resists the force exerted by the drive wheels either with a power absorber (eddy current, water brake, or friction brake) or solely through its own inertia. Chassis dynamometers with power absorption brakes are typically instrumented to measure torque *and* roll speed. Inertia-only dynamometers must be instrumented for roll speed, and do not measure torque, but the torque can be calculated from the known relationship of power, speed, and torque. In order to have good accuracy and make comparisons to other dynamometers, the exact inertia of the roll and drive system must be known.

Chassis dynamometers come in a variety of designs and are commonly either two-wheel drive (2WD) or all-wheel drive (AWD). In the case of motorcycles, there is typically only one roll for the drive wheel.

*Power-absorption chassis dynamometers* have some type of power absorber (water brake, electrical brake, or friction brake) attached to or driven by the roll(s) that are in contact with the tested vehicle's drive wheels. The load on the absorber can be varied by the control system in order to absorb power at steady speed or under acceleration. The load the absorber places on the system can be controlled in order to keep the acceleration at a constant rate. Power-absorbing chassis dynamometers can be programmed to allow simulation of many racetracks for either endurance or driveline and cooling evaluations. Some units can even be programmed to allow for the changing load on a test vehicle from the aerodynamic and driveline losses vs. vehicle speed.

Similar to chassis dynamometers are the brake testing types used in many countries and states as part of their ongoing vehicle safety inspections programs.

*Inertia-only chassis dynamometers* by design cannot measure power at a steady speed or simulate racetrack load conditions. The roll and drive system in contact with the drive wheel(s) of the vehicle must have a known inertia value for accurate test results. Because the roll system inertia is fixed, if the time is accurately measured during acceleration of the mass, then power can be calculated. Power is calculated on inertia-only chassis dynamometers by measuring the time it takes to accelerate the roll(s) driven by the wheels. Typical designs calculate the torque at each data point and assume a loss in the drive train to calculate engine power and torque. Higher power accelerates the roll in less time than lower power can. An exact measurement of inertia, time, and roll speed is very critical in order to have an accurate assessment of power. Inertia-only chassis dynamometers cannot be readily calibrated in the field, and accuracy depends on a *known* inertia (particularly when comparing data with other test sites and dynamometers).

## Horsepower: The Real Basis for a Power Struggle

*What is horsepower and where did it come from?*

James Watt, an entrepreneur and engineer in Scotland, first used the term horsepower (HP) in 1780. He had modified the steam engine so that it was substantially more efficient and therefore put out more power than other engines at the time, yet he was having a difficult time marketing his improved power source. He sought a simple way to express power so people could understand his machine's superiority.

Horses were a universal power source of the day, so Watt chose them to represent this concept (he used draft horses, which are larger and more powerful than the average horse). By watching horses work in the coal mines, Watt determined that they could move 22,000 pounds one foot in one minute on a sustained basis. Because the horses were not being worked to exhaustion, he added 50 percent to this observed figure, defining one horsepower as the power required to move 33,000 pounds one foot in one minute. One horsepower equals 550 ft-lbs/sec.

*This 1955 HRM article detailed building a dynamometer for anyone who was interested. This article and many like it spurred the interest of many youngsters and encouraged some to attend engineering school. The basic principles of the way that absorbers work have changed little since Froude's work in 1877.*

# INTRODUCTION TO DYNAMOMETERS

In engineering terms, a force times a distance is the definition of "work." Work is expressed in foot-pounds (ft-lbs). Work divided by time yields power. (Torque is also important in the performance arena. We discuss that in the following section.)

Because Watt needed to relate the horsepower of steam engines to their ability to move objects by dragging or lifting (doing work in some amount of time), it was necessary to convert rotation of the crankshaft to the distance moved. One full revolution (360 degrees) of the crankshaft is equal to 2π. Dividing the 33,000 by 2π (roughly 3.14163, times 2) yields 5252.113, and rounding that off becomes 5252, which is a constant that will be used later. This one tiny tidbit of information can gain you a lot of advancement on the dyno game board.

### What is torque, and how does that figure into the horsepower issue?

Torque is a twisting force expressed in pounds-feet (lbs-ft), or in Newton-meters (Nm) for metric measurements. The conversion values between the two systems are as follows: 1 lb-ft = 1.35582 Nm and 1 Newton-meter is equal to .737561 lb-ft.

Note that torque wrenches are quite often incorrectly marked as measuring foot-pounds when in fact they are showing *pounds-feet*, but now that you know the correct expression, you can know what you are talking about and can assist others in their own search for the truth. It is perhaps a minor point, but it becomes a major point if one is interested in the details, and it is the attention to the details that makes the difference in the long run.

Rocket engines, pistols, rifles, and artillery cannons are typically rated in foot-pounds of energy, or the amount of work that they can perform. As an example, an old Army Colt .45 pistol is typically rated at having 380 ft-lbs of muzzle energy. That is not torque! If you move 50 pounds 100 feet, you have done 50 x 100 = 5000 ft-lbs of work. That is a reference to work, not torque!

Now, if you moved 50 pounds 100 feet in 60 seconds, then the work divided by time is power. In this example, 83.33 ft-lbs/sec is the power produced. How much horsepower did it take to do that? 83.33ft-lbs/sec divided by 550 ft-lbs/sec equals only .152 hp! In fact, the daily average power that a human can produce is about .134 hp. So, continuing to carry 50 lbs for 100 feet in 60 seconds, all day long, would be a real problem!

### How is horsepower calculated?

Horsepower is equal to the product of torque multiplied by RPM, then divided by the constant from above, 5252. Stated mathematically:

$$HP = (T \times RPM) / 5252$$

Where HP = Horsepower,
T = Torque,
RPM = Revolution per Minute,
5252 = the constant that we proved existed in the earlier explanation.

If you apply a little algebraic manipulation to the basic equation for horsepower, you can quickly establish an equation for torque or RPM.

$$HP = (T \times RPM) / 5252$$
$$T = (HP \times 5252) / RPM$$
$$RPM = (HP \times 5252) / T$$

At 5252 RPM, the values for torque and horsepower are equal. On a graph where torque and horsepower are using the same scale, the two curves should cross at exactly 5252 RPM or something is not being calculated correctly. If the data is presented in a columnar printout as on a dyno sheet, then, at 5252 the plots for RPM, horsepower, and torque should be the same.

### What is the difference between horsepower and torque?

Enthusiasts and racers throw around horsepower and torque figures

*This sturdy piece is the inside of a DTS power absorber. It uses a dual-sided rotor (has vanes on both sides) and is made of cavitation-resistant aluminum bronze alloy. The hefty main shaft runs through the center of the rotors and is driven by the engine. The diameter of the rotors and stators establishes the torque capacity of the absorber. Photo courtesy of Dynamic Test Systems.*

*This power absorber is made by Saenz Dynamometers, and the photo shows the magnetic pickup mount and gear for measuring the RPM of the shaft. These absorbers are made of ductile iron for strength and for cavitation resistance. They can be equipped with multiple rotors to increase power capacity and can be matched to a particular application.*

# CHAPTER 1

*Almost anything that can turn the rolls on a chassis dyno can be measured for power output and performance. This Model T Ford was built as an over-the-road racecar by Steve Coniff. These cars have to meet certain restrictive rules and will produce about 25 to 35 Hp and attain speeds of 60 to 70 MPH! Spooky.*

*The photo shows an all-wheel drive (AWD) chassis dyno and is capable of either inertia only or loaded tests. The two eddy currents are under the covers off to the right. The popularity of chassis dynamometers is growing because of easy testing with the complete vehicle.*

*Also very popular are the motorcycle dynamometers. The designs vary from inertia only to fully loaded functions. Mapping EFI units effectively requires loaded testing. Take a close look at the photo. There is more than wheel bling to see here. Note the tire patch location and the chain drive of the bike. All are important to have good, reliable, and repeatable testing.*

to demonstrate their cars' prowess. Which number is more important for performance? Let's look at each measurement.

The engine generates torque when the ignited air-fuel mix forces the piston down and twists the crankshaft—torque, remember, is a twisting action. Not all of the fuel's energy is transferred to the flywheel, however, because some is lost to friction as the pistons move. If you want to get technical to impress your friends, the force on the piston top is the Indicated Mean Effective Pressure, or IMEP. What is lost to friction among the pistons, cylinder wall, crankshaft, and connecting rods is called the Friction Mean Effective Pressure (FMEP). The difference is what we have to work with at the flywheel, the Brake Mean Effective Pressure (BMEP). Engine torque measured on a dynamometer can provide a number for BMEP by multiplying the measured torque by 150.8 and dividing that value by the engine displacement in cubic inches, which yields BMEP in pounds per square inch (psi) for 4-cycle engines. Horsepower is a calculated number with a lot of emotion and unrelated baggage tied to it. As mentioned before, engineer James Watt coined the term in 1780 to relate the capabilities of his improved steam engine to the most popular mode of power of that day, the draft horse. The first reference to brake horsepower appeared in 1821. As discussed, horsepower = (torque x RPM) / 5252. In the horsepower formula, the RPM is entered as a time function. Because torque and RPM have equal positions in the formula (each is a multiplier), it takes *both* of them to produce a real horsepower number.

Horsepower describes the effort that pushes, pulls, shoves, or drags our vehicles and even aircraft through this friction-filled world. If we want to go faster, it takes more horsepower. Here's a way to compare horsepower and torque: If you raced two Corvettes that produced equal torque, but one made more horsepower, they would take off together—the launch being a function of torque (the force twisting the crankshaft, driveshaft and ultimately the drive wheels)—but the one with more horsepower would pull away as the resistance from friction began to slow the acceleration of the car with fewer horses. The extra horsepower keeps the other car accelerating as it overcomes a higher level of frictional resistance. Do we want to say that torque is the important number for drag racing and horsepower is the key figure for road racing? Not necessarily, but you can understand the logic of such a statement.

Here's a better observation. Faster and quicker vehicles have more *average* horsepower. Peak horsepower and peak torque are not the best performance indicators. It is the package with the greatest *area* under the horsepower curve that has the advantage. If a racecar drops

14     DYNO TESTING AND TUNING

# INTRODUCTION TO DYNAMOMETERS

*This particular chassis dynamometer is an AWD by Dyno Dynamics and has an automatic wheelbase adjustment. The dynamometer uses the cradle roll configuration, which essentially nests the tires. The red car on the dyno made some good power, as it had two turbos on board. Photo by Rob Kelly.*

*Typical of chassis dyno testing preparation is for the dyno operator to clarify some details with the driver of the vehicle to be tested. Photo by Rob Kelly.*

*A Subaru wagon on the rolls. It is operated by the dyno technician and watched by the very interested bystanders who use the vehicle to go to and from the grocery store. These Subarus make some serious Hp and because they are AWD, really like to put it down to the rolls. This was during an open house at Revolutions Performance, and they dyno tested all kinds of vehicles all day long and fed people too.*

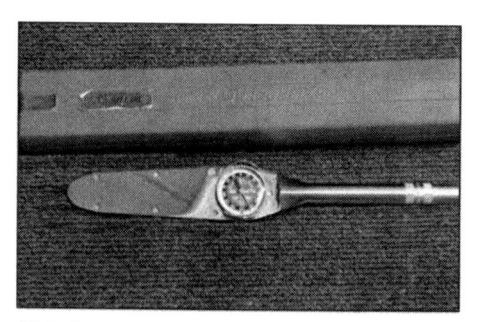

*This is a torque wrench. It is a precision tool that sees regular calibration (just like a dyno should) and when not in use is placed in the carrying case. The torque wrench is incorrectly marked in ft-lbs instead of lbs-ft. It is a common mistake because people do not generally (or specifically) know the difference in the terminology. In reality this tool is a friction wrench. If you tightened fasteners by using a stretch gauge you would know that.*

*This old Army Colt produces energy at the muzzle when it is fired. The energy is measured in foot pounds of energy (about 380 ft-lbs), and that is not torque! The energy is transferred to the slug from the burning powder in the fired shell, and the result is what is referred to as knock-down energy.*

below the effective power range on a gear change, it will lose speed and time. An engine with a broad power range is a real pleasure to race and tune because it is more forgiving in its shift points compared to a "peaky" or narrow-range engine combination.

Keep in mind that you can have torque without horsepower, but you cannot have horsepower without torque. Here's an example: A manual tells you to tighten lug nuts to 70 lbs-ft and tighten head bolts to 75–80 lbs-ft. The horsepower here is zero because you are not generating revolutions per minute with your wrench. Because HP = T x RPM/5252, we have a fraction with zero for a numerator, which equals zero.

Compare this example: Engine torque specs indicate 500 lbs-ft @ 4100 rpm (note it has an RPM reference). There is horsepower here: HP = (500 x 4100) / 5252 = 390.33 hp

There are all sorts of other references to horsepower and torque in engine terms. Terms such as FHP (friction horsepower), CBHP (corrected brake horsepower, OHP (observed horsepower), IHP (indicated horsepower), FT (friction torque), CBT (corrected brake torque), OT (observed torque), IT (indicated torque), and other such colorful terms are worthy of discussion and study. Before this book comes to a close, you will recognize and be able to talk about many of these numbers as you calculate and discuss the performance stats for your vehicle.

DYNO TESTING AND TUNING 15

# CHAPTER 2

# TYPES OF POWER ABSORBERS

Understanding the types of power absorbers and dynamometers and the differences between them will help you appreciate their capabilities and limitations. Some of these are more historical, while others are the very designs you will use to measure and develop your own engine's performance.

## Prony Brake Dynamometer

This is one of the very earliest (1820s) designs for putting a load on an engine or machine. The early designs used large wooden rubbing blocks around a rotating device such as a capstan pulley, a flywheel, or a sheave. Several versions of the Prony brake have been around since the mid to late 1800s and used in various applications. Rope dynamometers are included in this general category.

## Fan Dynamometer

This instrument is still in use in some specialty applications. In aviation, a "club prop" is a test load that is not adjustable (fixed pitch) and is used to break in newly rebuilt aircraft engines. However, this test does not produce a torque reading that would yield a calculation for horsepower. A true fan dynamometer would have a way to measure torque. Variable-pitch aircraft propellers have been used to vary the load on automotive

*This is the flight engineer's instrument panel on-board a Boeing B-29. This photo was taken before starting the four engines for a maintenance run-up cycle.*

*Also of the flight engineer's instrument panel, this photo was taken after the engines were started and running at 1,200 RPM. Notice that the photo is all blurred because everything shakes! There are 72 cylinders on this aircraft and huge props.*

## TYPES OF POWER ABSORBERS

*Starting the starboard inboard engine (#3) makes a sound that would thrill any gearhead. Smoke and noise and the occasional belching of fire signals that the dinosaur is awake once again. This aircraft is owned by the CAF in Texas.*

*These engines are all running clean, and all 72 cylinders are ready to answer the call for the wild blue yonder. After a run-in, the aircraft is either flown or sequentially shut down and returned to the hangar. Each R-3350 engine has 18 cylinders (2 rows of 9) that guzzle fuel and turn it into wonderful noise.*

engines with torque measured via an inline torque transducer or a strain-gauge-instrumented engine stand. Not a very popular solution, but some still exist.

### Eddy Current Dynamometer

The eddy current dynamometer has been around since its invention in the 1930s in the United States. Very precise load control and speed control (RPM) is possible. Manufacturers claim that RPM can be controlled to within +/- 1 to 2 RPM. In order to absorb a large amount of power, the eddy current has substantial inertia and, because of RPM limits, quite often requires being driven at less than engine crankshaft speed. This is not much of a problem when an eddy current absorber is used in a chassis dynamometer.

Sizes in field applications vary from tiny fractional horsepower electric motors to huge braking devices on drilling rigs and cranes. Eddy current power absorbers are also commonly used for additional braking assistance on large trucks, commercial buses, or school buses. Some very small eddy currents are supplied by Dyno-mite, allowing testing of

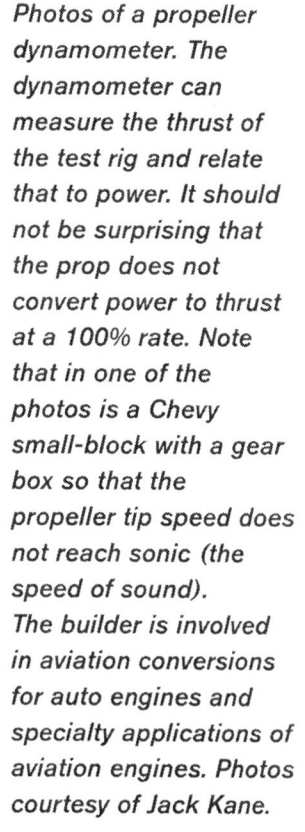

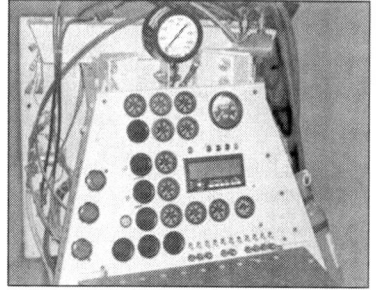

*Photos of a propeller dynamometer. The dynamometer can measure the thrust of the test rig and relate that to power. It should not be surprising that the prop does not convert power to thrust at a 100% rate. Note that in one of the photos is a Chevy small-block with a gear box so that the propeller tip speed does not reach sonic (the speed of sound). The builder is involved in aviation conversions for auto engines and specialty applications of aviation engines. Photos courtesy of Jack Kane.*

DYNO TESTING AND TUNING

# CHAPTER 2

*This photo shows a very small water brake absorber that is obviously connected to a Briggs and Stratton 5 hp engine. This engine produces about 7 Hp after dyno tuning and modifications. Small dynos similar to this one are used for modern-day UAVs (Unmanned Aerial Vehicles) with larger versions for larger engines. The principles remain the same.*

small radio-controlled racecars and aircraft engines.

One of the many advantages of the eddy current designs is that they can be supplied in both air-cooled and water-cooled configurations. The air-cooled units have the easiest application as they transfer the heat to ambient air and require no plumbing. That feature also makes them more affordable. Eddy current absorbers typically cost much more than their water brake counterparts.

## AC Dynamometer

The power absorber on this dynamometer is actually an AC (alternating current) motor. The advantage of this design is that the power absorbed can be dissipated into a local power grid, and some of the money spent in testing can be recouped by selling the absorbed power to the local power and utilities organizations. The type is more complex in actual operation and can also be used to power the non-firing engine in order to accomplish friction power studies. AC dynos are very popular, when many test cells are operated simultaneously for long hours, and it is sometimes more cost-effective to connect to the local power grid. Very rarely would this type be in use with most performance developers. It is very popular with the OEMs, however.

The AC dynamometers have fairly high rotational inertia values because the rotating element of the AC motor is very heavy and typically very large in diameter. This description holds for any AC dyno capable of absorbing any meaningful power.

As an example, the AC absorber to be used for 500 hp at 6000 RPM would probably weigh at least 2000 pounds, while a water brake absorber for the same job would likely weigh only about 150 to 200 pounds.

## DC Dynamometer

The DC (direct current) power absorber is just a large electric motor, but it has complex electrical control requirements. These dynos are essentially DC generators or motors, depending on how they are used. The rotational inertia values of the DC motors are typically equal to or higher than those for AC dynos. The overall absorbers are generally heavier than their AC counterparts as well as having a higher mechanical inertia when rated at the same torque, power, and RPM levels.

## AC/DC Dynamometer

No, it does not blare "Back in Black" when you use it. This specialty design uses the DC portion for motoring the engine or chassis dyno

*The highlighted areas in this photo are to point out a few things to consider when testing on a chassis dyno. The deflection on the tires is from the heavy load placed on the tie-downs. It is not a tire inflation issue although that is an item to keep track of. These turbocharged bikes need to be pulled down tightly or the tire slips on the rolls. A larger roll would be of some assistance, but these things can make in excess of 500 CWHp at the tire patch. Also note the color of the exhaust pipe vs some other photos.*

# TYPES OF POWER ABSORBERS

*This dynamometer tests some of the most powerful engines in all of performance. It is the setup that Kenny Duttweiler uses to develop lots of turbocharged engines that produce more than 3000 Hp! The unit is a Heenan-Froude absorber and has been specially modified to suit Kenny's requirements.*

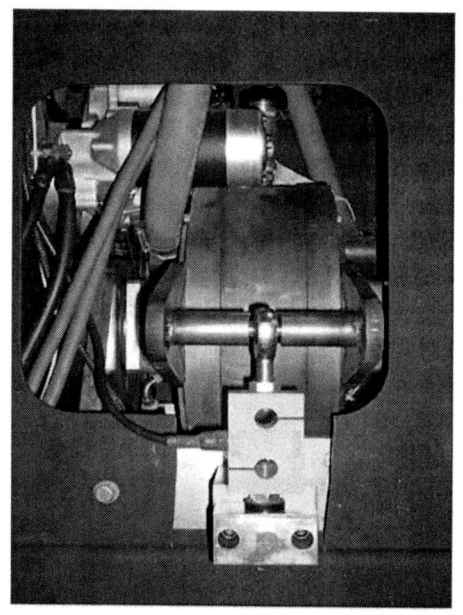

*This is one of the DTS PowerMark engine dynamometers for high Hp applications. It uses two control valves at the same time for rapid response to engine demands. The strain gauge is shown in this side view. This is one of the most popular dynamometers in performance applications today. Photo courtesy of Dynamic Test Systems.*

and the AC portion for absorbing power. They are very popular in OEM environments where test cells cost millions of dollars. The AC/DC dynamometers are very large and have high mechanical inertia. While in use as a dynamic or motoring package, they also provide excellent control of engine RPM or torque. These absorbers are typically only used in research and development because of their tremendous expense.

The AC/DC dynamometers can generally change from full motoring to full absorbing modes in fractions of a second. The units typically can operate clockwise or counterclockwise. The electric dyno absorbers can cost from 10 to 12 times the amount of an equally capable water brake.

## Water Brake Dynamometer

This type of power absorber is one of the least expensive to apply while maintaining good control characteristics. A very good water brake system can control engine speed to within +/- 5 RPM in steady-state testing. This absorber is the most popular in high-performance applications and is frequently used on engines with outputs between 3 and 3,000 hp (or more). Industrial-strength versions might handle in excess of 100,000 hp. The water brake dynamometers allow for easy testing if the control system functions properly. Controls may operate on the water inlet, on the water outlet, or in some cases both.

Water brake dynamometer absorbers with straight vanes are capable of both clockwise and counterclockwise rotations; angle vane absorbers can function in only one direction. Most domestic (USA) engines operate in a clockwise rotation as viewed from the front of the engine. Other countries' designs, as well as aircraft and marine engines, often turn counterclockwise.

## Chassis Dynamometer

A chassis dynamometer is one of the most popular methods to test the power a vehicle makes at the drive wheels—the actual, useable power available. This device takes up a lot of space, as it must accommodate the whole vehicle plus related safety features. Clayton Industries began developing the automotive chassis

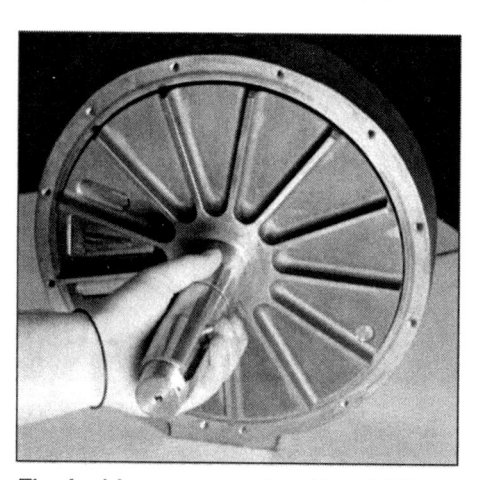

*The inside components of the DTS PowerMark are very beefy pieces. The large main shaft has proven to be nearly indestructible in field testing. These units serve many supercharged and turbocharged applications as well as large marine engine uses. Photo courtesy of Dynamic Test Systems.*

**DYNO TESTING AND TUNING**

## CHAPTER 2

dynamometer in the United States in 1938. The chassis dynamometer is currently very popular for motorcycle applications, and it was these inertia-only types that launched the Dyno-Jet Research company in 1972. DynoJet also introduced an automotive chassis dyno version in about 1992 or 1993. Today there are several domestic manufacturers to choose from as well as many international suppliers. The absorption method varies—some manufacturers use water brakes, others use eddy currents, while very few use an AC motor.

The types to consider are either single-roller, dual-roller (cradle rolls), or all-wheel-drive (AWD) versions that may be a combination of both types. The cradle-roll types distort the drive tires and make solid power numbers more difficult to maintain because the tires are also power absorbers.

*This engine and vehicle are just about to be tested on a chassis dynamometer at Revolutions Performance. The application is a small-block Ford in a Mustang for drag racing. As you can see, it is turbocharged and uses EFI. The intercooler is larger than the radiator, as is common with boosted packages like this one.*

### Towing Dynamometers

As the name suggests, this design is towed behind the vehicle tested. It is commonly used in tractor development and evaluation, and may also be used for tracked vehicles and railroad engines. The towing dynamometer measures power via a strain gauge, and the output data is normally called drawbar pull. This dynamometer provides the numbers for force, distance, and time so that drawbar power can be presented. They vary in size depending on vehicle types to be tested.

Towing dynamometers are typically used at road speeds between about 5 and 60 miles per hour (MPH). Some towing dynamometers are designed for off-road use only. Many of these have tracks instead of wheels so as to distribute the load in deformable soil over the area of the track.

### Inertia Dynamometer

This type uses a fixed mass as the load for the system. There is no control system and steady-state loaded tests cannot be done; only

*These shots are quite informative and show what can happen when lots of power is supplied to the tires. Many things in the drivetrain of a vehicle are power absorbers. This sequence of photos shows what happens as more and more power is applied to the tires on the Mustang. The test produced a maximum of 1,050 Hp at the tire patch! What that means is that on a larger-roll dynamometer it would have made larger numbers. The car went 8.56et at 160+ MPH at the drags a few days later. Rob Kelly photos.*

20     DYNO TESTING AND TUNING

## TYPES OF POWER ABSORBERS

*The most awesome of towing dynos is the "power sled" or the "dirt dyno" that is shown here. The truck was in a pulling competition and had been on a chassis dyno and the drag strip and produced almost 550 Hp at the drive wheels (rear). On the dirt all the wheels can be driven. As the vehicle moves forward, a huge weight is pulled forward and provides more weight to the pulling vehicle. Photo courtesy of Kathleen Henry.*

acceleration tests are possible on inertia dynos, and the rate of change always varies with the power. These are the simplest of all designs because they have few parts, no control system, and can be operated with little training. Inertia dynos cannot be calibrated or verified without extensive testing to determine the actual inertia value of the rotating mass. Inertia-only dynamometers were the basis of the DynoJet Research Inc. company, and its first products were for chassis testing motorcycles in the marketplace. The same basic concept also provided an opportunity for the company to grow into automotive chassis dyno applications.

### Other Dynamometers

There are more dyno designs out there. They include transmission dynos and drive axle dynos, camshaft break-in dynos and valvetrain dynos (a Spintron is an example), water-pump dynos, and dynos for testing electric motors. There are dynamometers for testing bicycles with riders, runners, and even swimmers. Some of these are in regular use at the United States Olympic Training Center in Colorado Springs, Colorado, and at other locations involved in training and testing athletes.

Inertia dynamometers can be connected to another absorber such as a water brake or eddy current in order to "trim" the inertia load. This additional absorber can add to the inertia load, but cannot decrease it. This type of dynamometer would be in the hybrid or specialty-applications category.

*This might be called a hybrid dynamometer. The unit uses a water brake and a massive inertia weight. This is the first dynamometer of this type to see application in the performance aftermarket. Typical variation (repeatability) in data is about .16% from run to run. The unit is making quite a statement with the folks who want to test the durability of components when it is programmed to duplicate race track loads in both acceleration and deceleration. Photo courtesy of Excellaration, LLC.*

*One of the Excellaration units during the fitment of a specialty starter and drive for sprint car engine applications. The sprint car type engines typically drive oil and fuel pumps from the rear of the engine and use no flywheel on the engine. Photo courtesy of Innovation Engineering.*

# CHAPTER 2

*Various chassis dynamometers allow either steady-state or acceleration-type testing. Some even use inertia only with mixed results. This vehicle has just set a standard of challenge for the other competitors in a diesel-only contest. These vehicles had to dyno test, drag race, pull a dirt sled, pull a loaded trailer on the drag strip, and go through a mileage test as well. Photo courtesy of Kathleen Henry.*

*The diesels can be seen from miles around when they drop the hammer on either the dyno or pulling or the racetrack. Fuel and more fuel makes the smoke. The guy in the cloud was trying to take a picture of the glowing turbos (this Cummins set up uses a tandem turbo package) just as the waste gates kicked open. What a snootful! Photo courtesy of Kathleen Henry.*

## Dynamometer Testing Descriptions

*Constant-Speed* or steady-state tests are taken at a fixed RPM rate. Constant-speed tests produce the best and most reliable data, though there are ways to gather data and get reliable results by other means.

### How is a constant-speed test used?

A constant-speed test is one of the most convenient ways to establish a performance map or establish the best mixture and spark requirements. Modern electronic fuel injection (EFI) systems need specific inputs at many data points in order to have data for the engine management system to work more effectively. In this test, the throttle increases or decreases torque while the dynamometer varies load to maintain constant RPM. Imagine going up and down a hill and having to supply more and then less throttle to maintain constant speed. At each of the various throttle positions, the parameters for engine control likewise vary.

*Constant load* reverses the emphasis. Rather than keep RPM fixed, increase the load, and increase throttle to keep pace, here the load is instead kept steady. This approach can be used with either engine or chassis dynamometers and is often called constant-torque testing.

As you can guess, the values that change under constant-load testing are throttle position and RPMs. Obviously the more powerful the engine, the more quickly it can raise RPMs under a given load.

### How is a constant-load test used and why?

Constant-load testing is common for diesel engines, but can be applied to spark-ignition engines too. In a constant-load test, the operator would select a load of a specific torque value, such as 350 lb-ft, and go through a series of tests that vary engine RPM. A manufacturer developing an engine for a particular job may want to run this test to determine how various engine setups handle a typical load encountered in the job in question.

*Acceleration testing* measures engine performance during a fixed rate of acceleration. The test produces a fixed and non-varying slope of either RPM vs. time, or speed vs. time. For accurate comparison across tests, the acceleration rate must be the same. This data is not very usefully compared against a steady-state test. Steady-state testing normally will produce higher brake horsepower (BHp) and acceleration testing will normally produce slightly lower BHp. Acceleration testing better duplicates the real world, where engines are seldom operated at steady RPM or load; they also allow an operator to get in more testing and data collecting per unit day.

### How is an acceleration test used and why?

Acceleration testing, sometimes called transient testing, has rapidly replaced steady-state testing as the preferred method.

An acceleration test is typically used to replicate the changes in RPM vs. load that an engine or vehicle sees in practical application. The rate

## TYPES OF POWER ABSORBERS

*The little street rod sedan is ready to be tied down before it is dyno tested. Regardless of the application, testing provides valuable data so that the package can be optimized. The tests on a load type dynamometer can produce configurations that supply a load that varies with speed or applies more load the faster the car goes (simulating the wind resistance of the vehicle). Photo courtesy of Westech Performance Group.*

*The testing that can be done on most modern-day engine dynos allows acceleration-type tests that get more testing done during the dyno day. Various rates of acceleration are used that normally settle on either about 300 RPM/sec to 600 RPM/sec for racing engines.*

selected will be one commonly faced by the engine in the vehicle; for example, 300 RPM per second acceleration from 3,000 to 7,500 RPM.

The major advantage of an acceleration test on an engine dyno is that you can run more tests and gather more data within a given timeframe compared to steady-state tests. Acceleration tests are much less abusive on the engine and components as well.

Most drag race engine builders will test their engines at 300 RPM/sec to 600 RPM/sec in order to duplicate what the vehicle might do in high gear. It is quite common for NASCAR engine builders to use rates of 600 RPM/sec for short track engines and 100 RPM/sec for the super speedway engine applications. There is no set rule or standard for the testing rate, but it should be done the same way and at the same rate if the data is for comparison purposes among engine components or engines. The faster an engine accelerates, the less power is available at the flywheel.

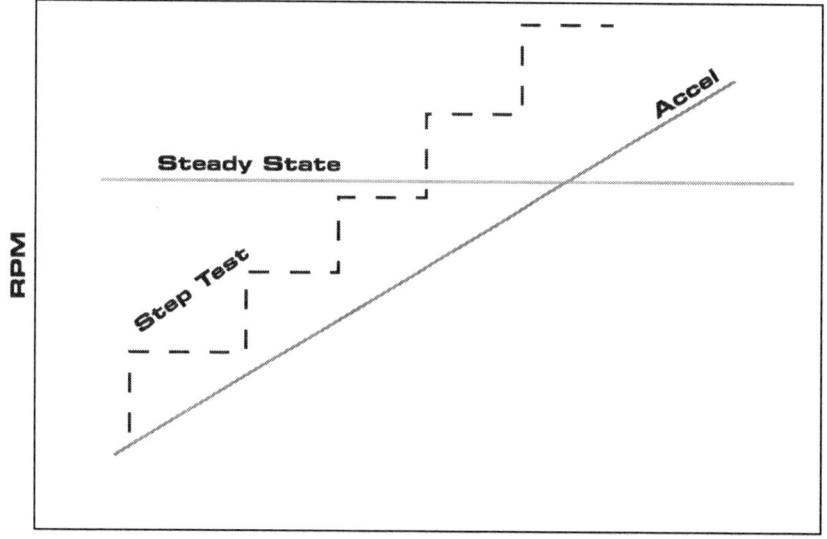

*Comparing RPM vs time shows that an acceleration test is at a uniform slope. Conversely step testing or simple steady state testing is also shown. There is not a simple way to compare the results of these tests unless the tests were the same type (such as accel or steady state) and only then when at the same conditions or rates of change. On chassis dynos, the comparison is typically done at speed vs time.*

*Inertia Testing* utilizes a fixed mass or inertia. Some chassis dynamometers do not have any way to apply a fixed load for steady-state tests or controlled rates of acceleration and rely on the mass of the rolls to provide a load for the vehicle power. Very few engine dynamometers are inertia-only designs, but some do exist.

**DYNO TESTING AND TUNING**   23

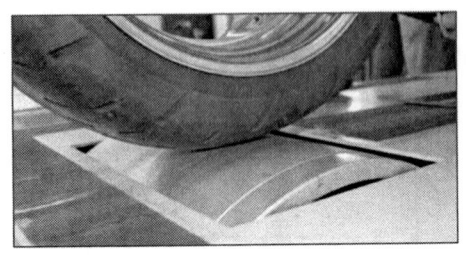

# CHAPTER 2

*Inertia-only testing can lead you astray if you are trying to find the best setting for both fuel mixture and spark advance. The inertia-only types accelerate faster when more power is applied, and that makes it difficult to compare all testing results on an even basis. The inertia of the system might or might not equal the inertia of the vehicle being tested. More variables to try to sort through ...*

*A well-informed dyno technician is a great help in sorting through any kind of tuning issue. Here a dyno test technician explains to a customer how the tuning has performed on his vehicle. Surprises are always good if they are on the higher-power side.*

One of the greatest caveats for inertia-only testing is that it encourages the tester to use more fuel and more spark advance than if the engine was tested at a slower and more controlled acceleration rate. One of the limitations in applying inertia-only test data to the real world is that it assumes a vehicle has fixed mass and inertia. In fact a vehicle on the road or track has variable inertia due to its aerodynamics and its rolling resistance and rotating parts, even though the overall vehicle weight remains the same. In practical terms, the power required to accelerate the vehicle and to attain various speeds is not linear. On deceleration, the same problem exists.

Some manufacturers list the inertia as some number of pounds, which is intended to relate to an equivalent vehicle weight (including driver). What this means is that if you are testing on a chassis dyno that is listed as 2500 pounds of inertia (incorrect units) and you are testing with a vehicle of some different weight, then the inertia load will not be the same.

You will probably get more reliable test results on an inertia-only dyno when the inertia of the system is *greater* than that of the vehicle you are testing.

If the mechanical inertia is *less than* that of the vehicle, the rate of acceleration is going to be faster, and that will perhaps not be in the best interest of the more discriminating tester who wants good data.

The ideal circumstance for the inertia-only dyno arises when the rate of acceleration on the dyno is very similar to the vehicle's acceleration rate on the racetrack.

"Resolution," or roll-sampling rate, is very important to precise data from inertia-only dynos. Some make only one or a few counts per revolution. If the roll counter is part of the calculation for power and the basis for timing the acceleration of the roll, then you see the problem that pops up here. With a roller, say, four feet in diameter sampled only twice per revolution, the error margin for a quarter-mile evaluation is wide. The very best resolution would be 6.28 feet per revolution. The circumference of the 4 ft diameter roll (C = π x D) = 12.5664 ft, divided by the two samples per revolution, would produce pretty poor data.

### How is an inertia test used and why?

The inertia-only test is one of the easiest to do because no control is involved. The fixed mass can be described as a flywheel, and if its mass is known, then the time is measured from one point to another and power can be calculated. The real problem with this test is that if the engine makes more power, then the fixed mass is accelerated faster. If the rate of acceleration is not at the same rate, there are many engine variables that have an effect on results. This type of test will not allow any accurate way to establish an engine map for spark and fuel if one is working with an electronically controlled engine. The critical details of electronic fuel injection (EFI) cannot be adjusted properly on an inertia-only dynamometer.

One way an inertia test might be more beneficial is for endurance testing of components so that the test is simply cycled over and over until a given amount of time is accumulated or something breaks; this will establish an endurance limit or a cycle limit for the vehicular system or an engine part. This type of testing is normally done to evaluate drivetrain components as well.

DYNO TESTING AND TUNING

# CHAPTER 3

# NUMBERS AND FORMULAS

A dynamometer is a tool, and most tools we use to fix and improve our vehicles do not require a theoretical background. We take it, we use it, we move on, and we are glad it was there in the toolbox.

Dynos perform important measurements, and to use them properly and understand the results they produce, you must know some foundational principles. They may look threatening to the non-mathematician, but there is no reason to fear. After all, the engineering that went into the rest of your car involved a lot of complex theory on aerodynamics, acoustics, ergonomics, and other specialties. You don't need to be an engineer to use something designed by one. You just need to learn enough to know what the tool does and how best to employ it.

Let's look at the basics that will help you get the most from your dyno time.

## General Formulas

Horsepower is an easy calculation, involving two variables and the constant 5252. Here's all you need to know:

$$Hp = (T \times RPM) / 5252$$

This relationship allows you to isolate each of the other values in the equation. Thus,

$$T = (Hp \times 5252) / RPM$$
and
$$RPM = (Hp \times 5252) / T$$

Where HP = horsepower, T = Torque (in lbs-ft), RPM = revolutions per minute

The calculation for Force is helpful in many situations:

$$F = ma$$

Where F = Force, m = mass, a = acceleration

This is the basic formula for all inertia-only dynamometers.

Here's how to calculate miles per hour:

$$MPH = (D_t \times RPM) / (336 \times G_r)$$

Where MPH = miles per hour, $D_t$ = diameter of drive tire in inches, RPM = engine revolutions per minute, $G_r$ = gear ratio

As always, we can rewrite this equation to isolate other values as follows:

$$D_t = (336 \times G_r \times MPH) / RPM$$
$$RPM = (336 \times G_r \times MPH) / D_t$$
$$G_r = (D_t \times RPM) / (336 \times MPH)$$

An engine's peak horsepower figure is useful to know and fun to throw around with friends and competitors, yet horsepower can be discussed in many contexts. Knowing the horsepower required to overcome various forces resisting acceleration will help you to understand and maximize your vehicle's performance capabilities.

Here is how you calculate the horsepower required to overcome aerodynamic resistance:

$$HP_a = (A \times C_d \times V^3) / 146600$$

Where $HP_a$ = Horsepower requirement aerodynamic,
A = frontal area of vehicle in square feet,
$C_d$ = coefficient of drag,
V = vehicle speed in miles per hour

The horses you'll need to conquer rolling resistance are determined like this:

DYNO TESTING AND TUNING

$$HPr_f = [(Rr_f \times V) / 375]$$

Where $HPr_f$ = Horsepower required to overcome rolling resistance, $Rr_f$ = rolling resistance force in lbs, V = vehicle velocity in MPH

If you need to calculate rolling resistance for the previous equation, do so as follows:

$$Rr_f = Cr_f \times W$$

Where $Rr_f$ = rolling resistance force in lbs, $Cr_f$ = coefficient of rolling friction (typical auto tires at normal inflation = .015), W = Vehicle weight in lbs

Hydraulic HP would be used for evaluating such things as water pumps, oil pumps, etc.

$$HHp = (GPM \times psi) / 1714$$

Hydraulic Horsepower
Where GPM = gallons per minute, psi = pounds per square inch

Acceleration Rate of the engine

$$RPM / time = accel\ rate$$

Where RPM = engine revolutions per minute, time = seconds

Acceleration Rate on chassis dynos may be determined by

$$Speed / time = accel\ rate$$

Where Speed = vehicle speed in miles per hour, time = seconds

To convert dyno figures to road stats, you need to equate the distance the wheels travel over the dyno roll to miles on a road:

$$Rev/mile\ (rolls) = 5280 / ((R_d \times 3.1416) / 12)$$

Where Rd = Roll Diameter in inches

BMEP is a way to effectively evaluate an engine's efficiency.

$$BMEP = 150.8 \times (T / D_e)$$

Where BMEP = Brake Mean Effective Pressure in pounds per square inch, T = Torque in lb-ft, De = Displacement of engine in cubic inches

The amount of fuel burned correlates directly to power produced and requires an amount of air suitable for efficient combustion.

$$A/F = Air / Fuel$$

Where Air = pounds of air per hour, Fuel = pounds of fuel per hour

The following four equations will help you calculate air density depending on what information you have available:

$$Air\ Density,\ \rho = 1.325\ (P_b \times T_{air})$$

Where air density, = weight of air in pounds per cubic foot, $P_b$ = Local barometric pressure, inches of mercury, "Hg, $T_{air}$ = °F + 460

$$Air\ Density\ \% = 100 \times (P_b - V_p / 29.92) \times (520 / T_{air})$$

Where $P_b$ = local barometric pressure, "Hg, $V_p$ = vapor pressure, "Hg, $T_{air}$ = °F + 460

$$Air\ Density = (P_b \times 1745) / T_{air}$$

Where $P_b$ = local barometric pressure, "Hg, Tair = °F + 460

$$RAD = ((P_b - V_p) / 29.92) \times (520 / T_{air})$$

Where RAD = Relative Air Density, $P_b$ = local barometric pressure, "Hg, $T_{air}$ = °F + 460, at 29.92"Hg, 60F, dry air, the RAD = 1.00

You ought to know this one too—we all talk about cubes; here's how to determine the number:

$$CID = B^2 \times .7854 \times S \times N_{cyl}$$

Where CID = cubic inches displacement, B = bore diameter, inches, S = stroke, inches, $N_{cyl}$ = number of cylinders

## Computer Simulations and Dyno Testing

There are many levels of computer simulation that are easily available and affordable in today's market. Unfortunately, the prices do not relate to how simple the program is to operate nor does it indicate levels of accuracy.

There are computer simulation programs that range from the simple to the exceptionally complex, and they vary in price. The OEMs use some very complex engine-simulation programs that cost hundreds of thousands of dollars, but the same OEMs also continue to use engine and chassis dynos in their overall planning and development routines.

Of the many engine simulations available for personal computers, there are a few that are very handy to use. Alan Lockheed's Engine Expert is easy to use, has been around a long time, and has proven to be reliable. Also handy is Kevin Gertgen's Performance Trends package called Engine Analyzer or Engine Analyzer Pro.

*Somewhere in all this stack of stuff there might be a trick answer to all the problems of the universe. However, one can get confused if all you look for is a few numbers in simulation programs. They all have their place and like most things all the inputs should be evaluated logically and completely before heading off in the dark without a flashlight.*

*This is what it is all about. All the planning and preparation and tuning might produce a very complementary package that is fun to drive and can even get good mileage too. Here the look on the dyno technician's face says thehard work has paid off—over 400 Hp at the tire patch. Photo by Rob Kelly.*

Another that is easy to use and has active graphics is Dynomation, sold by ProSim of Comp Cams. The Dynomation software has a great graphics display of intake and exhaust pressures as well as pressure in the cylinder and helps you to see and realize the importance of valve-event timing. Patrick Hale's Racing Systems Analysis software for engines is called EnginePro, and he has just finished a book that describes how he developed the software.

These programs are only as good as the data you feed into them. If you spoof the numbers or enter in wrong information, the reported figures may be impressive but they will not be valuable to you in improving your car's performance. Assuming you enter good numbers, most computer simulation programs can predict power accurate to within two to 10 percent.

Theoretical horsepower will probably only win virtual races, so at some point you will gravitate toward the real parts and pieces to build something to race. Do your homework and the results will be worthwhile. You may also enjoy comparing your "desktop dyno" data, or prefer to use "computer dyno" figures, to those you achieved from an actual run on an engine or chassis dyno. The software figures may be so far off that they're not much use; or you might discover your computer is so close to the real numbers, you may as well work there most of the time and part with real dyno money only when the best numbers are critical.

## Estimating Vehicle Performance Based on Dyno Testing

If you have some reliable engine dynamometer data, then you can estimate what the performance will be when the engine is installed in the racecar. However, it would also be necessary to estimate the losses that occur in the drivetrain before the power is delivered to the drive wheels. Some suppliers already do that with some easy-to-use software applications.

There are all sorts of computer simulations for vehicle performance if you have solid dyno numbers to input to the program. One of the best known is Patrick Hale's Quarter and Quarter Jr. Pat also has other programs for many other racing applications and a program for Bonneville racers as well. Performance Trends has several programs for racers and a drag race program that includes land speed applications for El Mirage and Bonneville, too. Another drag race performance prediction program is by Larry Meaux, from down in the bayous of Louisiana, and it is called MaxRace Software. Larry has many other programs targeted for the racer using both old- and new-style computers.

All of the programs will help you sort out gear ratios and converter choices. And all will break your heart if you use bogus or incorrect power

# CHAPTER 3

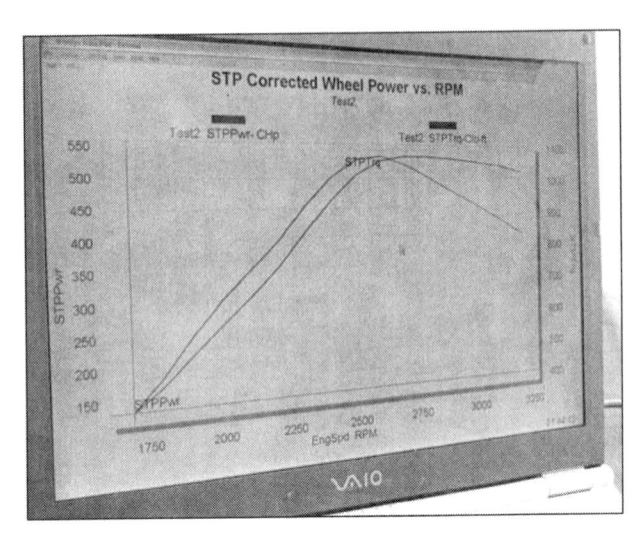

*Almost 550 Hp and over 1050 lbs-ft at the tire patch is one nasty over-the-road diesel pickup! And the thing got about 20+ miles per gallon at highway speeds. That is pretty good tuning in anybody's book. This is typical of information available from modern chassis dynos. Photo courtesy of Kathleen Henry.*

numbers or incorrect data about your vehicle. If you stay on the realistic side of things, the programs will get you very close to sorting the final details out at the track without taking a ridiculous amount of time.

There are even simple slide-rule calculators that can be used for some assistance. The Moroso Power-Speed Calculator has been around for ages. Iskenderian Cams has one that has been called a "dream wheel" since its introduction back in the early 1960s. Others probably exist as well and typically would follow the same process of number manipulation and relationships.

*This little pocket dyno book is long out of print but has many handy things inside its cover. It might be reprinted, and if it is it will become another speed secret that people keep in their toolbox.*

Another very handy reference for prediction of vehicle performance is the *Pocket Dyno*, originally published in 1975 by Dr. Dean Hill. Long out of print, it was based on an article in the *American Journal of Physics* by G.T. Fox, "On The Physics of Drag Racing," 1973. We are told that a revised *Pocket Dyno* book might be reprinted by AERA (Automotive Engine Rebuilders Association). Chrysler Corporation performance engineers used a very similar approach early on in their drag racing program. The simple equation stated that the horsepower produced at the track was a function of weight and the 1/4-mile speed. However, the equation equates to flywheel horsepower.

$$Hp = (.00426 \times MPH)^3 \times Weight$$
$$MPH = 235 \times \sqrt[3]{(Horsepower / Weight)}$$

In the 1960s, when Chrysler race engineers applied mostly the same techniques, they used a constant of a slightly different value (225), but the same arithmetic approach for calculation of estimated power. The horsepower numbers relate to flywheel-power numbers, however, not power at the tire contact patch. More will be presented on the two constants used at the end of this section on prediction of performance. It is important to note that when these empirical formulas were developed, top speed was measured over a 132-foot distance at the end of the dragstrip, beginning 66 feet before and finishing 66 feet after the quarter-mile mark. "Trap speed" refers to the speed "trapped" or measured over this segment.

Today's dragstrip top speed trap is somewhat different in that it covers only the last 66 feet of the quarter mile. What has changed is that in earlier times the trap speed was averaged to the end of the quarter mile and today its terminal speed is slightly less. When using the simple calculations, the indication is still more than adequate for prediction of estimated horsepower, but maybe not as accurate as in times past.

Although there are several computer simulation programs in use today that estimate the performance of vehicles in 1/4-mile acceleration contest format, simple calculations can be made with a handheld calculator.

Most of the popular computer simulations relate the power to engine flywheel horsepower numbers. However, if you are testing on a chassis dyno, then you can estimate vehicle performance with a few formulae.

### Estimated Tire Patch Horsepower Based on 1/4-Mile Trap Speed Applications of Chassis Dyno Data

The estimated horsepower at the tire patch that a vehicle has applied

DYNO TESTING AND TUNING

# NUMBERS AND FORMULAS

to produce any 1/4-mile trap speed can be calculated by using the following equation. This formula allows for some of the assumed losses in the chassis and for aerodynamic and driveline inertia.

$$Hp_{est} = (.0040 \times V_v)^3 \times W_v$$

Where $Hp_{est}$ = Estimated Horsepower (tire patch),
$V_v$ = 1/4 mile trap speed of vehicle in MPH, $W_v$ = Vehicle weight in pounds

For a chassis dynamometer only, because you are not pushing the complete vehicle through the wind and typically only half of the vehicle's wheels are rotating, the following formula can be used.

$$C_{dyn} Hp = (.0037 \times V_v)^3 \times W_v$$

$$MPH = 270 \times \sqrt[3]{(Hp / W_v)}$$

Where $C_{dyn}$ Hp = Chassis Dyno Horsepower at the tire patch,
$V_v$ = Velocity of the vehicle drive wheels, MPH, $W_v$ = Weight of the vehicle, pounds

The other issues of aerodynamic losses and traction limitations and the other detailed losses are not accounted for here. If you were using a dynamometer that has the capacity to apply additional load for an assumed aerodynamic load, this calculation would not be correct as written.

You can also use the horsepower numbers measured on a chassis dyno to predict top speed if the numbers were reliable to start with. Or, you can be creative and estimate the chassis losses by calculations based on comparison of the track and dyno numbers. It is a good way to appreciate that nothing is for free and the chassis has a loss associated with it.

Estimated Chassis Power Loss (track data)

$$C_{loss} = Hp - Hp_{est}$$

Where $C_{loss}$ = Chassis loss, Horsepower, Hp = (.00426 × Vv)3 × $W_v$, Horsepower, $Hp_{est} = (.0040 \times V_v)^3 \times W_v$, Horsepower

Or you can use chassis dyno data and track data

$$C_{L2} = Hp - C_{dyn}Hp$$

Where $C_{L2}$ = Chassis loss based on track and dyno tests, Horsepower, Hp = (.00426 × $V_v$)3 × $W_v$, Horsepower, $C_{dyn}$ Hp = (.0037 × $V_v$)3 × $W_v$, Horsepower

For the best answer, you can use engine dyno data (flywheel Hp) and subtract the chassis dyno data (tire patch Hp) to get a figure very close to the real loss for that particular vehicle. That can be done at various speeds, and you would have a representative curve that would be handy to use for other detailed applications. This is very valuable information for a specific vehicle and can be the basis for finding some free power by optimizing the chassis so that it consumes less power. All the horsepower numbers are to be the observed data and not corrected.

### Estimated Elapsed Time Based on 1/4-Mile Trap Speed

The estimated ET (elapsed time) that a vehicle might attain based on the 1/4-mile trap speed can be calculated by using the following formula. Notice that in the equation there is not a reference to horsepower, but to MPH ($V_v$), which is directly related to the horsepower produced to shove the vehicle to the end of the track.

$$ET_{est} = \overline{5.5 \times (235 / V_v) \times \sqrt[3]{[((V_v - 100 / 400)) + 1]}}$$

Where $ET_{est}$ = Estimated Elapsed Time in seconds,
$V_v$ = 1/4 mile trap speed of vehicle in MPH

Is there good reason to spend so much time and space on this performance estimation issue? Yes, there is. For example, if you have calculated

*This unassuming little red Rx-7 had two turbos and laid out some impressive numbers on the chassis dyno. It was fast and quiet, too. Dynos in the hands of effective tuners can produce some good results.*

that your car can go 145 mph in the quarter based on the data from a chassis dyno test or guesswork, then something is suspect if your car only produced 107 mph on its best run at the local dragstrip! Perhaps it is the dyno horsepower number that you used, or you need a much more accurate weight for the vehicle. Maybe it's something so simple as the throttle not opening all the way, or perhaps your crew did not check the distributor hold-down or something equally simple and basic. If everything else checked out, it is possible that you relied on some bogus dyno data. It happens all the time.

Using the simple equation listed previously, assume that your vehicle weighs 3237 pounds with you in it. Assume that you drove it down the local dragstrip at 108 mph and had an ET of 12.75 seconds. How much HP did that take to shove it that fast? The answer is, at least 261 horsepower at the tire patch. So if you test the car on a chassis dyno and the peak power number at 110 mph shows up to be 436 horsepower, then somebody probably has a very "happy" dyno. Or perhaps you were smoking the tires all the way down the racetrack?

Another scenario is that you test your vehicle on a chassis dyno and after tuning for an hour on the dyno, you end up with 225 horsepower at the drive wheels at a peak speed of about 104 mph. You might be disappointed because you thought for sure that your engine had more power than that rotating your tires. If your car weighs 3315 pounds with you in it, how fast do you expect to go at the local drag strip? Kicking the numbers through the calculation, it shows that you should expect a trap speed of about 102 mph.

This methodology is not perfect by a long shot, but it is just a simple way to relate performance to horsepower numbers and is a good way to keep a reality check on dyno numbers as well.

If the track performance of a racecar is not as fast as the dyno indicated from the horsepower numbers, then something is highly suspect. Conversely, if your track performance indicated that you should make more power at the drive wheels than the test systems showed, something might be suspect with the dyno numbers. It is all related, dudes and dudettes. Don't be for sticking pins in some voodoo car model or thinking about reinventing the wheel. Stick to the basics and think about the variables that have a very meaningful effect on performance.

If your computer simulation or calculation shows that you should be able to go 115 mph instead of the 100-mph performance that the vehicle ends up producing at the track, then check the logical things first. Is the throttle opening all the way? Don't laugh; that problem is more common than many would believe. The crankcase might even be overfilled with oil. It would not be the first time that enthusiastic crewmembers duplicated efforts at the cost of performance. This is one of many places where checklists work wonders in solving basic problems.

So, after all this description, what is the real deal here? Well for sure, if you have a vehicle that makes lots of power on the chassis dyno, then it should have a predictable level of performance on the dragstrip. Also, if you have engine dyno data that is very impressive and your vehicle does not perform well on the strip, then either there is a tremendous loss in the drive train or the numbers from the dyno might be suspect. Of course there is always that possibility the throttle was not at maximum opening. Details are neverending. Much of performance tuners' analysis time is spent checking the basics; they never assume that

*Kenny Duttweiler's dynamometer has seen some beyond serious horsepressure go across its measurements over the years. Notice that there is a lambda sensor in the exhaust collector. Even an experienced hand such as Duttweiler uses as many inputs as possible to tell him what is going on with the engine tune-up. When the engine comes off the dyno, the engine builder and tuner can feel more confident in the product.*

# NUMBERS AND FORMULAS

*The engine in this dragster was tested on an engine dyno even on nitrous with a 400 Hp shot of $N_2O$. This thing consistently goes 7.30s at 5880 feet above sea level (Denver). Various engine tune-ups have been tried with most based on the engine dyno testing information.*

anything is working to its potential until the function is verified.

## Algorithms for Application and Evaluation

If you have some decent chassis dyno data as outlined previously, how does that relate to track conditions if the weather is different? If you take a close look at the upcoming chapter on correction factors, you can learn about how to apply weather corrections. It will surprise you how closely the corrections can work.

The corrections for atmospheric changes (weather) can help with choosing a main jet for your track tune-up or can supply you with a difference in power between the chassis dyno and the track surface.

Much of the math is just simple arithmetic and should not intimidate you to non-action. The math is just another tool for you to learn in order to improve performance.

## Exhaust, Cooling and Energy Balance

An excellent reference on how influential exhaust systems are on vehicle performance is Jim Hand's *How to Build Max-Performance Pontiac V-8s* by CarTech Books. Hand's book goes into some very good detail on how the exhaust system affect 1/4-mile drag times and speeds. See below.

## Cylinder Pressure: Relationships to Torque and Power

The pressure in an engine's combustion chamber and cylinder is normally expressed in pounds per square inch (psi). As the fuel and air mixture begins to burn, this combustion exerts a great force on top of the piston. That pressure in a performance engine might be 1200 psi or higher and creates a force that can be called instantaneous torque as the force is exerted on the crankshaft.

The pressure on top of the piston is called Indicated Mean Effective Pressure (IMEP). There is friction within the engine, and what ends up

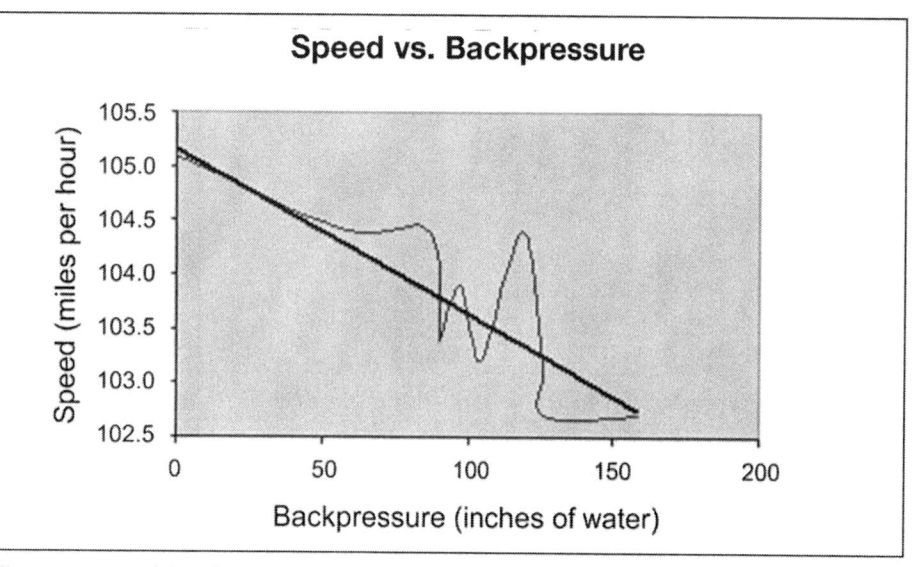

*The measured backpressure is inversely proportional to the trap speed of the test vehicle. Lower backpressure provided higher trap speeds. Graph courtesy of Jim Hand.*

DYNO TESTING AND TUNING

CHAPTER 3

at the flywheel to be put to work is called Brake Mean Effective Pressure (BMEP). The frictional elements are referred to as Friction Mean Effective Pressure (FMEP). So, BMEP = IMEP – FMEP.

In testing, the indicated mean effective pressure numbers can be measured per cylinder with pressure sensors and they are referenced with a shaft encoder for very accurate indications of what goes on within the cylinder. These methods are typically done on an engine dynamometer because the system needs to be worked against a load. Such systems are very expensive and typically require a pressure sensor to measure

## Exhaust and Cooling Must Work Properly

If in testing an engine on an engine dyno the exhaust system used was not what will be used in the vehicle, all sorts of difficulties can result. The problems arise as a result of the backpressure and exhaust-flow characteristics that various systems produce. This becomes a very serious situation when the engine is being tested with an electronic fuel injection and electronic engine management system. The electronic management system will try to change the tune-up map, and if the exhaust system is not the same as the one to be run on the car, then the system just might go nuts when the engine and the management system is installed in the vehicle. It's the details, folks; plain old details.

If testing on a chassis dyno or an engine dyno and the total airflow through the dyno room is poor, then there is the great possibility that the exhaust gases will recirculate back into the airstream that also supplies the combustion air to the engine. EGR (exhaust gas recirculation) is great for emissions applications, but it's a killer when you're trying to really make some horsepower.

*The exhaust air and the exhaust gases must get out of the dyno cell without re-entering the air intake. Exhaust gas recirculation is great for emissions, but it costs power. This dyno room uses simple racecar-type mufflers with some success and still has happy neighbors.*

*The exhaust system and airflow across and out of the dyno cell are absolutely important in achieving good results during the dyno testing sessions. An engine will lose power from too much backpressure in the exhaust and it will not like anything but fresh air in the inlet of the engine. Studying what happens on the exhaust side is a critical detail.*

*One way to get representative results on the engine dyno is to use the same exhaust system that is used on the car. As this photo shows, some packages just can be nightmares. However, in this case, it was accomplished by a serious tester. Somewhere in that bundle of tubing is an engine. Photo courtesy of R&R.*

DYNO TESTING AND TUNING

the pressure inside the cylinder. The systems are referred to as invasive systems because of the need to get a pressure tap into the cylinder.

Assuming the IMEP might be 1200 psi as listed above and the bore size is 4.030 inches, then an initial force of over 15,000 pounds of force pushes the piston down the bore. Multiplying the 1200 psi times the square inches of piston area yields this calculation. However, there is a rapid decay of the pressure as the piston moves down the cylinder. So, it is not just the instantaneous torque that we can either analyze or put to work in the engine, but also the average torque. That average torque is multiplied by RPM and, of course, it is average horsepower that moves the load down the road or racetrack.

The exhaust system for an engine dyno cell is an important part of the system because if the backpressure is too high, it costs horsepower. A good general rule is that the first 1 percent power loss happens when the backpressure on the exhaust system is 1" Hg or 13.6" H2O. Note that many vehicle exhaust systems have restrictions that amount to many psi, which causes horsepower loss. The best circumstance in testing is to have the same exhaust system in place during testing as will be used on the racecar.

Engine cooling can be approximated by estimating that *at least* one third of the flywheel power goes to heat that is carried away in the cooling system and through the radiator or water-cooling system for the dynamometer cell.

Reciprocating internal combustion engines are not very efficient (thermally), and the amount of power that gets to the flywheel is less than 30 percent of the energy that the fuel initially provides. Diesel engines are a bit more efficient by a few percentage points. Pressurized engine cooling is typically a better choice for duplicating the operation that the unit sees on the racetrack. The pressurized system helps to keep down the problems of bubble generation on the backside of the combustion chamber, which leads to random detonation in some chambers. Bubbles are great heat insulators and can cause all sorts of problems on long dyno pulls or tests.

The engine uses fuel to burn and turns some of the energy into usable horsepower. Evaluation of this process is called energy balance. The fuel provides a given amount of energy typically in BTUs (British Thermal Units) and each type of fuel has a rating in BTU content per pound. After combustion, the engine liberates and transfers an amount of heat energy to the air surrounding the engine, the cooling system, the oiling system, the exhaust system; what is left is used to power the transmission and drive axle through the tires. After all that, what is left over is what powers the racecar down the track.

**Where does the fuel energy go in a spark ignition engine at WOT?**

Fuel energy (~115,000 BTU/gal) .... 100%

Heat to cooling water ................... -28%

Heat to engine exhaust,
Heat to convection
and radiation, Heat to oil .............. -40%

Heat to pumping and piston friction .. -2%

Usable power at the flywheel ......... ~30%

**Chassis and Drivetrain Losses**

IF the engine power at the flywheel is at best tune
- Clutch or Torque Converter Loss (Friction and Heat)
- Transmission Loss (Friction and Heat)
- Driveshaft Loss (Friction and Heat)
- Drive Axle Loss (Friction and Heat)
- Tire Distortion Loss (May come from Tie-downs and Tire Growth or Air Pressure)

What is left over is power at the tire patch, which is the power left for propelling the vehicle.

# CHAPTER 4

# GOALS AND OBJECTIVES

*Dynamometer testing by nature is potentially very dangerous. Please read all the information in this book on safety before attempting any testing.*

Dyno testing for engine development is about exploring different parts combinations to maximize performance where you want it for your purposes. To get the information you need on the parts you're considering, you have to enter the testing day with a detailed plan. You'll be hiring the dyno for a set period of time, and you want to use those hours in the most efficient way possible to secure the data you need. A drag racer, for example, may want more off-the-line power—but not produced in such a way as to encourage random tire spin; the circle track racer may want smoother power delivery and better gas mileage for one less pit stop on race day. You're not just after "more power." Instead, you're after more power in particular places on the tachometer or the race track.

To get the essential information, you must enter the test with the parts you've selected and a careful plan for testing them in an orderly fashion. You don't want to spend the time and the money only to realize on the way home that you forgot to do one of the tests you wanted for comparison.

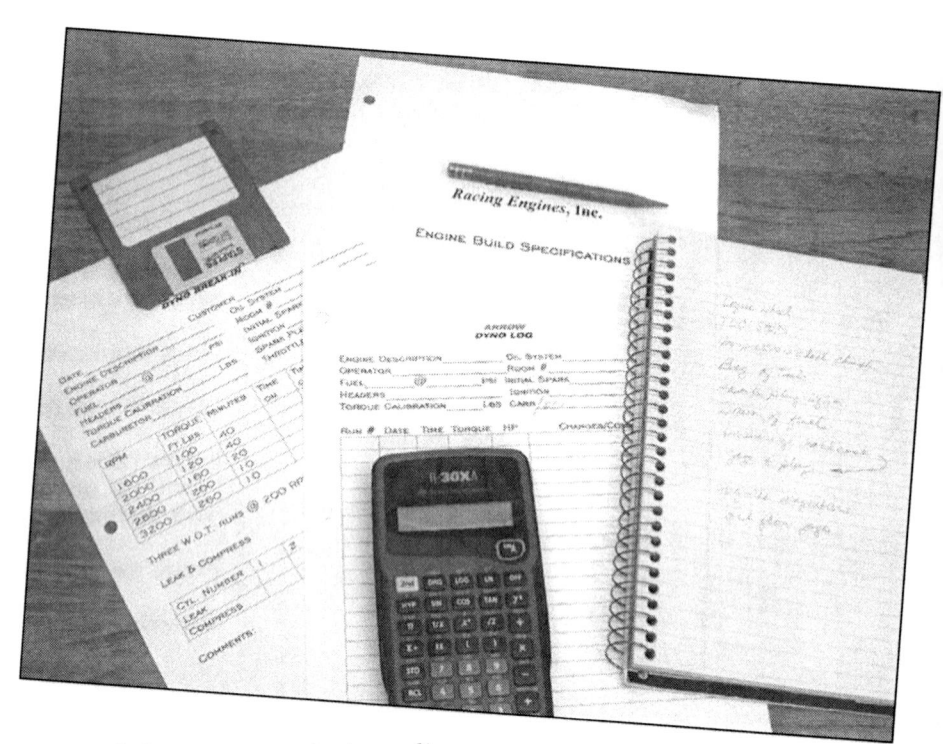

Start your test plan by writing down your goals and objectives for the test. Be as specific and detailed as you can, but above all, be honest with yourself. Try to imagine the best path to follow, and then make sure you have all of the necessary parts, and special tools, so your time on the dyno will be productive. An outline, flow chart, and/or a test plan is a good method to help you to visualize the test. Follow along as we plan a test for a daylong rental at an engine dyno shop. We will test three cams and two sets of headers in an attempt to improve our engine's performance.

## Our Primary Goal: Improve Our ET or Lap Times at the Race Track

We will accomplish this goal by raising the torque and horsepower

## GOALS AND OBJECTIVES

output while getting rid of dips and peaks in the torque curve that cause tire spin and traction loss coming off the line or coming off the corner. We would like an engine combination that could be flatfooted off the corner, or not overload the tires coming off the line at the drag strip. A smooth, predictable torque curve makes a racecar much easier to drive, and hence faster. With a peaky torque curve, the driver has to gently get in and out of the throttle. This is walking the tightrope between spinning out and bogging down. We will show how selecting the proper camshaft and tuning or refining the combination of camshaft and headers can usually correct this problem. After these new torque values from camshaft and headers are established, the fuel and spark requirements must be reevaluated to ensure that they are still optimal. By looking at our goal we list the objectives: Test three cams, and test two sets of headers. We start with what is called the test matrix. In this case it looks like this:

| Cam | Header A | Header B |
|-----|----------|----------|
| A   | Test 1   | Test 2   |
| B   | Test 3   | Test 4   |
| C   | Test 5   | Test 6   |
| A   | Test 7   | Test 8   |

**Each Test has peak Hp and Peak Torque**

We have to fill in 16 boxes in our matrix with answers. This will take a minimum of eight tests, since each test will give us a peak torque and peak horsepower figure. You will notice that we have Cam A twice. Why is that? See the sidebar on this page.

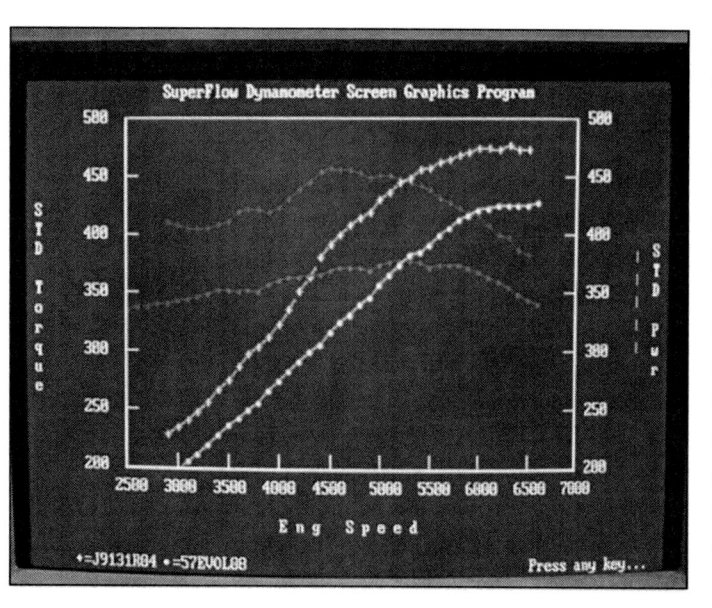

*Here we see how different the torque curves are. Although higher, the top torque curve has some fluctuations that would make the vehicle difficult to drive, or at least to be fast in. The lower curve is much smoother and would be easier to drive.*

## The ABA Method of Testing

We test by comparing the results of parts or systems run on the dyno. We generally use a test technique called the ABA method. This means we test a particular part (A) in the first test, and then we exchange only that part for the other test part (B) and re-run the entire test again under exactly the same conditions. At this point, it would seem like we would be able to draw a concrete conclusion defining which part produced the best performance. In some cases that is true, but in many more cases something may have changed with the engine condition or the test conditions, which in either case might increase or decrease the performance. By going back to the original parts and repeating the test exactly for the first part (A), you verify that the performance for the first configuration or part confirms the earlier data. This re-testing procedure is called "closing the loop."

When you can close the loop you have much greater confidence that what you found to be true for part A is still true. If, during the course of testing, the engine became worn or suffered some hidden damage like a scuffed piston or broken valve spring, the second part (B) might show a negative result when compared to part (A). But if a re-test of part (A) does not confirm the original performance figures, you know there is a problem inside the engine and that your part B numbers may not be good. Stopping with part B would leave you convinced that it was at fault for the lower power showing. You might then have reinstalled part A, gone to the track and had a bad race because damage was the cause of the figures, not a performance advantage in the part A configuration.

DYNO TESTING AND TUNING

# CHAPTER 4

## What is a Spintron?

Think of a Spintron as a dynamometer for valvetrains. Manufactured by Trend Performance Products in Warren, MI, it typically has a 100-horsepower variable-speed AC motor that drives the valvetrain. It incorporates a laser to measure valve lift and a high-resolution rotary encoder that continuously monitors crankshaft position. Crankshaft position and valve lift are then fed to a computer that plots a curve of valve lift versus crankshaft position.

Through the magic of high-speed data acquisition and laser accuracy, this machine can capture the actual motion of the valve at speeds in excess of 10,000 RPM. This data lets the engine developer graphically analyze the valvetrain dynamics and make improvements to enhance and literally tune the dynamic stability of the valvetrain.

The Spintron is able to identify and measure infinitesimally small anomalies that contribute to valvetrain instability. Except in rare instances, the overall goal for the valvetrain is to have the lifters or valves follow the camshaft profile by staying in contact with the lobe, since the lobe design ultimately dictates the engine performance. In some stock or lower-class applications, where lift or duration is limited by the rules, or a stock cam is required, lobes from some camshaft designers are actually designed to float or "loft" the valve over the nose in what can best be described as controlled valve float. In reality this can also be viewed as uncontrolled variable valve timing. This dynamic lofting creates a larger camshaft that will still pass the sanctioning body specifications, which are measured statically.

Inherent in any of these applications is the ability to carefully tune the performance to operate within a much wider band than a normal valvetrain. This capability means that the valvesprings must be carefully selected,

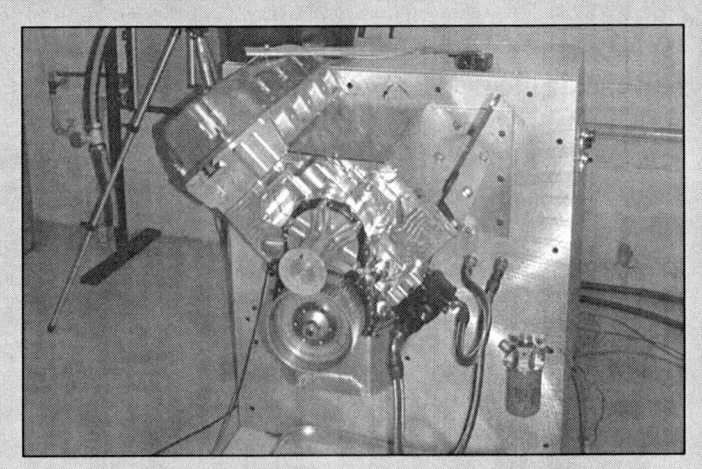

*The Spintron is a wonderful tool to analyze the valve train motion and evaluate the changes necessary to tune the camshaft and valvetrain dynamic stability. It can also be used as a component dynamometer to measure power required on various individual components.*

## Baselines

We start the ABA process with a series of runs that should have very repeatable results. Typically we like to see three runs with less than 1–2 percent full-scale variance in torque all made under the same test conditions. These runs are then averaged and this set of data becomes what is known as the baseline for part A. Once a baseline is established, the test part or system is changed and the test is repeated exactly. The closer you come to making the test conditions identical, the better your comparison will be.

It is perfectly acceptable to test other parts or settings such as spark advance in between the first and last tests. In those cases, the test order becomes ABCDA. There are some cardinal rules we like to follow when testing.

## Testing Individual Parts versus Systems

Camshaft comparisons are rarely as simple as swapping camshafts and making a second set of power runs. Horsepower, but not always torque, is typically improved by adding more lift (raising the valves higher) and duration (holding them open for a longer period of time). This increases the area under the lift curve. Adding more area under the curve is often referred to as *expanding* the cam. This expansion puts additional demands on all of the valvetrain

# GOALS AND OBJECTIVES

*The Spintron crankshaft has no throws, since it only transmits the power from the electric motor to the camshaft. It has sufficient mass to prevent bending and to dampen some camshaft torsional vibrations.*

qualified and maintained. Because it is designed to have low stress levels, a production valvespring has a relatively wide range where it can operate successfully with excellent durability. On the other hand, a pro stock drag racing spring, which is very highly stressed, has a very limited life and must be made of absolutely flawless material in order to prevent a costly failure. As a result of this higher demand, racing valvesprings are frequently replaced to maintain peak performance.

Ultimately, the Spintron allows a sharp operator to tune the valvetrain to move the harmonic or nodal points (places where the valvetrain resonates) to a region where the engine does not spend any appreciable time. Being able to speed through these resonance points and not have to spend any time there greatly extends the valvetrain life. Something as simple as changing the mass or the bending rate of a pushrod, or the inertia of a particular rocker arm, can make an otherwise unstable camshaft a race winner. The Spintron analysis will sometimes prove that lighter is not always better.

Since the Spintron actuates only the valvetrain, it allows an isolated analysis within the engine's working environment. While possible, performing this type of dynamic analysis in a running engine is very difficult and quite expensive. It must be noted that although the Spintron provides excellent dynamic measurement, it does not replicate the working system in an engine because gas dynamics are not taken into effect. To better understand this, consider a supercharged engine with high boost. In this application, the intake valve has pressure pushing on the back side, trying to lift it off the seat. This means that additional seat pressure must be designed into the engine to compensate for this variable offsetting load.

*A laser measures the valve movement from within the cylinder bore. Placing this inside the cylinder necessitates cutting a hole in the side of a worn or damaged block to turn it into a development part.*

components, especially the valve springs. Typically, new springs with greater seat loads and lift capabilities are part of any camshaft upgrade. So now our simple camshaft swap includes changing springs as well. The next step may involve going from a solid lifter cam to a roller cam. Again, this means two sets of hardware. Each set or combination of parts is called a system. In this instance, we would be comparing two systems—two camshafts, each with its own valvetrain. This is no problem as long as we carefully document what is in each system and we

## Testing Rules

- Never base a decision or comparison on one run.
- Change only one part or test condition at a time.
- Always try to test under similar conditions. Avoid comparisons made with widely varying weather conditions.
- Always close the loop
- Create a solid baseline—typically a minimum of three runs
- Always try to graph the three-run results for each part to spot trends and to highlight differences in the parts or systems.
- Never make an evaluation by looking only at the peak numbers; look at the overall picture. This is where graphing your data really helps.

# CHAPTER 4

make all of our comparisons from one system to another system.

You may have some intuition about which system will provide the best results. In that case you may want to test that combination last—which means you will also test it first, because the last test you run is a re-test of the initial setup to confirm that no major changes took place within the engine to skew your results. (See sidebar 4-1.) When your guess is correct, this approach allows you to keep the best system in the engine after a tough day of testing or before going to the track. Once you have some testing experience, this intuition becomes easier. If you start with the "A" cam, then you should finish with the "A" cam to close the loop.

Dyno time is not cheap, so prepare the engine and your components before you go. If something doesn't quite fit, you will be paying for dyno time in addition to whatever costs you incur for other parts or modifications. In most cases it makes sense to prepare for the test with the biggest cam in the engine. In most cases, if the one with the highest lift and most duration will fit, then the others you want to test will too. When checking cam fit, make sure that you test the minimum valve-to-piston clearance at both extremes of the range of cam centerlines you plan to use in the engine. You don't want to lose a day's dyno time and rental fee when you damage the engine because the valves hit the pistons.

If the cam is unusual, or from a lesser-known cam grinder, it may not have been thoroughly or dynamically tested and refined. As you begin to use higher performance camshafts, it really pays to run the cam—and the exact valvetrain you'll dyno it with—on a spin fixture like the Spintron prior to running the combination in your engine. This testing helps to ensure that the valvetrain you have chosen will run smoothly to the maximum RPM without encountering false motion or valve float. If you are unable to run your combination on a Spintron, stick with the cam manufacturer's recommended list of matching valvetrain components.

Today, virtually all top engine builders will have or use a Spintron to validate their valvetrain combinations before installing them in an engine, since an engine that suffers valvetrain failure at high RPM is typically a total write off.

## Choosing a Test

Next, we have to decide what type of test to perform. We should try to replicate the engine running conditions for our chosen track as closely as possible. In our example, we will use a constant acceleration test. If you have in-car data acquisition capability and some relevant past data, go to your database and get the engine speed range from some race conditions. Let's assume this data reveals we will run at WOT from 4,500 RPM to 7,500 RPM, or a 3000 RPM spread. The data also shows the car takes six seconds to get from 4,500 to 7,500 RPM. We will choose a 500 RPM/second rate, since at that rate an acceleration test from 4,500 RPM to 7,500 RPM will take 6 seconds (3000 ÷ 6 = 500).

## Engine Accessories and Support Equipment

There is a great benefit to testing the engine and actual accessories and support hardware such as the fuel pump, water pump, distributor, ignition system, and vehicle headers and exhaust system you use on your vehicle. *Always* use the fuel system you are using in the vehicle when you test on the dyno. In case the new cam makes more horsepower, we must be able to feed enough fuel to the engine to maintain the correct air-fuel ratio. By carefully monitoring air-fuel ratios during testing, you will be able to catch a shortfall on the fuel delivery. If you test with the dyno facility fuel pump alone, it might easily feed each of your test cams. Once the test is over and the engine is back in the car with the new higher-horsepower cam, the original vehicle fuel system might not be able to keep up with the new higher fuel demand created by the newfound power. You might incorrectly assume that since the new cam performed so well on the dyno that it will do so in the car. You could then spend a whole season trying to find this poor-fuel-delivery problem. If you tested on the dyno with the vehicle fuel pump, and analyzed the data correctly, you would know instantly that there was not enough fuel flow coming from your present system to support the additional horsepower. In some cases, you must remember to include the G-load demands in your fuel system requirements.

Careful testing on an engine dynamometer can pay great dividends. An engine dyno is not subject to track conditions nor does it have a driver, who may not take the same line thru the corner each lap. As dyno operators like to say, "the dyno has no conscience." The dynamometer will give you as good an answer as you let it. If you feed it poor data or practice poor testing techniques, you will get erroneous results. Ultimately, if you don't employ proper testing

GOALS AND OBJECTIVES

# On-Board Data Acquisition

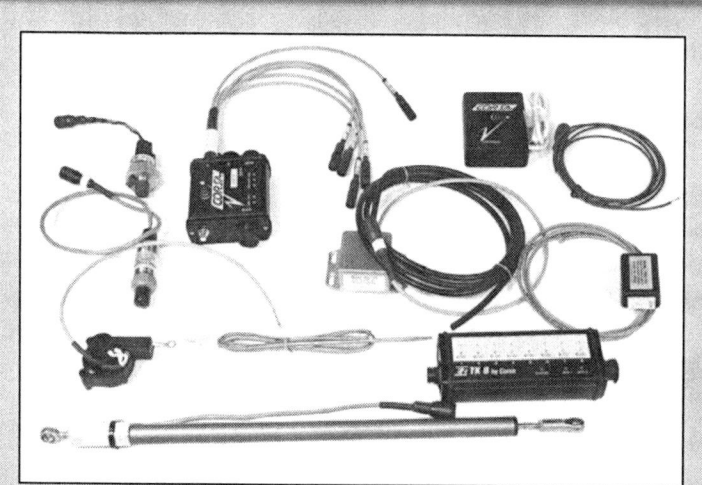

*An on-board Data acquisition system, like this one from CORSA, is a key to vehicle & engine development. It allows virtually any pressure, temperature, or movement to be recorded, measured and analyzed. Sophisticated dynos can use this data to map and replicate race-track conditions for the dyno.*

Think of on-board data acquisition systems as tape recorders or an instant-replay capability for data. In some cases, these recorders are no bigger than a pack of cigarettes and allow you to record virtually any form of data useful in analyzing an engine or vehicle. While these systems have been around for a while, most notably as the fabled Black Box or Primary Flight Data Recorder found in all commercial airplanes, they have only recently become economical for the performance user. The more sophisticated ones such as the CORSA system use GPS positioning to enable the user to see where they are on the course as well as analyze or map motion between different points.

By mounting pressure transducers, thermocouples, G meters, and linear potentiometers, you can track the simultaneous pressures, temperatures, G loads and movements of virtually anything in the entire vehicle or drivetrain. You can even evaluate the driver! It has always been interesting to compare a driver's opinion of their performance to an unemotional data system's printed record of the driver's performance. By recording this engine and vehicle data while you are operating the vehicle at speed and under racing conditions, you can capture data not able to be seen by the driver (hopefully they are focused on winning). Once you have this data, you can play it back, graph it, or (in some cases by clever manipulation) import it into the dyno to allow the dyno to replicate the on-track engine settings.

Endurance race teams, for example, will "tape" a course like Daytona or Sebring and then program the dyno to replicate the entire 24-hour race, including pit stops. It lets you get valuable race durability mileage without the expense and hassle of having to go to the race track.

If you have one of these systems, by all means, be prepared to run it in conjunction with your dyno testing to allow you to correlate and calibrate it against the dyno. Once the engine is back in the car and the car is at the track, you will be able to take trackside data and confidently relate it back to your dyno data.

Quite often these systems are used to augment the dyno data acquisition systems, since the dyno systems are often limited in the number or type of variables able to be tracked. As an example, it may make sense to look at exhaust gas temperatures as a function of G force, or hood scoop pressure as a function of vehicle speed. The more you can learn about the actual in-car conditions, the better you can prepare to test or replicate them on the dyno.

techniques, you will end up paying the price by racing with a part or adjustment that produces inferior results.

## Data Requirements

We should start planning any test by logging all of the engine configuration data. Much of this data will have to be entered into the dyno computer prior to starting the test to enable the dyno computer to make its various performance calculations.

The configuration data is also important when you review the test, so you can remember just what was in the engine and what subtle adjustments were made between each run. These notes become really important when you are reviewing the data six months or two years later, when all of the subtle details and changes are no longer crystal clear.

Configuration data identifies your engine and combination. Here

DYNO TESTING AND TUNING

# CHAPTER 4

are some of the basic engine configuration requirements.

**Displacement**
   Bore
   Stroke
**Compression ratio**
**Fuel system**
   Type-Brand
      Specific gravity
      Octane rating
   Fuel pump(s) and line pressure
**Induction system**
   Heads
   Manifold
   Carburetor(s)
   Air cleaner
**Ignition system**
   Plug heat range and gap
   Hardware
   Spark advance
**Camshaft and valvetrain system**
**Cooling system**
   Radiator
   Pump and drive ratio
**Exhaust system**
   Header type and dimensions
   Tail pipe(s)
   Muffler(s)
   Backpressure
**Oiling system**
   Pan
   Pump and drive ratio
   Cooler
**Accessories**
   Vibration damper
   Accessory drive system

The typical configuration data is shown on the sample run log in the appendix. You can create your own level of detail here. It is easier to write it down at the time than *repeat the entire test* later because you can't remember. If you fail to keep good test records, you may have to repeat the test.

## Initial Data

Prior to testing, some initial weather data must be taken to initialize the correction factor process. The following should be taken and maintained throughout the test:

Mercury column barometer reading
Wet bulb temperature in the cell
Dry bulb temperature
Calculated Vapor pressure

## Data For Every Run

Let's look at the minimum data required to make a good decision. In the case of our cam test, our dyno data acquisition system should take the following data for each run:

RPM
Torque
Horsepower
Oil pressure
Manifold vacuum
Dry bulb temperature, also known as carburetor air temperature or simply CAT
Inlet air flow
Exhaust backpressure
Exhaust gas temperatures (EGT)
Lambda (fuel/air) or air/fuel ratio for each bank minimum, preferably each cylinder
Fuel flow
Barometer
Wet bulb temperature
Humidity
BSFC (brake specific fuel consumption)
BSAC (brake specific air consumption)
Oil temperature
Water temperature in and out of engine
Correction factor

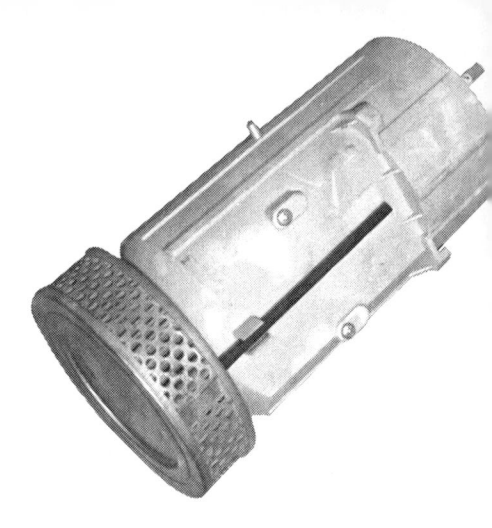

*An electric in-tank fuel pump is found on virtually all cars today. It replaces the old mechanical diaphragm pump. These pumps require a decent amount of current and produce the much higher pressures required for electronic fuel injection.*

*If you use a mechanical fuel pump, make sure it is capable of delivering the correct amount of fuel for the entire operating range of the engine.*

*This older sling psychrometer relies on two mercury bulb thermometers, one with a wet sock covering the bulb and the other without to give "wet bulb" and "dry bulb" readings. Once you have the two temperatures, relative humidity can be calculated using the sliding scale in the handle.*

## GOALS AND OBJECTIVES

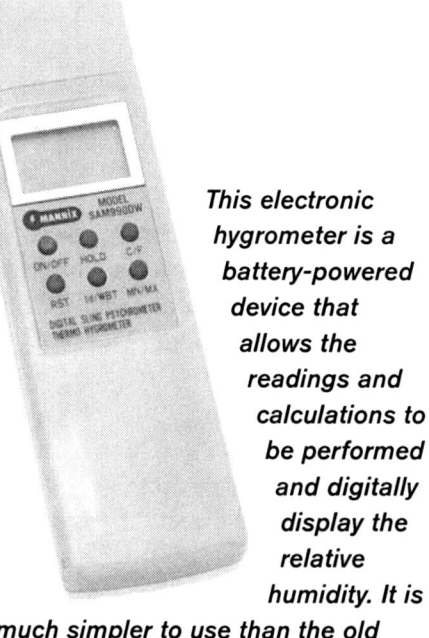

*This electronic hygrometer is a battery-powered device that allows the readings and calculations to be performed and digitally display the relative humidity. It is much simpler to use than the old sling psychometers.*

```
                              ARROW RACING ENGINE INC.
                                 3811 INDUSTRIAL DRIVE
                              ROCHESTER HILLS, MI  48309

Test Number:      12
Date (M/D/Y): 6-12-07  Time (H:M:S): 02:52:55 Operator: DALE MATTHEWS
Engine description: 460 FORD FE DUAL CARB HOLLEY 2" HDRS 36 DEG TIM
Test description: BREAKIN & POWER RUNS  80/76 - 70/70 JETS

Test:   200 RPM/Sec Acceleration  Fuel Spec. Grav.:    .751   Air Sensor: 6.5
Vapor Pressure:    .32            Barometric Pres.:  29.32    Ratio: 1.00 TO 1
Engine Type: 4-Cycle Spark        Engine displacement: 460.0  Stroke:  4.000

Speed   Trq    Pwr    FA     A1    A/F   BSFC  BSAC   Man-P   Oil  CAT Fuel Oil Wat
 rpm   lb-Ft    Hp   lb/hr  scfm        lb/Hphr      In Hg    psi   F    F  Out Out
 2800  402.7  214.7   99.5   .0    .0    .46   .00    -1.4    51.7  85      90 147 157
 2900  400.0  220.9  105.4   .0    .0    .48   .00    -1.4    51.8  87      91 147 157
 3000  397.8  227.2  123.6   .0    .0    .54   .00    -1.5    52.4  89      91 147 156
 3100  397.8  234.8  115.9   .0    .0    .49   .00    -1.5    52.8  89      89 148 156
 3200  407.1  248.0  112.4   .0    .0    .45   .00    -1.5    53.0  90      89 147 156
 3300  406.8  255.6  113.9   .0    .0    .45   .00    -1.5    53.1  90      90 147 157
 3400  414.2  268.1  114.4   .0    .0    .43   .00    -1.5    53.4  90      90 147 157
 3500  423.7  282.4  124.2   .0    .0    .44   .00    -1.5    54.4  90      90 147 157
 3600  425.4  291.6  126.4   .0    .0    .43   .00    -1.5    54.2  90      90 147 157
 3700  424.9  299.3  134.9   .0    .0    .45   .00    -1.6    54.4  90      90 147 157
 3800  428.8  310.3  135.5   .0    .0    .44   .00    -1.5    54.9  90      90 147 158
 3900  439.8  326.6  143.5   .0    .0    .44   .00    -1.5    54.7  88      90 147 158
 4000  448.1  341.3  147.1   .0    .0    .43   .00    -1.6    55.1  89      90 147 158
 4100  451.5  352.5  154.9   .0    .0    .44   .00    -1.6    55.3  89      90 147 160
 4200  457.4  365.8  159.5   .0    .0    .44   .00    -1.6    55.3  90      91 147 161
 4300  457.9  374.9  163.5   .0    .0    .44   .00    -1.6    55.6  90      91 147 161
 4400  460.6  385.9  168.3   .0    .0    .44   .00    -1.6    55.5  90      91 147 161
 4500  470.3  403.0  177.0   .0    .0    .44   .00    -1.6    55.8  90      91 147 162
 4600  471.8  413.2  189.4   .0    .0    .46   .00    -1.6    55.7  89      91 145 163
 4700  474.5  424.6  197.9   .0    .0    .47   .00    -1.6    55.9  88      91 146 163
 4800  477.9  436.8  204.2   .0    .0    .47   .00    -1.6    56.2  88      90 146 164
 4900  484.3  451.8  210.8   .0    .0    .47   .00    -1.6    56.3  88      90 146 164
 5000  484.0  460.8  218.1   .0    .0    .47   .00    -1.6    56.4  89      91 146 165
 5100  478.9  465.0  224.4   .0    .0    .48   .00    -1.6    56.2  89      91 146 165
 5200  484.3  479.5  222.7   .0    .0    .46   .00    -1.6    56.8  89      91 145 166
 5300  486.0  490.4  224.8   .0    .0    .46   .00    -1.6    56.8  88      91 146 166
 5400  486.2  499.9  237.7   .0    .0    .48   .00    -1.6    57.1  88      91 147 166
 5500  484.0  506.9  247.1   .0    .0    .49   .00    -1.6    57.3  88      91 147 166
 5600  483.5  515.5  248.0   .0    .0    .48   .00    -1.7    57.5  88      91 147 166
 5700  482.8  524.0  253.6   .0    .0    .48   .00    -1.7    57.0  89      91 147 167
 5800  484.7  535.3  257.4   .0    .0    .48   .00    -1.7    57.3  90      91 148 168
 5900  480.8  540.1  256.1   .0    .0    .47   .00    -1.7    56.9  91      92 148 168
 6000  474.7  542.3  260.9   .0    .0    .48   .00    -1.7    56.4  92      92 148 168
 6100  470.3  546.2  261.1   .0    .0    .48   .00    -2.1    56.4  90      92 148 168
 6200  469.1  553.8  263.5   .0    .0    .48   .00    -1.8    55.9  90      94 148 168
 6300  465.0  557.8  271.6   .0    .0    .49   .00    -1.8    53.9  91      92 148 170
 6400  460.1  560.7  266.4   .0    .0    .48   .00    -1.8    53.8  91      92 147 170
 6500  455.4  563.6  262.9   .0    .0    .47   .00    -1.8    53.2  91      92 147 170
 6600  451.0  566.8  256.8   .0    .0    .45   .00    -1.8    53.9  90      92 147 170
 6700  419.3  534.9  259.9   .0    .0    .49   .00    -1.8    52.3  90      93 148 171
```

*This is what your data for a power run will look like from a SuperFlow dynamometer. At first all of the columns and all of the values are confusing, but once you become accustomed to reading the data, it all makes sense.*

*It is highly recommended that you use a mercury column barometer to establish and monitor your room pressure. All of the correction factors rely on the barometric pressure as a basis for the calculations. While most modern dynos have an internal barometer, you must be able to check the calibration.*

### Primary Goal

We take data for many reasons, with engine safety among the most important. Our primary goal should always be to protect ourselves and the equipment that we are testing. If, for example, we are running an engine too lean, we could burn a piston, which might cause the engine to explode and cause a room fire. To prevent this, the safe operator carefully monitors the air/fuel ratio. Do this by watching the air/fuel ratio or lambda readings as well as the individual Exhaust Gas Temperatures (EGTs) during a run. If the mixture runs lean, and the temperatures increase, we are headed for trouble. Stop immediately and correct the problem by enriching the mixture in the affected load zones or RPM ranges.

### Secondary Goal

The second goal of testing, after safe operation, is to enhance the

---

DYNO TESTING AND TUNING                              41

CHAPTER 4

# Records and Data

Except for a lighter wallet and a little wear on the tested componentry, all you leave the dyno with is data. Simply having 10 separate tests on sheets is not enough information. You need detailed notes on all the relevant conditions, components, settings, etc., if the generated data is really going to help you improve your engine's performance. Even adding digital photos can be useful—anything that helps you recall each test's specific details.

Make and keep lots of notes and sketches so that you can easily recall what the test data means and what the results were at the track. There is nothing more frustrating than trying to sort through 10 or 15 tests that did not have adequate notes of what changes (if any) were tried. The details on changes you made to timing, jet selection, exhaust-system components, and so on are so important that it is worth the time to make notes to jog your memory. Invariably, you won't have as much time to review your notes and prepare for a race as you would like, so make sure your notes tell you everything you need to know. Good notes allow you to compare experiences easily so that you can consistently move ahead in your development program.

Your memory is not nearly as reliable as what gets written down. Those who learn this key fact last will lose in more ways than one.

## Data Acquisition and Data Averaging

You would think (based on high school math) that you could take the high numbers and the low numbers and half way between would be the average. It is not that simple, but close. You see, it depends on how many samples there are to average. You should also be aware that there are about a zillion methods for averaging data. Yes, that is a bit of an exaggeration, but taken on the average it is somewhat true. Oh…hey, lighten up and enjoy this stuff!

### Data Rate (Sometimes Called Sample Rate)

Over the course of any test, values are changing, whether they are RPMs, torque, load, or all the other electrical and mechanical events inside the engine. The more frequently the data is sampled, the better it is at telling you exactly what is going on.

When attempting to compare data from one place to the other, it is important to know if both places were using the same testing scheme, including data rates and data averaging. More often than not, things are not as simple as they seem.

### Data Averaging and Statistics

The numbers the dyno test gives you use data averaging. This is because a table or graph of results, plotting every single sample the dyno's sensors take, would be overwhelming. Instead, it provides only incremental figures, each of which represents an average of the information the sensors detected within that period. For example if it provided figures for every second, each of those figures would average the many samples per second the sensors actually took. The very best comparisons of dyno data come when the tests to be compared use the same method of data averaging. Unfortunately, since there are many ways to do this math, and dyno programmers often do not or will not share their method, comparisons are limited by the differences the methods represent. All facilities put out numbers called horsepower, yet some will not measure up to the real standards of full-size horses that are ready to race.

Remember that there are all sorts of ways to average data and you need to know which scheme is in place at each facility at which you might spend your valuable time in testing.

*Don't rely on your memory to provide you with all the details about several different tests. Most modern dynamometers (engine or chassis types) can supply you with a CD and printouts including graphics of all the variables that were measured or calculated during dyno testing. It is always easy to remember peak numbers, but the peak numbers do not prevail in the overall scheme of things.*

DYNO TESTING AND TUNING

## GOALS AND OBJECTIVES

performance of the test engine whether by improving the power output or by changing the shape of the torque curve to make the torque more effective and hence make the car go faster. Neophyte tuners all tend to focus on horsepower and peak numbers; in most cases it is more productive to focus on torque and more importantly the shape of the torque curve and the overall area under the torque curve.

Remember that horsepower is calculated from the torque produced. Almost any sharp dyno tuner would give away 2% of their peak power to gain a better torque curve. On the other hand, if the torque is not sacrificed, more horsepower is always better. Our goal here is to "shape" the torque curve by optimizing all of the tunable systems in the engine and make sure that they are within the vehicle capability envelope. What does this mean? Put very simply, it does not matter if you find another 20 lb-ft of torque at 4500 RPM if the tire combination you are forced to run can't handle the extra torque. In fact, the vehicle will always slow down when you produce more torque than the tires can handle. In this case, an engine dyno test would have highlighted the increased torque difference, yet when we go to the track and go slower instead of faster, it should send the strong message that the car is traction limited. Sometimes a simple trick, like changing the final gear ratio to lessen the torque that the rear tires have to handle, can verify the poor traction capability.

After a dyno test is over, you will want to sit down and carefully arrange all of the data so you can make a logical decision that will satisfy your goal of reducing your lap times. It is therefore important for you to take all of the data you will need while the test is running. If you fail to take the data or to get good data, you will have to go back and repeat the test as well as possibly pay an additional dyno fee! It usually costs no more to take all of the basic data for each run the first time. There is no requirement that you use the data, but it is certainly difficult to go back and repeat a test if you failed to take the data or didn't log the changes as you made the comparison tests. There is nothing worse than finding a winning combination and not remembering what you did to get it.

Graphical analysis is perhaps the best way to visualize and understand your data. Today's PC-based dynamometers allow virtually any imaginable comparison between data inputs. These variables can then be easily graphed against each other. Looking at a series of numbers in columns does not lend itself to good data interpretation. *Always* graph the variables against each other. When you do this, relationships start to

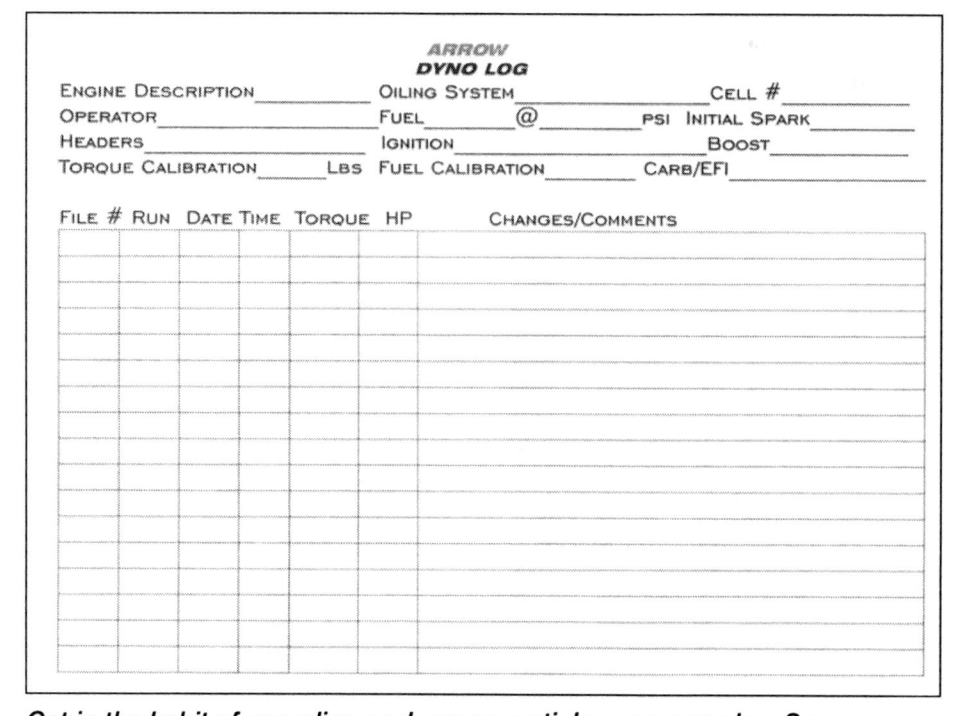

*This thermocouple allows temperature to be read as a voltage, which is then converted to a temperature for the data printout. This one is suited for higher temperatures and hence used to monitor the exhaust temperature.*

*Get in the habit of recording each run or partial run on a run log. See Appendix B for one you can copy and use. Later when you are looking for your data, it will greatly simplify data analysis and document the changes from run to run.*

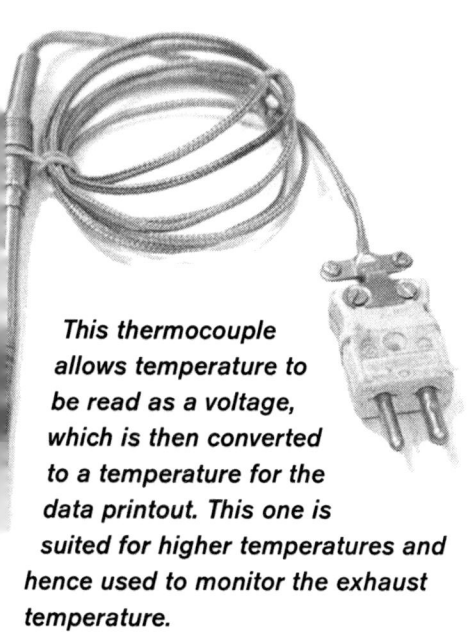

DYNO TESTING AND TUNING　　43

# CHAPTER 4

# Vibration Dampers

While we are on the subject of endurance engines, we should mention vibration damper tuning. Any time you alter or change the crankshaft and its attached components such as rods, pistons, and flywheels, you change the natural frequency of the system and should consider retuning the vibration damper. If you could accurately and discretely analyze the rotary motion of the crankshaft you would find that, rather than smoothly rotating in the bearings, it actually ratchets, going forward and backward as it makes its way around the firing order. As each cylinder fires, the power pulse accelerates the crank in a positive direction. As this power pulse dies, another rod journal sees a negative load from a rod that is trying to force a piston upward in the cylinder bore to compress a mixture of incoming air and fuel. This constant ratcheting effect, called torsional vibration, is ongoing; because of the components involved and the nature of the motion, certain periods or resonance points occur. At certain discreet points in the operating curve of an engine, all of the various frequencies come together to form a nodal point. This may be described as everything going the wrong way at once. Left to vibrate in this way, the crankshaft will fracture and fail. How do we prevent this?

The vibration damper, or harmonic balancer as it is sometimes called, consists of a mass, called an inertia ring, suspended by a torsional spring. In a production engine, this spring is often a layer of bonded rubber connecting the outer inertia ring to the inner crankshaft hub. By carefully varying the mass of the inertia ring and natural frequency of the rubber, a skilled technician can tune the damper to move the destructive harmonics to another portion of the operating curve. It should be pointed out that nodal points cannot be eliminated, only moved. The trick is to move the nodal point to a place in the operating curve where you don't operate for any significant amount of time. A nodal point may occur at 8400 RPM where the engine spends a lot of time. You may want to move this nodal point so that is at 7,800—well below the power peak where the engine never spends any time.

Damper tuning requires sophisticated measuring equipment and complex calculations. It is an area in which only a few specialized companies, such as ATI, have the expertise and equipment to perform the analysis as well as make the specifically tuned dampers. Today most of us use explosion-

*An explosion-proof damper, like this one from ATI, is highly recommended for any high-speed testing. Any time the output or components are significantly changed in an engine, you should consider re-tuning the damper.*

*A torsiograph is a high-resolution rotary encoder mounted on the end of the crankshaft to record the crankshaft movements for analysis. Once analyzed, a new damper can be tuned for your engine. If you are going to run at sustained high speeds, such as in marine or endurance racing, damper tuning becomes a must.*

proof dampers, but we run whatever damping factor is recommended by the damper manufacturer. If you are planning an endurance-racing venture, it would pay to enlist the aid of a damper manufacturer to tune your damper for your program. While it is not inexpensive to have the work done, it is far less expensive than losing an engine.

There are a number of manufacturers today who produce performance dampers. These dampers employ several different strategies to damp the vibrations. No matter what, as a matter of safety, always consider running an explosion-proof damper. If a damper explodes during a dyno test, the shrapnel can cause injury on its own as well as sever a fuel line and possibly start a fire.

A few engine builders will hone a damper so that it is no longer an interference or press fit on the front end of the crankshaft in order to speed cam changes on the dyno or at the track. This negates the dampening characteristics and is a dangerous practice. If the damper comes off the crank, it will fly into the dyno room and strike something or someone. Make sure there is adequate press fit, and a properly torqued retaining bolt, securing the damper to the end of the crankshaft.

## GOALS AND OBJECTIVES

emerge. For example, everybody knows that as air/fuel ratio increases, so does exhaust gas temperature. Or does it? If we follow the curve out, as the air increases and the fuel decreases, the EGT's actually cool off.

Let's say we spot a huge hole or dip in the torque curve of an acceleration run. If we graph fuel flow versus torque for that run, we quickly notice that the fuel flow started going away well before the engine fell on its face. This points us toward the fuel curve. Either the supply was inadequate or the fuel metering or management system didn't deliver the correct amount of fuel required by the engine.

This is also an example of where an acceleration test will uncover flaws that a steady-state run (a run where the RPM is held constant) would not find. In steady-state running, the engine is slowly and carefully brought to a specific RPM at a specific load or throttle setting. The engine is allowed to stabilize its temperatures and then the readings are taken, after which the engine is returned to a lower RPM and load until the next point to be taken. Steady-state testing is quite important because we need to know what the engine sees at a given load and RPM. A NASCAR engine, for example, may cycle (vary) only a few hundred RPM at Talladega for 30 laps. We want to make sure that the engine is happy when it does this. Passing through this point on an acceleration run is far different from "living" there all afternoon.

### Preparing for the Test

Use your written test plan and flow chart and rehearse the steps while trying to think beyond just the test parts. Try to include everything, such as spare gaskets and special tools that will be needed to work quickly and efficiently.

Before we can run our test, we must ensure that both sets of headers fit the engine and clear the dyno and that the new cam has sufficient valve-to-piston (V-to-P) clearance to run in the engine. If we don't have enough V-to-P clearance in the engine we want to use for the cam test, we will probably bend all of the valves and damage the pistons. Learn of any clearance problems

*Perhaps the most critical measurement before trying a new camshaft is valve-to-piston clearance. Unless there is sufficient clearance, the valves will hit, bend, and eventually break.*

*A large degree wheel like this one is essential to get accurate readings when changing the camshaft centerline. The readings go from 0-180-0 degrees.*

before you arrive so you don't waste paid dyno time disassembling the engine and notching the pistons. One approach for avoiding this problem is to build up the engine with the largest or worst-case cam before you arrive at the dyno facility. If that setup fits, then you should be confident that the others will too. For added insurance, check the camshaft at both extremes of the installed centerlines to be tested.

Before the big day, pack all of your equipment and special tools. We make sure we have the cams, but also have the cam specs, a degree wheel, offset keys or bushings to set cam centerline, and whatever parts are required to go with each system. Make sure you have spare gaskets and spare small parts, such as valve springs, keepers, and lash caps. Ask yourself, "What are we likely to break, and what is unique to my engine?" Most dyno shops are willing to loan or sell you parts to enable you to keep testing, but what if they don't have what you need? Your day will be much more productive and rewarding if you are equipped to test all of your parts and get the answers you came for.

### Fuel

Which fuel and how much of it will you need? Decide whether to bring your own fuel. Many dyno shops require that you bring your own fuel; others want you to buy it from them. Some include the fuel in their rental fee. The shop should be able to estimate how much you will need for your testing. Here are some simple general rules for determining fuel requirements. If you are going to break in a gasoline engine and do some dyno testing, multiply the

DYNO TESTING AND TUNING

# CHAPTER 4

*Pack a tool bag with what you will need in the dyno room. Often there is not enough room to roll in a full toolbox. If the engine requires too much work, the best bet is to pull it off the dyno and put it on an engine stand.*

*These offset bushings and offset keys allow you to incrementally advance or retard the camshaft relative to the crankshaft for tuning.*

projected horsepower times .044 times the number hours of run time, to get the gallons of fuel needed. For example, if we were going to run a 400 horsepower engine for variable speed and load running for a total run time of two hours, we could plan on using approximately 35 gallons of fuel. (400 hp x 2 hours x .044 (factor) = 35 gal of fuel).

Be prepared to enter the specific gravity of your fuel into the computer. Many systems require this number to be input in the initial data entry to calibrate the flow meter. The specific gravity can also be a measure of your fuel's potency. Make sure that you have the fuel manufacturer's data for specific gravity. If your fuel doesn't measure up, don't use it. While it may not hurt your engine, you will base your tuning around fuel that will not be available at the race track. Conversely, you should always check your fuel at the point of purchase to ensure you are getting the correct fuel. If fuel loses its potency or resistance to knock, it could potentially hurt your engine. Most of us who have been around for a while tend to use only fuel from well-established suppliers and only from "sealed" drums. These are some of the only ways to ensure fresh fuel. The only quick point of sale test is a hydrometer, which is a bobber to measure specific gravity, or a dielectric fuel tester, which measures the electrical resistance of the fuel. The dyno facility should have a hydrometer to test your fuel for specific gravity. You will need to enter this measured specific gravity value to calibrate the dyno flow meter.

Once a barrel of fuel is opened, try to use all of it. Half-full barrels of fuel, unless tightly sealed and stored in a climate- and temperature-controlled environment, will "breathe." With each breath, the barrel exhales the light ends of the gasoline vapors and inhales cool air, usually filled with moisture. When you come back 6 weeks later and try to reuse the fuel, you will be faced with fuel that has lost significant potency and may have water in the bottom of the barrel.

While some racing associations use a dielectric test to qualify fuel and discourage cheating, this resistance test may be inadequate to bet an engine's performance against. A few unscrupulous fuel outlets have cut or mixed their fuels, which results in lower octane for the user and increased profits for the seller. Unless you know your fuel supplier

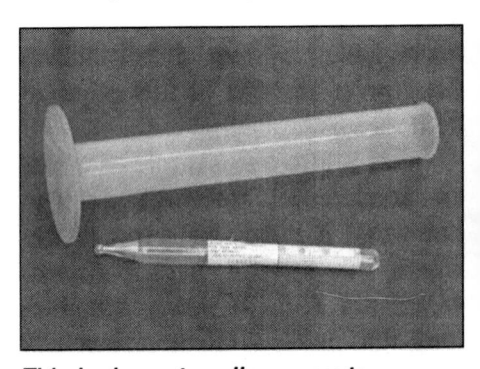

*This hydrometer allows you to measure the density of your fuel, which will be needed to calibrate the fuel flow meter. Be sure to also take the temperature of the fuel and apply the temperature correction factor.*

*To ensure fuel quality, it is recommended never to purchase fuel unless this seal is intact. If fuel is in a sealed drum from a well-known manufacturer, chances are that it still retains its original quality. Once a drum has been opened, the fuel should be used promptly. Never return old fuel to a drum.*

DYNO TESTING AND TUNING

## Tracking Wear

If an engine is experiencing high wear or bearing failure, the first clue will usually be debris in the oil. Therefore it pays to use several filters in series and inspect these filters frequently. You should use a lighted magnifier to view the debris. Once you find it, try to identify the source of the debris and make a decision either to proceed or stop the test and look deeper into the engine. Write a test plan that has reminders to check things like filters and oil levels built in so you don't skip these important checks.

Crankshaft end play is important to monitor, especially on cars with automatic transmissions. Always measure the end play prior to installing the engine on the dyno or in the car. Once you are ready to run, check again. If you don't have the same clearance, stop and find out why. If you have improperly assembled the engine on the dyno or in the car and all of the thrust clearance is taken up, you will immediately ruin a thrust bearing and usually lose a crankshaft in the process when you first start the engine.

Every time you drain the oil or inspect the filter, look for debris. Try to identify the debris. If you see bearing material, stop and find the cause. Remove the oil pan and inspect the bearings.

If you see brass or bronze, it may be a bushing or a bronze distributor gear grinding itself up. If left unattended, it will change the spark timing and ruin your test.

Small steel O-rings may come from the valve stem seals or roller lifter or roller tip rocker axles. This would indicate you have over-traveled the valves and crushed the seals or one of the lifters has lost a retaining ring

---

## Compression Ratio versus Cranking Compression

Quite often there is confusion about these two terms. Let's see if we can put this one to rest.

**Compression ratio** is the ratio of two volumes within the cylinder.

The volume above the piston when the piston is at TDC is called the compressed volume. When the piston travels down the bore on the intake stroke it adds the swept volume to the compressed volume to form the total volume. The total volume in the cylinder above the piston when the piston is at BDC is the compressed volume plus the swept volume. Total volume divided by the compressed volume is the compression ratio. Imagine placing your engine at BDC with both valves closed and filling it with some light engine oil through the spark plug hole. This amount of oil would be called the total volume. Then rotate the engine 180 degrees, stopping the piston at TDC while collecting the oil coming out of the spark plug hole. This volume of oil is called the swept volume. Subtract the swept volume from the total volume used to fill the cylinder in the beginning to get the compressed volume. Divide the total volume by the compressed volume to get the static or mechanical compression ratio. The swept volume times eight is the displacement of a V-8 engine. Displacement is typically measured in cubic inches or liters.

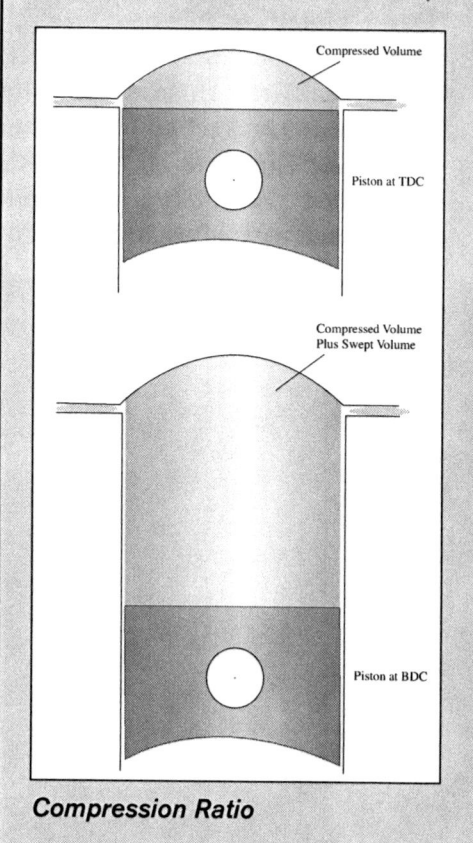

**Cranking compression** is a pressure. It represents the peak pressure attained in a cylinder while cranking without firing the engine. Although compression ratio does certainly affect cranking compression pressure, it in no way can be accurately measured by cranking compression pressure. In practice, cam timing affects cranking compression more than static compression ratio does. As an experiment to get a better understanding of valve events, try measuring the cranking compression on the same engine with two camshafts having different event timing.

**Compression Ratio**

# CHAPTER 4

*This filter cutter makes short (and clean) work of cutting an oil or fuel filter to examine the paper element for debris. Never hacksaw one open, since sawing puts more debris in the filter.*

*This is what an oil filter paper element looks like when it has been removed from the filter can and cut from the base plate. Look carefully between the folds for harmful debris.*

*Mount a dial indicator on the end of the crankshaft, then gently pry the crank forward, zero the indicator, then push it back to get the total end play movement.*

and an axle may be coming out. If one of these O-rings gets sucked up into the oil pump, it will almost certainly jam the pump, in which case you will lose oil pressure and hence an engine.

These are just some of the many things that can happen to an engine. The plan is to be careful, take time to inspect filters and the engine, especially in the beginning and later during the testing.

## The Engine

If you are going to do extensive dyno testing, you may want a dedicated engine for this purpose. Top teams and engine development shops have dedicated engines called "Dyno Mules" or "Dyno Queens," which are engines that rarely, if ever, see a car. These engines are fully instrumented and set up to replicate the vehicle engine in all ways with the added capability for rapid changes and easy adjustability. Quite

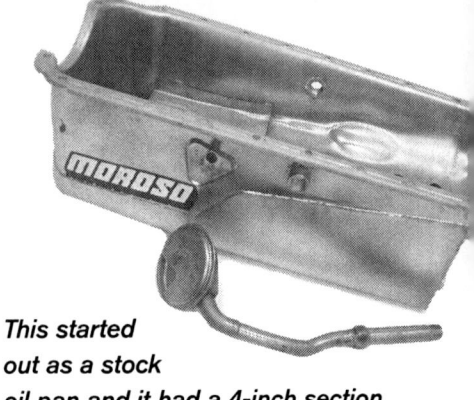

*This started out as a stock oil pan and it had a 4-inch section welded it to lower the oil level far below the crankshaft and rods. Note that the pickup tube was extended an equal amount.*

often they have adjustable cam gears that allow cam and cam centerline changes to be performed in minutes rather than hours.

They often have deep-sump dyno oil pans designed to remove all windage considerations, easily adjustable header systems, and remote spark timing adjustment. Once the development process is completed, a car engine is built and the concept engine is tested in the car under race conditions. Sometimes the car test will uncover the need for additional dyno testing, such as cooling-system development, which needs to be addressed before the overall dyno development project is complete.

Engine selection is very important. If you are not using the engine that you plan to race, then take care in designing or choosing a dyno engine as your "mule." In order to make a good test engine, it should have very close to the same specifications as the engine you want to race. Displacement, bore and stroke, rod length, compression ratio, combustion chamber shape, head flow capability, and choices such as aluminum heads are important factors. In the hunt for horsepower, as you improve your output, it gets progressively harder and more expensive to make

## GOALS AND OBJECTIVES

*This slip-on collector along with short primary tube extensions allow incremental length changes to the primaries for tuning. Collectors can be extended by a similar method.*

*This connection between both banks is called an 'H' pipe and has proven to be quite a good tuning aid to even out and smooth the shape of the torque curve.*

*These weld-on bungs allow you to outfit your headers for pressure taps as well as $O_2$ sensors. Most header manufacturers have the $O_2$ sensor fittings. Hardware stores have steel pipe fittings.*

incremental gains. Somebody just starting a testing program with a street-driven car can easily expect to find some fairly large percentage gains. On the other hand, NASCAR teams often win races with a .2% torque advantage over their nearest competitor.

If you build a dyno mule, make sure that you equip it with a deep pan, adjustable timing gear, and several sets of headers for dyno tuning. The headers should be adjustable in both primary and secondary length (for a Tri-Y design) and be able to take different collectors and "H" pipes and vehicle exhaust systems including mufflers if they are required. The headers should have bungs for thermocouples as well as $O_2$ bungs if you are going to measure Air / Fuel ratio or if you have $O_2$ sensors in your engine control system. Bungs for backpressure testing are important if you plan to do any exhaust system development.

### Break-in

If the engine is new or freshly rebuilt, you should plan on a break-in period. Bypassing a break-in could save some time in the short run but cause you to miss a performance gain in the long run. As a new engine runs, the piston rings wear in and lap themselves to the bore surface, creating a better seal between the combustion gases and the crankcase. Skipping the break-in could result in engine damage such as scuffed pistons or rings. A similar but smaller improvement in sealing occurs as the valves run in. After a relatively short period, the overall engine sealing is at its performance peak and should operate in this state during its useful life.

As the engine approaches the end of its intended life cycle, the rings, cylinder bores, valves and valve seats fall victim to accumulated wear, and their performance rapidly diminishes until the engine won't make rated power or torque. If you decide to test with either a fresh engine that hasn't been broken in or a worn-out engine, you will produce questionable results. For example, if you develop the fuel and spark curve for a worn engine and apply this tuneup to a fresh engine, it may run lean and possibly burn a piston because the fresh engine will pump more air. Always test and tune on a race-worthy engine that is healthy. Specific information on how to run a break-in cycle is detailed in the appendix. Obviously, a Top Fuel engine, or a Pro Stock drag race engine will not be a candidate for a break-in, but any endurance and lower-class drag racing engine will benefit from this.

### Spark Plugs

Because performance dyno testing typically takes an engine to the edges of the operating envelope, the spark plug requirements are usually different from those used in a vehicle. Always remember to use colder spark plugs for your test engine until you are satisfied that the spark plug heat range is correct. All of the spark plug manufacturers offer brochures and learning aids to enable the novice tuner to stay in a safe area. If a spark plug runs too hot, you run the risk of pre-ignition. On the other hand, if the plug runs too cold, you may fail to fire the mixture and foul the plug. A cylinder that is not firing will soon become loaded with fuel and "wash" the lubricant off the walls, often

DYNO TESTING AND TUNING

# CHAPTER 4

*This is a variety of gapping tools used to measure the spark plug gap as well as adjust it.*

*The planning time before the dyno session is important. It is more time effective and more cost effective to go to the dyno with a plan so that everyone is on the same page. No panics. Methodical work toward a goal. These turbo-boosted bikes can regularly make over 500 Hp at the tire patch and still live.*

*This is an R gap plug, which requires a special tool to set the gap. These plugs are used in applications where additional clearance is needed as well as a very cold plug. Supercharged engines running nitromethane often use this type of plug.*

*This is a typical side gap spark plug. Make sure that you remember to put plugs at least one range cooler in your engine before doing any extended WOT testing on the dyno. On the street and on most race tracks, you run out of talent or race track before you can hurt your engine with spark plugs. Marine use and dyno use as well as places like Daytona and Talledega are the exception to this.*

resulting in a scuffed piston and worn rings

Get in the habit of looking at the plugs to recognize any signs of distress before they become a major issue. As long as you "sneak up" on fuel, air, and spark, you will be able to catch impending disaster before it becomes a reality. If you get carried away or hurried, you may for example find yourself adding 2 to 3 degrees of spark in an engine with a sensitive chamber. Your first clue that you have stepped out of bounds will be a distinct loss of power. Investigation may reveal a broken top ring land and/or scuffed piston, or sagged piston top Never keep testing when you have a sudden unexplained loss of power. As you progress through your testing, re-baseline your engine by returning to the "A" configuration that we discussed in the ABA testing method description.

## Spark Plug Boots

Spark plug wires and boots all too often become a casualty of dyno work. Because the engine is stationary and no cooling breeze is flowing over the engine from the vehicle motion, the spark plug boots and wires often burn or melt. Once this happens, the spark is grounded and a misfire will result. There are a number of solutions such as high-temperature sleeves and socks in addition to wire looms designed to keep the wires away from all the high temperature areas. Find a solution that works for you, but never test with a dead or non-firing cylinder.

GOALS AND OBJECTIVES

## Planning a Dyno Test

*Go with a plan, because wishes won't work when it comes to testing.*

Before we get into the specifics of goals and objectives, be aware of one thing when you are renting a testing facility or service. You are the customer! Because you are going to be paying for the test, try and get the most out of the time and dollars expended.

Talk with the test facility coordinator before you go to the test session. Find out what parts they expect you to bring to the test session. Bellhousing? Headers? Your own shop rags or paper towels? Know before you go. If you have a flat-tappet camshaft in the engine, what is recommended for a break-in procedure? Soft springs need to be changed after break-in! Different rocker ratios after break-in? Remember that you also might be required to re-torque the heads after the break-in.

Make a list of your tuning objectives. The list helps make up the plan. Don't go into a dyno test session with three carburetors, five manifolds, three camshafts, and two separate ignition systems and expect to get it all done in one day on the dyno. Prepare the parts and make sure the engine is capable of accommodating the new or upgraded parts. Have the support equipment, parts, and spares ready to take to your test session. Make sure you have the proper fuel and that the fuel you have is fresh. Be realistic and be methodical. Be very rigid about keeping notes and work at creating good documentation of your testing experiences. This process alone (if done well) will help move your testing program forward.

## Goals and Objectives Summary

Part of the plan should outline what you want to test and what specific parts you want to test. Sequences are important so that you can get the best bang for your buck. Most testing services start charging once you and your engine or chassis are on site.

If you require a particular fuel, you need enough for the tests or you will be paying for down time while waiting on more fuel. The same goes for specific lubricants. If you intend to break in the camshaft and then change oil, as is the common practice, then you need to have your brand with you. If you don't, you are still on the test facility's clock while someone chases the things that you forgot to bring.

Plan to keep the water temperature, the oil temperature, and the A/F ratio as controlled as possible. If testing on a chassis dyno, the temperature of the bearings on the dyno, the temperature of the transmission, and the temperature of the drive axle should be controlled as much as possible. Even the inflation pressure and the temperature of the drive tires are important variables to control if dependable results are the goal.

Put in some time creating a plan that will help you keep focused on the real target of the testing: to gain more useful data to convert to meaningful information. Test first and analyze later.

*The ignition timing is a very critical part of engine tuning. Each engine will have a "sweet spot" that is preferred relative to its use of fuel and combustion characteristics. The timing light being used in this photo is not the best one to use. The "spark search" method of timing is time consuming but is worthwhile. The text covers how to establish MBT in Chapter 7.*

DYNO TESTING AND TUNING

# CHAPTER 5

# LET'S TEST

## Get Serious

Dyno testing should be treated as an exact science, so some preparation must precede any attempt to fire the engine, especially for the first time on a brand new engine, or for the first time on a particular day when everything has previously been completely shut down after testing.

There are four areas in which you should pay particular attention: The test plan, the test cell, the dyno and, of course, the engine. In the case of a chassis dyno, the vehicle must also be included. Since there are numerous items, all of which are important, most dyno operators make a checklist for each category or one major list.

There is a sample checklist in the appendix that can serve as a template for your list. Let's review the items and talk about their importance. As with all activities, safety is the most important area and should be addressed first.

Let's begin with a test cell checklist:

### Fire

Fire can be deadly as well as devastating. Make sure that you have the proper fire extinguishers in sufficient quantity to put out any fire that you may encounter. The preferred fire extinguisher to use is an ABC type; however, if you have flammable metals on hand such as magnesium, be sure to use a type D extinguisher. Keep both types on hand for safety. Prior to getting started, review where the fire extinguishers are and make sure they all have current inspections. If you are renting time in a cell, make sure you know where the closest extinguisher is, just in case you have to find it in a hurry. If a fire should occur in the cell, immediately turn off the fans to cut off the supply of fresh air and oxygen. Once the fire is fully extinguished, you can turn on the fans and remove any remaining smoke.

If you have a fire, call 911 as soon as possible. Get everybody to a safe area, then shut off the fuel. Having a fuel shutoff outside the test

*Make sure you know where these are located before you need them! A type ABC is the best bet for extinguishing anything outside of flammable metal. Magnesium, a flammable metal, would require a type D.*

52  DYNO TESTING AND TUNING

# LET'S TEST

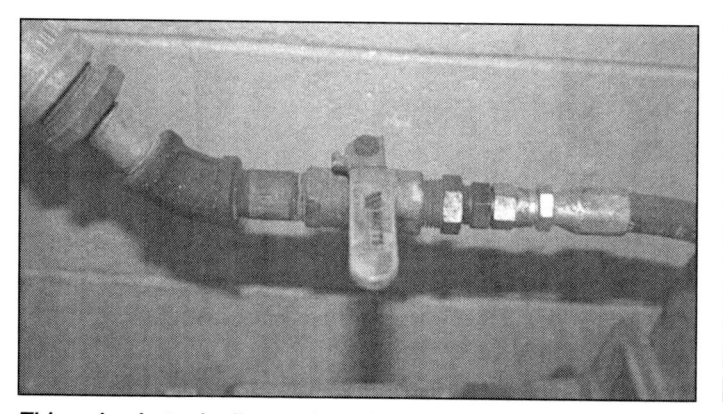

*This valve is typically used to shut off the fuel entering the test cell. Whenever the dyno is not running for a period of time or shut down at night, or whenever the engine fuel system is disconnected, make sure this valve is shut.*

*This valve is designed to close automatically if the fusible link gets hot. In a fire, this valve is designed to close when the heat reaches it. Make sure your room has one of these.*

area really pays big dividends here. Nobody wants to charge into a room filled with smoke and fire to look for a shutoff valve. Remember: until you can remove the fuel, air, or ignition (heat in this case), the fire will continue. To be effective, review these steps to familiarize yourself with the location of fire extinguishers and fuel shutoff valves, *before* a fire occurs. Dyno testing can be inherently dangerous since gasoline, heat, sparks and air can all come together to create an unplanned fire.

## Safety Is Our Primary Goal

In all of our testing, our primary focus should be on performing a safe test. A test that destroys an engine or causes damage is dangerous and costly. Hence we must be extremely careful at all times to ensure that we are following all of the safety rules and precautions as well as not taking any unnecessary risks.

### General Cautions for Chassis Dynamometer Testing

Potential problems from tire destruction and flying debris from

*This non-pressurized cooling tower is valuable when you want to run an engine with modified cylinder heads. This system does not build pressure and merely exchanges the hot water for cool water.*

driveshafts and other whirling things should be carefully addressed and planned for before a problem happens. Caution is the standard to apply when engaging in any kind of dynamometer testing or racing process.

Safety in chassis dynamometer applications is a very serious issue. If a tire disintegrates or a driveshaft exits the vehicle, there might be a

*This liquid-to-liquid heat exchanger uses pressurized recirculating coolant just like the engine in a vehicle. Be sure to use a pressurized system for any final calibration work.*

real problem with various shrapnel in the test area. A very careful inspection of the vehicle should be done, and it is certainly between the owner of the vehicle and the owner of the dynamometer facility as far as warnings and responsibilities. However, it is important for us to make very clear that this can be dangerous stuff, and

# CHAPTER 5

# Safety Limits

New dyno operators often confess to becoming overwhelmed by the sheer amount of data blinking and cascading madly down the computer screen during a run, while fearing that their prized engine may be roaring away headed toward certain destruction. To the uninitiated, it can be an awe-inspiring experience. Fighter pilots, who certainly have an even greater set of data inputs and consequences to deal with, have named the massive data overload a "helmet fire." Today, with our advanced data-gathering technology, we can bombard the brain with more simultaneous data inputs than it can possibly manage.

What should we do? How do we protect ourselves, our engine, and the dynamometer equipment while conducting a test that gathers data and hopefully yields the meaningful answers to our questions? Start by carefully setting the internal safety limits so that the same system that can shoot out streams of data can also keep a watchful eye on the results, and when they stray out of bounds, take the appropriate action to protect us and our engine in a split second.

For example, set the range of acceptable RPM to an upper and lower limit. This will protect the engine should something fail in the drivetrain, like the dyno input shaft. A computer-controlled safety-limit system simultaneously shuts off the ignition and fuel and then applies full load to quickly stop the engine. It can head off trouble faster than any operator.

In this case, we start the safety limit selection process by choosing the RPM range for the test, then designating the action we want to take should the range be exceeded. In this case, we want to shut the engine down and print a record on the screen telling why the engine was shut down. This note serves as notification to the operator, who might not be present during the event. In the case of a less extreme event, such as rising coolant temperature, you may elect to sound an alarm on the console, print a warning, and continue running since rising temperature happens at a much slower pace than a runaway engine. This warning alarm might allow the operator to increase the cooling or reduce the load to scrub off some heat but not lose the test by stopping in the middle.

Modern dynos allow the user to choose safety limits for virtually the entire range of engine operating functions. By merely selecting them and then designating an appropriate action, we can protect ourselves and our engine, providing we engage them prior to the start of a test.

Make sure you turn the limits on or engage them before starting any test. If you carefully select the limits but fail to engage them, they are just along for the ride. Think of this as failing to wear your seat belts in your car. The only time we should disengage the safety limits is possibly when we are trying to fire a totally new engine. If it is slow getting oil pressure, the timer in the oil pressure shutdown mode will kill the ignition just as it has been programmed to do. It is OK to do this as long as you remember to reset the limits once the engine starts, and prior to starting any testing.

Since the initial firing of an engine is by far one of the most critical points in an engine's life, most professional engine builders will prime their engines with a pressure primer before ever firing them for the first time. This ensures that all of the internal passages are filled with oil and there will be no critical time with no oil pressure or no oil flow to the bearings.

*This tank is filled with the required amount of clean oil and used to pressurize an engine through the oil gallery before the engine is fired. Rotate the engine with the starter but do not fire it as the oil is being fed to it.*

careful inspection of the tie-downs and the vehicle itself are absolutely imperative in order to try to keep safety at the forefront. Just having floorsweep handy is not addressing the potential problems with adequate caution.

One of the most important issues might be driveshaft failures and containment on the chassis dyno applications. If the dyno is below ground, the driveshaft parts might exit the vehicle and have only the space between the bottom of the vehicle and the floor to ricochet around. However, if the vehicle and dyno are above floor level, the exiting parts might have an easier path of potential destruction. Some allocation should be done for absorbing the potential energy of broken parts exiting the vehicle. Some type of protective barrier should be used between the vehicle and bystanders or observers.

*Caveats for Engine Dynamometer Testing*

Testing on an engine dynamometer can be just as dangerous as on a chassis dyno, but the areas of focus are a bit different. If the dyno that you are to test on uses a driveshaft, be very careful around the things that spin at high speed. The driveshaft should be covered with a guard in case of failure so that the shaft pieces are contained.

The same is to be said of the bellhousing area. Make sure that the flywheel and dyno drive coupling are tightened in place and are in good condition.

Also be aware of the potential for problems concerning the balancer on the front of the engine, or any mechanical blower drive belting. Anything that can go wrong normally does so at the wrong time, so be careful and fully aware that safety is critical around machinery of any sort.

Be particularly aware of the airflow through the room so that if you are in the cell and checking ignition timing, etc., you do not get exposed to carbon monoxide any more than necessary. Clip-on personal CO monitors are not terribly expensive for the safety warning they provide, so be aware of them as a good safety tool.

## Engine Cooling Systems

Dyno engine-cooling systems generally fall into two types: pressurized and non-pressurized systems. Both systems have advantages and disadvantages.

## Pressurized System

Pressurized cooling systems operate as they do in the vehicle, and in some cases allow you to employ the vehicle system in its entirety. By using the complete vehicle system, the final dyno tuning will be that much closer to what is required in the vehicle, thus allowing more efficient use of valuable track time for

*Before testing any engine, it is highly recommended that a high-performance SEMA-rated safety bellhousing be used to prevent flying debris in the event of a drivetrain failure.*

additional areas of tuning. Most engines run with pressurized cooling systems, which maintain coolant in sufficient quantities around the combustion chamber to prevent formation of steam pockets that inhibit proper cooling and result in detonation. Unless you race a vehicle with no cooling system (like a dragster), the sooner you test with a pressurized cooling system, the sooner you will get close to your final fuel, air, and spark map. Spending too much time early in a development program without using a pressurized cooling system means having to repeat all of the testing again with the pressurized system. If a pressurized system is required, a heat exchanger is typically used to transfer the heat to the dyno water. The heat exchanger must also be used if anything other than water is used as a coolant in the engine. The heat exchanger acts as an engine-coolant-to-dyno-water radiator. The coolant in the engine circulates under pressure throughout the system as it does in the vehicle. Instead of exchanging the heat with outside air like a traditional car radiator, the heat exchanger transfers the heat to the cool dyno water supplied to the dyno cell.

## Non-Pressurized

Non-pressurized cooling systems use the dyno water feed pumps to supply cool water to be circulated throughout the engine under very low pressure. A cooling tower acts as a reservoir of cool water to be exchanged for hot water coming out of the engine. The flow from the dyno-feed water system is controlled by a mechanical valve relying on a mechanical thermostat. This thermostat modulates the correct

# CHAPTER 5

*This shows a DTS dyno, which uses a separate driveshaft. Be sure to enclose the driveshaft, adaptors, u-joints and connections before firing the engine.*

*This Mustang is about to be tuned on the dyno in order to get the power curve in line with the chassis capability. This kind of chassis dyno does not use any kind of gears or transmissions, but uses an eddy current absorber driven at roll speed. The unit is capable of 225 MPH and 2,400 Hp! Photo courtesy Dynamic Test Systems*

amount of incoming water to maintain the selected engine cooling system temperature. This valve is often referred to as the foot valve or "Johnson" valve. Non-pressurized systems are valuable for engines that have been highly modified and have less than optimum cooling-system integrity. For example, cylinder head modifications often break through the existing port walls, and the resultant holes are repaired with various patching methods such as fiberglass or epoxy glue. These repairs will be replaced by virgin metal in a new casting if the proposed modification works, but first the modification must be validated. The method here is to make some power runs with very low pressure in the cooling system to avoid filling the engine internals with water leaking from the cooling jackets.

Most sharp dyno operators will be extremely careful when trying to run a prototype set of heads where water may leak into the combustion chamber. The recommended procedure is to remove all of the spark plugs prior to every run and gently rotate the engine first by *hand*, and then with the starter to ensure that no water is in the cylinders. If water is in the cylinder, the room gets sprayed, but a rod or cylinder wall is saved. The trick is to rotate the crank by hand for several revolutions prior to turning the ignition on just to ensure that it is not going to lock up. These engines with fragile cooling systems should be completely drained before going to lunch or before going home at night.

Also remember to drain all engines in winter months in case the building loses heat and the water in the cooling system freezes during the night or weekend.

Let's look at the dyno next.

## Engine Mounting

Mounting the engine on the dyno is critical. There are two types of mountings on engine dynos that we will consider. The first mounting is the traditional method where the engine is held stationary in at least three points, and typically four, on a bedplate while the engine's crankshaft is connected to the dyno or absorber by a traditional driveshaft. The dyno is typically mounted securely to the same bedplate as the engine. The engine torque reaction is typically taken in the same locations on the block as it is in the vehicle.

The second method of mounting involves bolting an absorber to the engine bellhousing and taking the reaction torque through the bellhousing. In this configuration, the weight of the engine block is merely supported in the front, and the absorber is typically hung from the dyno cart. Since all of the torque transfers through the bellhousing to the absorber, the installer must be sure to use all of the correct bellhousing bolts and dowel pins when using the bellhousing to transfer the torque.

Regardless of which type of system you use, there are several areas of importance. Always make sure that the carburetor mounting pad is level side to side and front to rear. If you are using a driveshaft, make sure there are at least 2 degrees of angularity between the shaft and engine or dynamometer at each universal joint (U-joint); otherwise, the u-joints will fail prematurely since they will not actively rotate the needle bearings. By all means make sure you have a very robust driveshaft guard

56  DYNO TESTING AND TUNING

system in place that not only covers the driveshaft but also extends well past the universal joints. This is as important as a driveshaft loop in a car. The rollers and parts from an exploding U-joint or driveshaft can be lethal.

When you are using a clutch or drive plate to transmit the torque from the flywheel to the dyno input shaft, there are several important measurements to take. Prior to mounting the clutch or drive plate, you should check the engagement of the dyno input shaft into the crank pilot bearing hole. Aside from the fit, which should be free but without excessive clearance, check the spline location on the shaft relative to the spline location on the clutch disc or drive plate. You should ensure that you have used the entire spline in the drive disc without either bottoming the spline or pilot bearing. Once this measurement is taken, mount the bellhousing and measure from the bellhousing face to the face of the input shaft hub. Adjust the depth of the input spline to ensure that you are using all of the available spline. Avoid bottoming on the splines or pilot bearing, which would create an axial preload on the thrust surface of the crank when the engine-flywheel, clutch disc, and bellhousing are all assembled and the engine is mounted on the dyno.

When the engine mounting is completed, install a dial indicator on the front of the crankshaft and make sure that you are able to move the crankshaft fore and aft by the full amount of end play built into the engine. Make sure that this check is made before ever firing the engine! If you cannot move the crank back and forth, this means the driveline is loading the crankshaft axially and you are setting yourself up for a thrust-bearing failure in the engine. Typically, the input shaft is hitting the pilot bearing or the crankshaft and forcing the crankshaft into the rear of the thrust bearing. Not having enough spline engagement is just as bad, since all of the load will be carried by a small length of clutch and input shaft splines. The spline will typically shear when overloaded. When the shaft breaks, or the splines shear, the engine instantly over-revs. This situation illustrates why you always want to make sure that you have set and engaged your safety limits prior to making a run.

## Throttle Control

Whether you use a cable or a rod, make sure that the throttle and linkage has free movement and does not contact any other items during its full range of motion. Just like a vehicle, we should check for a potential over-center condition that would prevent the throttle from closing and essentially hold the engine at full throttle until it either blew up or was shut down by lack of ignition or lack of fuel. Make sure that accessories such as the air cleaner, wiring, thermocouple leads, or hoses do not contact the throttle linkage throughout its range of travel. Most important, verify that you are getting full throttle. When the throttle is fully advanced at the console, you want the throttle blades to be fully open.

## Air Flow Meters

Make sure these meters are correctly installed and properly calibrated. Several of the critical performance ratios such as air/fuel ratio, brake specific air consumption (BSAC), and volumetric efficiency (VE) rely on knowing how much air is going through the engine. Make sure you maintain the air flow meters to ensure not only their accuracy but also their air flow capability. Plugged or bent vanes will redirect the air, causing improper air distribution in the manifold or carburetor. If you tune the carburetor with an airflow meter that is damaged, you will

*Looking through the top of the air flow meter, all of the fan blades are in place and the honeycomb air straightener is open. If these features are not intact, don't plan on accurate results. Broken or missing blades will cause imbalance and inaccurate readings.*

*Make sure the air flow meter is properly mounted and supported. Also make sure the thermister (temperature sender) is in place and calibrated as well.*

run a risk of either tuning around this deficiency or creating a flaw in the airflow that will cause the carburetor to malfunction somewhere during the run. Broken or missing flow meter fan blades will cause vibration in the flow meter leading to inaccuracy. Also, if you use an air cleaner on the engine in the vehicle, it is *very important* that you remember to install it prior to completing your tuning session. Quite often, an air cleaner will affect the air flow and distribution, causing the fuel curve to change. See Chapter 9 for information on calibrating the flow meters.

*These bungs can be welded onto virtually any place where you need them to enable you to mount a thermocouple, O₂ sensor or pressure tap.*

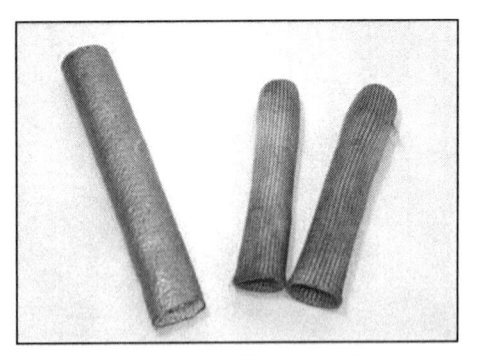

*Since there is little if any underhood air moving around during a dyno test, spark plug boots are more likely to burn or melt than when they are in a car. Use glass fiber or Kevlar socks to gain some safety margin.*

### Fluids

Whatever your engine pumps in the vehicle, you want it to pump in the test. If those fluids are oil, coolant, power steering fluid, and gasoline, remember to turn each system on, check fluid levels, and ensure adequate and correct levels prior to testing. That may be the time to calibrate the dipstick on a new engine with a new oil pan that has never been used before. It is important to have the correct oil level in the pan, and also important to be able to check it accurately. Additionally, the engine should be carefully filled with oil and pre-lubed in a manner to ensure that when the engine fires you have oil pressure immediately instead of waiting until the oil pump purges the air from the filter and oil galleries of a fresh engine. Once the engine has started and run at low speed briefly (no more than 1 to 2 minutes), you should shut the engine down and recheck the fluids to ensure that they are still at the proper levels with no leaks.

Filling the coolant is especially tricky in some engines. These engines

## Exhaust Backpressure

While testing exhaust systems, it is important to measure and control exhaust backpressure. Traditional thinking says that backpressure is bad, but this is not necessarily so. We all know too much backpressure is not good, but in many cases, some backpressure is very effective. Backpressure benefits exhaust-gas scavenging by creating a negative pressure wave that travels back through the exhaust system to the cylinder, where it helps draw out exhaust gases and draw in the fresh air-fuel charge. Camshafts and valvetrains are often developed for engines that have to use limited camshafts (modest lift and duration). If you remove the backpressure by using a low- or no-backpressure system, you will actually lose horsepower. In order not to get trapped in this phenomenon, make sure that you measure and record your backpressure for each set of changes you make.

The easiest way to measure backpressure is to weld or drill and tap a steel fitting into the headers, exhaust manifold, or exhaust pipe ahead of the muffler and tailpipe. Run 10 feet of brake line steel tubing away from the fitting on the exhaust system before going to a traditional rubber flex hose to avoid having the heat ruin the hose or pressure gauge. If you have a spare pressure channel in your data acquisition system, use a pressure transducer and arrange the reading to be shown as a function of the RPM. If you don't have digital capability, you can use a simple analog pressure gauge mounted in the dyno room window and take the readings manually.

If you use an "H" pipe (a pipe connecting both banks of a vee engine's dual exhaust system), make sure to take the pressure both in the H pipe itself and before it. H pipes are quite effective and have become a common tuning tool in all types of engine combinations. They serve to reduce the peaks and valleys in the torque curve, making the power curve more predictable and smoother while raising it.

tend to have hidden pockets of air that prevent the water passages in the engine from filling completely. Once the engine starts circulating coolant, either they "burp" themselves or, in some cases, the trapped air heats up, expands, and literally blocks the coolant from entering some areas of the engine. Be especially careful when you change heads and use different head gaskets. Head gaskets have many small holes in them, which serve to vent the steam and allow coolant to displace the steam. These holes are carefully engineered to ensure the correct coolant flow distribution, which ensures equal cylinder cooling. If a combustion chamber is surrounded by steam, it will not cool properly and detonation will occur. It pays to look inside of each cylinder head casting to see if any casting flash or core sand may be blocking the coolant path. A few top engine builders actually port the individual coolant passages to ensure that they have equal coolant distribution with no blockages.

### Exhaust System

Make sure you have installed all of the fasteners and correctly installed all of the exhaust system components. Make sure all of the heat shields are in place and no loose or stray items such as wiring harnesses or hoses can come in contact with the hot exhaust pipes. Exhaust systems run hotter on the dyno than in the vehicle because there is virtually no air stream cooling since the dyno is standing still. Some chassis dynos have large fans available for this purpose. Spark plug wires, fuel lines, oil lines, and vibration dampers are especially vulnerable to excess heat. Some companies make special fabric socks or metal shields to protect the plug wires during the times of high heat. Placing fans with explosion-proof electric motors in the dyno room aimed at things like spark plug wires may help matters immensely.

The lambda or $O_2$ sensor bungs and thermocouple bungs will have to be added to your exhaust system if you plan to get accurate temperatures and fuel air readings.

Make sure that you have an adjustable set of dyno headers, which will allow you to make small changes in the primaries, secondaries, collectors, or tailpipe length. If you run mufflers or a long tailpipe, make sure you have bungs correctly placed to take backpressure readings

### Belts and Coolant Hoses

The engine accessories are typically driven by a belt or series of belts. In order for the accessories to function properly, these belts must be correctly aligned and properly tensioned. Be sure to check the speed of your accessories, because quite often the modifications we make increase the upper RPM limits, and unless you change the drive pulley ratios to reduce the accessory speed, the accessories will see this same proportional increase in speed. You should carefully recalculate these accessory speeds to ensure that you are not over-speeding these components and ruining them. As a general rule, never turn the water pump any faster than it does in its production application to avoid cavitation and loss of flow. If the water pump cavitates, it not only inhibits moving coolant through the engine, but the impeller usually suffers some damage. The alternator and power steering pump are also speed limited.

Coolant and fuel hose selection is extremely important. Not only must these hoses hold the pressure without leaking, but they must not restrict the flow. They must be resistant to whatever chemicals they encounter from either the inside or the outside. The hose must be compatible with the fittings or pipe it is joined to. The internal transitions should be smooth so flow is not restricted and remains streamlined throughout its journey. Specific hoses are designed to be used as coolant hoses and have many features such as embedded reinforcing wire to prevent the hose from sucking shut under lowered pressure like a soda straw in a thick milkshake. Always try to use molded hose since it has a constant section throughout the entire length of the hose to prevent it from necking down and causing a flow restriction. Be sure to use hose in your fuel system that is chemically compatible with your fuel requirements and whose pressure limits exceed your fuel system's maximum pressures by a reasonable margin for safety.

### Oil Pans

Special dyno-only wet sump oil pans are often used for oiling studies and windage testing. These absurdly deep dyno pans would never fit in a vehicle but they serve an important function on the dyno. The deep pans typically position the engine oil 6–8 inches below the crankshaft counterweights, which allows the crankshaft to run in relatively clean air free of oil spray. Decreasing the torque resistance from the drag associated with running the crankshaft through the oil is like finding free horsepower. Crankshaft windage tray and oil pan design allow the engine to use this

# CHAPTER 5

free horsepower. If the oil droplets returning to the crankcase fall on the spinning crankshaft, it slows down the crankshaft and robs power from the engine. If the crankshaft actually runs in oil like a lawnmower engine with a dipper rod, it will rob an incredible amount of horsepower while frothing and heating the oil.

The crankshaft and its associated parts find themselves wrapped in a film of oil whenever the oiling system does not properly manage the return oil flow, or, when the G forces cause the oil to leave the oil pan and submerge part of the crank in an oil bath. The G loads imparted to the oil by violent vehicle maneuvers cause the oil to stack up and wrap itself around the crankshaft more often than we care to admit. If you ever think that this force is insignificant, get a friend with a fast drag boat to take you for a ride across the river. At top speed reach over the side and stick your finger in the water. Now calculate the velocity of a rod nut on a crank that is spinning at 9000 RPM. Hint: the answer is over 94 mph for a small-block engine. Now imagine the power loss from dragging 16 rod nuts through the oil with every revolution! As an experiment, build a deep oil pan and make a series of runs to establish a baseline, then switch pans to your "race" pan, fill with oil to the correct level and repeat. Chances are you will be unhappy with the performance of your pan. Now get to work and build an oil pan that doesn't rob power.

## Dry Sump Oiling Systems

These systems use a shallow oil pan and a multistage oil pump, which is typically comprised of one pressure section and a series of suction sections. The suction sections keep the oil pan and engine scavenged with very little oil remaining in the pan or sump itself, hence the name "dry sump." The suction sections deliver the mixture of oil and air from the pan through a coarse screen filter back to a remote tank where the oil is stored. The oil then is drawn from the tank and through the pressure section where it is pressurized and passed through a traditional paper oil filter before entering the oil galleries of the engine where it lubricates the bearings and other parts. Once this is accomplished, the oil returns to the pan where it starts the cycle all over again. These systems require a fairly sophisticated hose layout in order to be effective. One of the places people tend to make a mistake is in sizing the hoses leading from the oil pan through the oil pump and to the oil tank. Because these hoses carry far more air than oil, it is important to make them much larger and have more of them in order to allow this mixture of oil and air to be returned to the tank where the air is removed before it is returned to the engine. This process, called de-aeration, is critical; otherwise, the oil film strength becomes compromised, looks like root beer fizz, and as legendary engineer and father of the 426 engine, Tom Hoover, once said, "Aaa-Haa! Once again we have performed yet another test in our never-ending quest to perfect the Air Bearing." Make

*This is a classic deep wet-sump dyno oil pan. It allows you to see what the engine will produce by getting the oil away from the crankshaft and eliminating windage.*

*Play with the section lengths and pump speed to minimize the horsepower loss. Remember, any additional oil delivery in excess of the true requirements just makes heat and takes power.*

*This dry sump pan incorporates two pickups to allow oil volume to be kept to a minimum in the pan. Be sure to incorporate screen filters in the pan to keep engine debris out of the pump in the event of an engine failure. A non-critical failure such as a pop rivet head can jam an oil pump and cause the belt to break, ending your day.*

DYNO TESTING AND TUNING

# LET'S TEST

fully controlled baseline runs, all at the same engine oil temperature, and then switch to the proposed-car dry sump system. In almost all cases, the dry-sump system will be a power loss compared to the dyno deep pan wet-sump system. The loss occurs because of the extra power required to drive the additional dry sump pump stages that are used to empty the pan and deliver the oil to the oil tank.

A good dry sump will probably be a significant gain over a typical wet-sump car pan, however, since the "wet pan" has a significant amount of windage losses. The deep wet-sump dyno pan, while a great development tool, is impractical since it could never be run in a vehicle because of ground-clearance requirements.

In reality, the vehicle may speed up when the dry sump is used—through better handling due to a lower center of gravity and less frontal area—compared to a wet sump. The object here is to improve the dry sump so it becomes less of a power loss and speed up the vehicle even more. Slowing down the pump, eliminating stages, or shortening them can reduce the pump power requirement. Remember, in theory all an engine needs is one more drop of oil at 1 psi more than required at each point on the oil-demand curve. Anything after that is just going to be sent back through the relief valve to the oil pan as excess.

If you are running around the race track with 90 psi of oil pressure and spinning five suction stages in a dry sump, chances are you are heating the oil and wasting valuable horsepower that could otherwise be put to the ground.

You should have a way of cooling the engine oil as well as accommodating an auxiliary oil filter. This will mean plumbing the engine block to accept external fittings to route the oil to and from the oil filter and oil cooler. Most builders like to use a screen filter in addition to the paper filter to enable them to quickly and inexpensively look at the debris coming out of the oil pan through the oil pump.

Spend time analyzing the debris, since it will give great clues to how the engine is faring internally. Sudden high concentrations of cast iron picked up on a magnet may indicate

*This tank is handy for running in the dyno room. If you are renting dyno time, make sure the tank and lines are thoroughly cleaned before use.*

sure you review the recommended layout and hose sizing for your dry-sump system with your pump and system manufacturer.

Engine dyno testing is an excellent way to evaluate oil pan designs. Most engine builders go to a dry sump in order to allow the engine to be run closer to the ground. As the flywheels and clutches become smaller, the rod bolts become the limiting factor to lowering the engine in the chassis. If the rods are the lowest point in the engine, there is no room for a traditional oil pickup, so a dry sump becomes a necessity. To develop a dry-sump oiling system, run the engine as a traditional wet-sump engine with only a single-stage pressure pump that draws oil from the bottom of the deep (8–10 inches overall) dyno pan and delivers it to the engine in the traditional way through a filter and then to the oil inlet to the engine. Get some care-

*Use one of these on the oil line before it enters the dry sump tank, or on a wet-sump engine in between the oil pump and the paper filter. These can be quickly taken apart to check for debris. The screens come in a variety of meshes. Never use only a screen filter. Always incorporate a paper filter to trap the 10-15 micron-sized particles just before the oil enters the engine.*

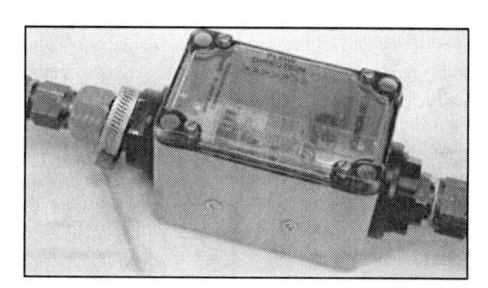

*When you start developing a dry sump system, use an in-line flow meter to monitor oil flow. Be sure to compare only runs with equal oil temperatures and pressures.*

DYNO TESTING AND TUNING

# Oil Coolers

Oil coolers become a necessity in most performance applications with perhaps the exception of marine usage, where care must sometimes be exercised to prevent the oil from running too cold. It is important to keep the oil temperature above at least 212 degrees F during normal operation to prevent water from forming and collecting in the crankcase. Sizing and selecting an oil cooler is an important part of basic engine development. There are many factors that determine the capacity of an oil cooler. Some high-performance street vehicles use relatively small oil coolers, while some off-road heavy equipment utilizes oil coolers that are huge. In high-performance vehicles, four primary factors determine the oil cooler:

How much heat do we need to lose?
How efficient is the oil cooler?
How much room is available for the oil cooler in cool high-velocity airstreams?
How much oil-flow restriction does the cooler contribute?

Don't just pick an oil cooler based on size or weight. Inquire about the flow rate and pressure drop across the cooler. Look at and compare the BTU rating and see how that rating was obtained. Understand how the cooler was rated and comparison-shop.

Unless you have a very expensive take-apart unit, do not try to clean an oil cooler. Internally, most typical oil coolers have a labyrinth of hidden passages that cannot be effectively cleaned short of taking the cooler apart. We have seen people clean, flush, blow, brush, and immerse coolers in sonic baths only to miss a piece of hidden debris. In the end you bet a $100 cooler against a $50,000 race engine. This is not a good bet! Get a new cooler, and crush the old one so you won't be tempted to reuse it. For the same reason, never buy a used oil cooler!

If you plan to race with an oil cooler, by all means, test with one. You will have to build a water-bath system large enough to submerge the cooler, since there will be no effective air stream in the dyno room. Sometimes you can immerse the oil cooler in the incoming dyno-water supply tank and, by adjusting the water flow to the bath,

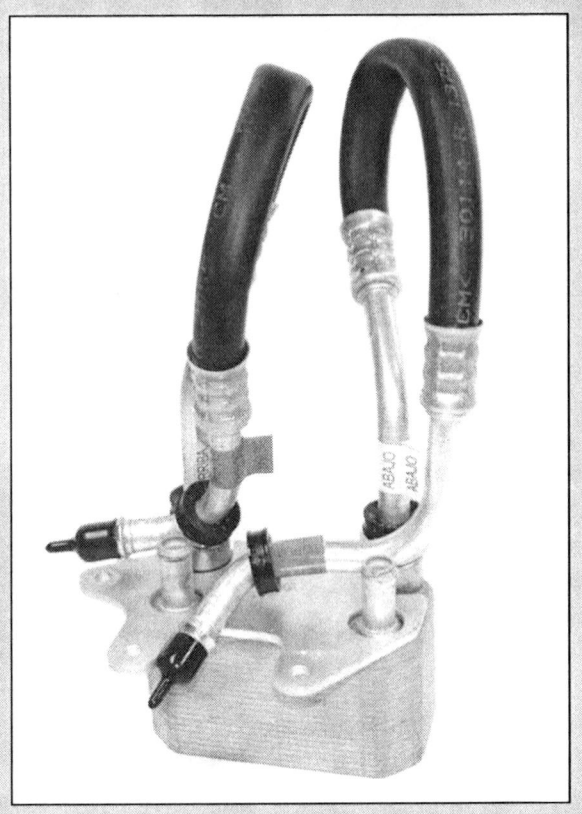

*If you run an oil cooler in your race car, always test with the vehicle cooler. Run it in an open tank of circulating cool water. This will give your oiling system the correct pressure drop that it sees in the vehicle.*

you can produce the temperature drop across the cooler found in your vehicle. This temperature drop is simply the entrance temperature minus the exit temperature and is often referred to by engineers as the thermal delta, temperature differential, or simply "Delta T." When you run instrumented vehicle tests, this is one of the parameters to measure so you have it as a reference point for dyno test and development. Testing with the cooler will replicate the pressure drop your engine oiling system has, and will let you optimize the oil flow and pressure to compensate for the flow losses through the cooler and associated fittings and lines. If you plan to run a cooler, plumb in a screen take-apart filter ahead of the cooler to trap any larger harmful particles that may try to enter the cooler.

a cam lobe wearing off; small bits or chunks of bearing material signal a bearing problem. A silvery cloud in the drained oil is quite normal for a new engine.

## Paper Oil Filters

Traditional paper-element oil filters still offer the best filtration. They routinely trap particles in the 10–15-micron range. (A micron is .00004 inch in diameter.) Under no circumstances should a screen filter be used in place of a paper filter. A paper filter can be cut for internal inspection using a filter cutter shown on page 48. A filter cutter should be used to prevent introducing any additional debris into the filter. Never use a hacksaw or cutoff wheel to open a filter, since either method will result in debris not related to the engine's operation entering the filter. A filter cutter leaves no debris since it functions like a rotary can opener or tubing cutter. Once open, the filter material can be opened by carefully using a razor knife. The paper can then be spread out like an accordion and carefully inspected for debris. No matter how carefully you clean and inspect an engine during assembly, there will usually be "surprises" in the filter. Bits of silicone sealer can be devastating if they end up in the oil-pressure relief valve. There, they can jam the relief valve causing the pressure to rise and possibly burst the filter canister. For this reason, most serious engine builders use very little silicone sealer and always use high-pressure filters.

After a traditional paper-filter canister is cut open it is no longer useable. The removable-screen filters, however, offer a quick look and the ability to be cleaned and reassembled with no additional cost. Always thoroughly clean the screen before reassembling the filter whenever they are inspected. The screens are cheap enough to allow frequent replacement if they cannot be properly cleaned.

## Flywheels and Clutches

Flywheels and clutches play a critical role in dyno testing. First and foremost, always think about safety. Never use a damaged component. All you have to do is look at the aftermath of an explosion in a dyno room and the typical ensuing fire to understand the importance of this. At the speed these components turn, the centrifugal forces are enormous. The centrifugal force combined with the torque carried at the same time make these parts highly stressed. For this and a hundred other good reasons, avoid going into a dyno cell with the engine running.

Always use an approved "explosion-proof flywheel and clutch assembly" and an appropriate, approved scattershield in any type of dyno testing. While the production flywheel and clutch may be fine for the intended output, the focus of this book is to improve on production power output. It should stand to reason that if we raise the output of the engine, we will increase the stress on all of the parts. Increased RPM plays a significant role here, since centrifugal force dramatically increases as the square of RPM, potentially causing stock flywheels and clutches to burst. While the explosion can be disastrous, the possible resulting fire can be devastating. Hot pieces of a flywheel loaded with energy can penetrate a dyno cell wall or sever a fuel line very easily. You must take all of the necessary precautions to prevent this.

## Starters

It is important to get the engine started immediately. One of the underlying causes of early engine failure is oil dilution. This phenomenon occurs when an engine is cranked too long before firing, and during this period the throttle is pumped to get fuel to the intake manifold. The engine catches, but can't seem to stay running, so the cycle is repeated. Eventually the engine stays running long enough for the timing to get set and the float bowls to be adjusted and the break-in cycle begins. Unfortunately, by now the crankcase oil is diluted with gasoline, which effectively reduces the lubricating capability of the oil. The cylinder walls may have been prematurely scuffed when they were washed down with fuel during the cranking cycles. It is just a matter of time before this engine fails.

A starting system that will rotate the world will save many engines. It stands to reason that you must also have a fully charged battery and good cables. The one caution here is an engine that might experience a hydraulic lock due to a cylinder filled with water or fuel. Even though fluid does not compress, the engine may fire, resulting in a bent rod or a broken cylinder wall.

## Fuel Pumps

Fuel flow is all-important in making power. For the best fuel-delivery performance, use the exact fuel pump on the dyno test that you intend to use when the engine is in the vehicle. You should pre-qualify the pump itself even if you have been running the engine prior to testing on the dyno. Never use the dyno fuel pump if you

# CHAPTER 5

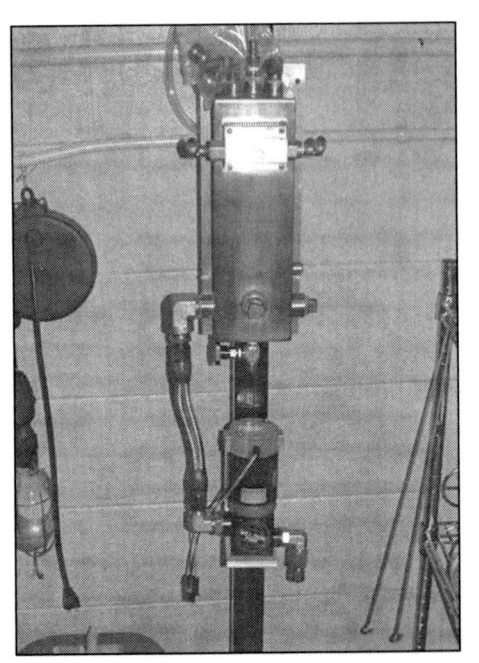

*A float can uses a float assembly from a carburetor and acts as a small reservoir for fuel. Locate this in a protected area, away from heat and flying debris.*

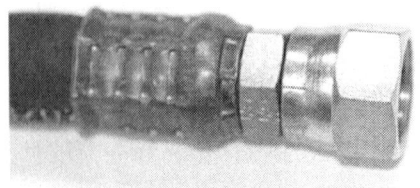

*Whenever you plumb a high pressure fuel system, make certain to use only fittings and compatible hose capable of handling the fuel and operating at the pressure you are testing. Most of the fittings will be crimped onto the line or hose permanently like this one.*

*These fittings are fine for low pressures when used in conjunction with properly sized lines and clamps. Never rely on just the barbs alone to hold the hose on the line. Make sure all hose is rated for the fuel you plan to use.*

can help it. The dyno pumps are sized to cover most applications and typically support far more horsepower than is expected. When you leave the dyno, after having made some new-found horsepower, the plan is to take all of your hard-earned gains with you. If you reinstall the engine and use the same old low-output pump in the vehicle, you may not be able to make the power you saw on the dyno. In fact, you may run lean and burn the engine down from lack of fuel. Fuel systems for fuel injection are also critical. Not only do they have higher pressure and flow requirements, but some of the systems also incorporate sophisticated regulators and return lines. When you encounter a fuel system with a fuel return, be especially careful to plumb the system through the fuel-flow turbines in such a way as to ensure that the fuel leaving the engine and returning to the tank is subtracted from the flow entering the engine; otherwise, your fuel-flow numbers along with your air/fuel ratio and your brake specific fuel consumption will be wrong.

Sometimes you may want to use a float can, which is a small-volume reservoir where the excess fuel from a fuel-injection system is returned from the engine to be rerouted back to the engine. The net flow into the can from the feed line is measured to determine the overall fuel flow. Take extra care to place the float can in a safe place away from hot areas and potential flying debris.

Another important factor to remember about high performance electric fuel pumps is their high current draw. They pump a greater volume of fuel at higher pressure; therefore they use more power, which translates into high current flow. Be sure to have an electrical system and wiring that will support the higher amperage required by these high-performance pumps. In an effort to save switches and relays inside the dyno, many people use starter relays to switch the high current running directly from the battery to the fuel pump(s). This ensures that the fuel pump will get the needed current to perform at its peak and the dyno wiring harnesses will not be burned up from high current draw. Remember, in the car, any voltage drop the fuel pump experiences results in less flow and pressure, thus changing your fuel curve.

## Fuel Hoses

Be sure to use only hose properly rated for the fuel you will be using. Also make sure that the hose is rated for the pressure you intend to run in your system. Many aftermarket fuel systems run at significantly higher pressures than their production counterparts. Never use hose clamps and low-pressure barbed fittings to make connections in a high-pressure application. You don't want a hose separating, spraying fuel across hot and electrical parts and the dyno room, and depriving your engine of fuel while it may be running at WOT. Use only approved, specially-crimped, high-pressure hardware and hose assemblies. These assemblies can typically be made at race shops and larger auto parts stores or heavy equipment dealers.

DYNO TESTING AND TUNING

# CHAPTER 6

# TUNING

Tuning is a large part of dyno testing. Next to endurance testing, tuning or calibrating, as it has been called, has easily become the second largest use of dyno time. Tuning is really all about adjusting all of the variables in the engine so they work together to fulfill your development plan's diverse goals and requirements. Let's explore how this is done.

## Tuning Basics

Tuning can best be defined as optimizing the key components of an engine within the limits bounded by principles of physics, thermodynamics, engineering, and chemistry, while recognizing the limits dictated by sanctioning bodies, durability, cost, and common sense. Creating an engine in which everything is properly sized and aligned to function in harmony is the goal.

Successful engines begin with a design or component selection scheme carefully created for peak efficiency. In the racing world, outside the premier groups using purpose-built power, most vehicles are propelled by adaptations or permutations of passenger car engines. The vast majority of these engines started life on a drawing board or computer as a high-volume, low-cost solution to power a four-door family car, SUV, or light pickup truck. When this general-purpose engine is suddenly called upon to displace more cubes, rev much higher, and produce more power, builders must make certain changes and compromises. Hopefully there is enough room left in the design to accommodate these changes. If, after increasing the bore size, the cylinder walls are too thin, nothing short of a different block casting will help. If you increase the stroke too far, the rods will eventually hit something and the crank won't turn. Sometimes the obstacle can be removed, but in some cases, it has to stay. The OEMs and the performance aftermarket have come to the rescue in some cases by producing specialty parts that allow the envelope to be expanded.

Although few of you readers will be working with purpose-built power, you will be surprised and pleased to learn that you can reach almost the same efficiency as a Formula One engine by carefully dyno-tuning your production engine. For example, by comparing Brake Specific Fuel Consumption (BSFC), we can show how a well-tuned passenger car engine can produce just as much horsepower per pound of fuel and hence have the same efficiency as its Formula One counterpart. In other words, each tuner got the same horsepower per pound of fuel per hour. This comparison obviously diverges when you realize that the Formula One engine burns a lot more fuel per hour and hence is able to make incredible horsepower. This is, in part, because of its incredible RPM, which produces many more power strokes per minute than a modified passenger car engine.

We will assume that you have carefully chosen your engine for a variety of reasons and are reading this because you want to utilize a dynamometer to get the most power and useable torque possible from your engine while still maintaining some level of durability and fuel economy. Begin your tuning plan by understanding the limiting factors for engine performance.

### Displacement

The old saying "there is no replacement for displacement," holds a great amount of truth. Obviously certain physical dimensions of an

## CHAPTER 6

engine set a series of limits for performance. A 200 cubic inch engine is not going to make 5,000 horsepower. Depending on the state of tune, a typical production-based variant will probably produce between 1 to 2 horsepower per cubic inch. This ratio is sometimes referred to as the power density. The displacement is defined by bore size, stroke length, and the number of cylinders. These dimensions are always limited by the physical layout or architecture of the engine. Always try to understand the limitations of the layout. For example, if you heard about a 998 cubic inch overhead cam twin-plug hemi, you might have visions of a current, no-holds-barred, match-race drag engine. In fact, the engine in question is an in-line Hall-Scott 6-cylinder engine designed and manufactured in Berkley, California, around 1930 for boats, trucks, and buses. It was rated at 175 hp. The power-density therefore was .1753 hp/ CID (cubic inch displacement). This is a far cry from a current SRT Dodge Neon producing 275 hp from 2.0L (1 Liter = 60.5 cubic inches, therefore: 2.0L= 60.5 x 2=121 CID), which has a power density of 2.27 hp/ CID or almost *thirteen* times better than the Hall Scott! See how we just compared a current 2.0L engine to an antique 16.5L engine by using a power density factor. By the way, the 2.5L V10 Formula One engine making 900 hp has a power density of 5.95, or over twice what the Dodge Neon engine does!

### *Piston Speed*

Piston speed is defined as the average velocity of the piston measured in feet per minute through its travel up and down the cylinder. Except in very specific highly-refined applications, 5,500 feet per minute (fpm) is considered an optimistic upper limit for most reasonable engine combinations. If this speed of just over 60 miles per hour sounds slow for a piston in a whirring engine that might be moving a car at 180 miles per hour, remember that it is average speed and that a piston comes to a full (if very brief) stop twice during each engine revolution.

Piston speed in feet per minute can be quickly calculated with dimensions in the English FPS (foot-pound-second) system by multiplying the stroke times the RPM times a constant of .16667. (S x RPM x .16667 = Piston Speed avg. in FPM.)

Generally, above 5,500 fpm average speed, the engine's oiling system has a hard time maintaining the hydrodynamic film of oil between the piston and the cylinder wall. When this film breaks down, the piston tries to friction-weld itself to the cylinder wall, and we have engine failure. This friction welding is sometimes called piston scuff. Obviously, piston scuff can occur at lower speeds if the hydrodynamic barrier is broken down by having the oil too hot, or using the wrong oil, or if the oil becomes diluted and loses its lubricating properties. It can be diluted by fuel resulting from an air/fuel mixture that is too rich, or rings that have lost control and are unable to keep the fuel and air mixture above the piston. Piston-skirt shape also has a lot to do with piston scuff. Pistons that have a high unit loading in the skirt area will build localized heat much more rapidly than a piston that spreads the loading over the entire skirt area.

### *Inertia Loading*

Twice per revolution each piston in a reciprocating engine comes to a complete stop; once when it reaches TDC and changes directions, and again when it reaches BDC. Imagine a piston racing toward the top of the cylinder where it has to stop, change direction and then get yanked toward the bottom of the cylinder. When the crankshaft reaches the top of the stroke at TDC, the piston wants to keep on going. The only thing preventing the piston from crashing into the head at this point is the rod. If the piston is too heavy or the rod is too weak, the rod will fail in tension, or the pin will pull out of the piston pin bores. Conversely, if the rod is loaded too highly in compression—when the engine detonates, for example—the rod will bend or buckle in compressive failure, or the top of the piston will cave in. When you are selecting a rod for your engine, be careful not to forget about inertia factors and keep the rods properly sized for both the weight of the piston and the RPM you expect to turn. Some high-end engine performance programs such as Engine Expert, will actually give a value for rod tensile load.

### *Brake Mean Effective Pressure*

BMEP is the mean pressure developed in a cylinder during the power stroke. This pressure multiplied by the area of the piston is the average force pushing on the top of the piston during the entire stroke. Force applied through a distance equals work. This work is transferred through the rod to the crankshaft and creates torque, which is passed through the crankshaft ending at the flywheel. The engine, as a whole, must have the structural integrity to be able to withstand the highest stresses imparted during the normal operating cycle. If the engine detonates, for example, this would be considered abuse and outside of the normal operating parameters, and all bets are off. Detonation is the uncontrolled violent pressure rise (this *is* an explosion) in the cylinder resulting from two separate flame fronts colliding within the cylinder. Detonation results in severe damage to the piston, rings, connecting rods, and bearings.

Remember, an engine is merely a chain of parts whose strength is determined by the ultimate strength of its weakest part. If a connecting rod cannot withstand the inertia loading imparted during the high-RPM portion of the operating curve, the rod will break. If the oiling system cannot deliver enough oil at sufficient pressure to lubricate and cool the bearings during the highest load encountered, bearing failure will invariably result. Unfortunately, just changing a camshaft or adding a ported set of heads does not make a performance engine. Having an improved oiling system will not make any more horsepower; however it will allow the engine to operate safely at the new increased power levels. The goal of any performance upgrade should be to choose a carefully coordinated set of parts and tune them to work together to create a true and sustainable net gain. Creating increased power is an opportunity, while making the engine last with all of the newfound power becomes a challenge.

## Spark Timing

Spark advance is the number of crankshaft degrees before Top Dead Center (TDC) when we introduce the spark to start the controlled burn in the combustion chamber. Consider this no different from cooking a steak dinner. If we want to eat at 6:00 PM, we should start cooking the steak at 5:45 PM, to ensure it is ready and properly cooked. This plan falls apart if you miss the start time but still want to eat at 6:00 PM. Many would-be tuners think that they can just turn up the heat at 5:50 and the steak will cook faster, and still be ready at 6:00 PM. As any good cook or our own experience tells us, this method will merely produce a burned steak that is raw in the middle. The trick with spark timing is to start the fire early enough so that the piston is already on the way down the cylinder when the controlled pressure peak occurs. As the engine increases in speed, we need to start the fire earlier since the piston is traveling faster. This advancing of the spark usually continues as speed increases. Interestingly, some engines actually require that the timing advance be reduced or retarded at higher RPM. This reduction or spark retard becomes necessary because the incoming charge gases in the cylinder are swirling around so violently that they spread the fire faster or much more efficiently than they normally do at slower speeds. The way the fire spreads in a cylinder is called "flame propagation."

Many people think that there is an explosion in the cylinder that pushes the piston downward. Nothing could be further from the truth. In a properly tuned engine, the mixture of fuel and air actually burns rapidly, creating a controlled and hence predictable pressure rise from the rapid expansion of the products of combustion. If an explosion does occur, your engine is in deep trouble, and is in imminent danger. Detonation can be thought of as a rapid explosion with a violent pressure rise staged too early in the cycle. The pressure rise is so violent that it damages the structural components like the piston and rings very rapidly. This event can be caused by improper timing, wrong compression ratio, poor fuel, or hot gases remaining in the cylinder that were never purged from the previous exhaust cycle. This last item, unpurged gases, explains why an engine with a worn exhaust lobe or broken exhaust rocker arm will backfire through the intake. Think of an engine as a campfire: as long as it burns, it can be fed fuel and put out heat to serve its purpose. If the fire turns into an explosion, the camping trip is over.

*Spark Mapping* Proper spark timing becomes a delicate dance between firing too early and possibly detonating or firing too late and wasting some of the valuable piston travel by not pushing on it. To properly tune the spark, you must adjust the spark for each point of the spark map. To visualize the spark and fuel map, think about an engine running at 6000 RPM. In neutral, it would require very little throttle opening to maintain 6000 RPM. However, if you were in a car pulling a trailer up a mountain, as you went up the hill, you would have to apply more throttle to maintain the same RPM. As you continue to open the throttle the manifold pressure would fall until it was zero, which would indicate the throttle was at wide open (WOT). If we graphed the spark advance for each 10-percent range of throttle opening at 6000 RPM, we would have 10 values for spark advance for the throttle-opening range; from 10 % to 100 %. While initially some of these values quickly increase, others would remain the same; finally, less

# CHAPTER 6

*Be careful of timing lights with a dial-back feature. They may not be accurate. Try instead to use a conventional light on a damper that has been marked and calibrated on your engine to be sure that TDC is accurate.*

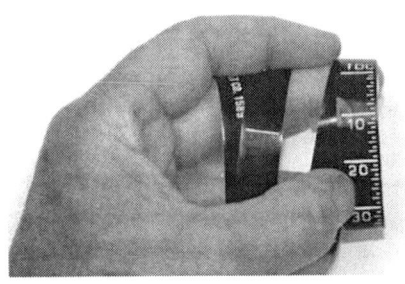

*A simple tape can be applied to the damper. Make sure you have the correct-diameter damper and tape for the application.*

incremental spark would be required as the load increased.

To select the proper spark at each of these points, we typically start very conservatively and ease our way into the spark curve. Here it really helps if you have some way to detect knock. Knock is the pressure rise resulting from lighting the fire too early, such that the pressure created by the ignited fuel-air mix collides with the upward traveling piston, which is further increasing the pressure in the cylinder. Most of the current production vehicles have knock sensors that electronically "listen" for knock and automatically start incrementally retarding the spark as they sense borderline knock. This knock control is coupled with oxygen sensors that measure the air/fuel ratio and allow the engine to be controlled in what is termed a closed-loop mode, resulting in engines that are incredibly efficient at all loads and at all speeds.

Many of the current aftermarket fuel-injection systems employ some very powerful and sophisticated electronic control units (ECUs) that rival and in some cases exceed their production counterparts in sophistication. Most of the aftermarket systems are laptop compatible, which means that you can manipulate a variety of variables, ranging from spark and fuel to start-up enrichment, to suit your own requirements. These engine controllers range from the very basic to something just short of the space shuttle in complexity. Today, what used to be referred to as the computer in a production vehicle is no longer merely an engine control unit; it has become a vehicle-control computer. It is a series of microprocessors that effectively control the engine, transmission, theft system, air conditioning, dash, and a host of other functions. When diagnosing these systems, be aware that all of these individual systems constantly communicate with each other. For example, an engine that will start and not stay running may actually be reacting to a signal from the theft-deterrent system, which is not happy with the signal from a key being used to start the vehicle. When the computer senses a potential unauthorized user, it triggers a shutdown relay to kill the spark and fuel.

This internal protocol presents a problem when you try to run an engine with this type of controller on an engine dyno using a vehicle harness. In this case, you would have to start the dyno with a key that had been preprogrammed into that particular computer. Aside from having to deal with all of the ancillary problems such as overriding the various internal features, it is becoming increasingly difficult and in some cases downright impossible to manipulate the fuel, air, and spark on the production controllers. On the other hand, any decent aftermarket controller has a simple user-friendly system, which, after a little practice, will become a joy to tune with. These systems are designed by tuners and engine people who are good with computers, contrasted with some of the first aftermarket attempts, which were designed by computer engineers who really didn't understand engines or tuning. When selecting one of these computers for a current late-model vehicle, make sure that it will "piggyback" or overlay the production system, otherwise you may lose the various non-engine functions such as the electronic dashboard (speedometer, gages, and odometer), and automatic transmission control. In the piggyback mode, the new controller overlays the current harness and allows you to modify the critical tunable engine functions such as fuel and spark.

If you are tuning a carbureted engine, always try to use a digital ignition system. It will allow you to incrementally create a spark curve using knock sensors and air/fuel ratio readings from a laptop computer at the console or in the vehicle riding down the road. This is preferable to constantly removing the distributor to change springs and weights as well as total advance. If you are unable to use a digital spark control system, use a production

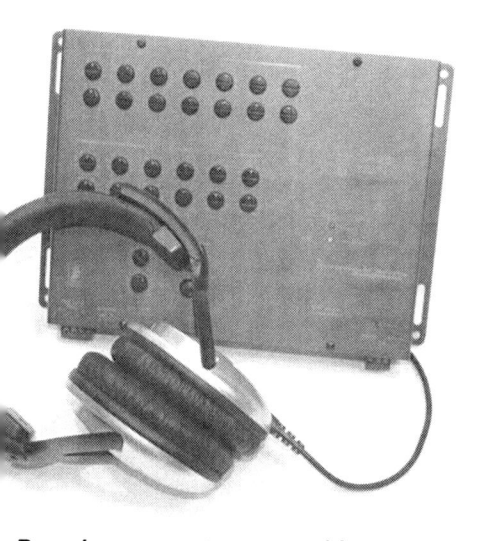

*By using a car stereo graphic equalizer to select the range for knock noise, you can listen for knock while running the dyno. Mount the knock sensors in the block and connect them to the input and gently drive into knock to learn to distinguish the sound. It typically sounds like a snapping noise through the headphones.*

knock sensor from either an aftermarket spark control or make one using a graphic equalizer and a set of headphones so you can listen, literally, for knock as you run your engine. The location of the knock sensors is important, and will vary for each engine. Experiment with sensor placement to find the best location. For example, there are some valve-train noises that mimic knock frequencies.

The other option is to do the old school routine and just watch the torque as you increase the spark while holding one throttle setting. As the engine passes from the correct spark advance to too much advance, the torque falls off. You simply note the advance, and typically subtract two degrees (for safety) and call it good. This becomes what is called max power spark. This method sounds simple enough until you are at the controls with a fully loaded engine screaming away for what seems like forever while you are gently playing with the spark. One false move here and you will buy a set of pistons. Remember that max power spark values change as engine speed or load changes. On the other hand, the ECU will sense the knock and automatically pull the spark back and create a graph showing where the knock occurred and how severe it was. Once you use this method, it will be hard to go back to the old way.

Using ignition systems available from MSD, for example, you can change individual cylinder timing to compensate for cylinder-to-cylinder differences. A spark curve can be developed quite readily that will address the needs of a traditional distributor-based system. When using a current engine, which employs a crank triggered coil-on-plug system in conjunction with multiple-point fuel injection, an AEM or FAST engine management system has a host of neat features that accept a wide variety of inputs allowing a tuner to effectively tune one of these engines.

*Optimizing Spark Timing* Be especially careful when optimizing spark timing and air/fuel ratio, since some of today's best and most efficient combustion chambers have very little margin between maximum power and instant destruction. The so-called fast-burn chambers produce some fantastic power numbers at great efficiencies, but they are extremely knock sensitive. A slow-burning chamber may progress from maximum power spark to damaging knock in four or five degrees, while a fast burn chamber is very sensitive and only takes one or two degrees to go from good to bad. The fast-burn chambers also take far less overall timing than conventional combustion chambers. Engines with multiple spark plugs per cylinder also take far less timing. This should be obvious because there are two plugs starting the fire at two different locations, so you can wait much longer to light the fire.

When you finally do reach your optimal tuning on your engine, it will develop the peak cylinder pressure at approximately 15–17 degrees after TDC on the power stroke. Interestingly, this is universally true for all well-tuned engines. In fact, some production engines will soon start employing in-cylinder pressure sensors to enable the computers to adjust fuel and spark to achieve this peak-pressure timing under all circumstances. By comparing a theoretically perfect cylinder pressure trace to the pressure trace from the previous cycle for that cylinder, the variables will be manipulated to produce an optimal pressure trace. Almost always, the peak cylinder pressure will occur at between 12 and 20 degrees ATDC, regardless of the engine design.

### Air/Fuel Ratio

Mixture, or the ratio of air to fuel in the combustion chamber, is the next tunable property. If there is too much fuel for the amount of air delivered to the cylinder, then we say that the mixture is rich or simply fat. If there is not enough fuel for the air in the cylinder, or conversely too much air, we call this mixture lean. Our goal in tuning the air/fuel mixture is to have a safe mixture that will allow us to make the maximum amount of power while not causing the engine to damage itself due to the high heat of lean burning. Just like spark advance, we try to start out with a conservative mixture that is decidedly rich.

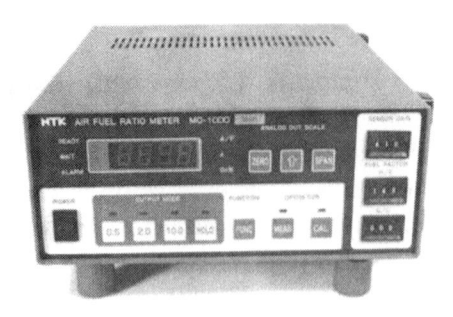

*While somewhat pricey, this meter will give you very good results for air-fuel, fuel-air, and Lambda. It even works on 12V, allowing it to go for a ride in the car. Remember to use only unleaded fuel. Leaded fuel will eventually kill the sensors.*

Some tuners use the ratio of fuel to air as opposed to air to fuel. Think of this as looking at a glass and viewing it as half empty versus half full. Neither convention is incorrect or inadequate. It boils down to personal preference or what you are used to. Most of the performance world uses air/fuel, so we will try to do that in this book. To make matters even more confusing, we have lambda (λ), which is yet another way of looking at rich and lean in precentage of stoichiometric.

### Lean Best Torque (LBT)

While watching the exhaust-gas temperatures for each cylinder and the lambda sensors (wide range $O_2$ sensors), if you have them, gradually increase the load by opening the throttle, while holding the RPM steady. At each throttle opening, take away fuel until the power falls off, then richen back up until you reach maximum torque by adding more fuel. This will establish the lean best torque (LBT) for the engine.

By now you should have figured out that the tuning process is a long and laborious task. It typically takes months to establish and validate a final calibration for an OEM production engine. Unlike performance engines, production tuners or, "calibrators," as they prefer to be called, have the additional challenge of having to balance performance, driveability, fuel economy, and emissions concurrently.

Our job as performance tuners or dyno testers is easy compared to that of a calibrator. This book will attempt to outline the steps necessary to increase power and prevent you from hurting your engine. Obviously, the top teams in all forms of motorsports spend days (and months, in some cases) on the dyno developing their competition engines, where just a few horsepower can be the difference between winning and not even qualifying. Today's sanctioning bodies all want to equalize the competition and thereby intensify the show. They do this by carefully regulating the performance characteristics of the vehicles to ensure very equal competition. This means that we all have to work very hard to be competitive.

When looking at the air/fuel ratio, remember several concepts. It would seem that we would want to provide the perfect mixture ratio of air and fuel to promote complete combustion at around 14.7:1 (stoichiometric) depending on the fuel used. In reality, we want to run an air/fuel ratio somewhere around 12.7:1. We choose to run richer, which enables us to run cooler and to provide a safety margin. While running at stoichiometric may seem to be where you want to be, the engine will typically make more power at 12.7:1. As you get leaner, obviously the fuel economy gets better, but the engine will lose power. Top teams in segments of motorsports where fuel economy plays a critical role will often spend months refining their fuel economy strategy while still trying to maintain adequate power. Obviously it becomes a balancing act. In any event where pit stops are required or overall fuel mileage is a factor, fuel economy becomes critical. One less fuel stop as the race unfolds can virtually guarantee a win in some cases.

## Stoichiometric

As we mix fuel with air to form a combustible mixture, there has to be an optimum mixture. If we start with the chemical reaction, we find that gasoline reacts with air in a ratio of 14.7 parts of air to one part of gasoline by weight. This says that if we were to burn 1 part of gasoline with 14.7 parts of air there would be no excess air or fuel left. Only the byproducts of combustion would be left. If a mixture of fuel and air has excess air remaining after combustion, it is said to be lean. Conversely if there is excess fuel after combustion the mixture is defined as being rich. Think of "Stoich" as being the dividing line between rich and lean.

When using other fuels, obviously the value of stoich changes. Alcohol, ethanol, or methanol, for example, has a ratio of 6.33 parts of air for every part of alcohol. Obviously, when testing, you will have to adjust your inputs to reflect the change in fuel density to enable the fuel flow meter to measure correctly the pounds per hour or fuel flow rate.

# TUNING

## Tuning Order

As an example, let's begin with a totally new engine in a class and type of racing we have competed in before. Where do we start, and in what order do we accomplish the tuning?

For this example we will use a small-block pushrod V-8 drag motor with an aftermarket laptop-programmable fuel injection system. We will assume that we have built the engine using good advice from knowledgeable sources, a fair amount of research, and a computerized study from an engine simulation program. We have rented some dyno time and we are going to see what happens. At this point, the question becomes "where to start?"

## Engine Break-in Conditioning

Since we are starting with a green engine, we will need to break it in. The first part of the break-in is fairly easy, since it is done at relatively low load and at low RPM.

Most aftermarket ECU systems come with a preloaded calibration that is fairly generic. Be sure to consult your manufacturer to ensure you pick the correct calibration. Some companies are able to download a calibration through the Internet right to your control unit. Make sure your checklist is complete (see Chapter 4) and fire the engine. Gently run the engine while checking all of the various readings. If everything is in order, proceed. Do not move on unless the engine is behaving correctly. A few minutes spent here checking and correcting minor problems could save your engine later. Fluid leaks and sensors that don't read must be fixed before you proceed.

Once the timing and air/fuel ratio are set at safe values, fire the engine and watch the EGTs and listen for knock, then run the first step of the break-in and shut the engine off to run your preliminary engine health checks. If the engine is healthy, proceed to the next step. In this step, you will need to validate the next speed and load setting to ensure you are running in a safe mode. While keeping the EGTs cool by running more fuel (1100–1200 deg. F), make sure that you do not run too rich, in order to prevent washing the cylinder walls down with raw fuel, which will dilute the oil and almost guarantee scuffing a piston. It helps immensely to have at least one good wide-band $O_2$ sensor on each bank of the engine to comparatively monitor the air/fuel ratio from side to side. Note: Most $O_2$ sensors cannot tolerate leaded fuel. If you must run leaded fuel, you may have to forego using $O_2$ sensors.

If you see one bank with values differing significantly from the other side, stop the test and find the cause. Set the spark timing to give you adequate power with little or no chance of knock. You should avoid overly retarded timing since this will create a lot of heat in the cylinder. Timing set at three to four degrees less than max power spark should be sufficient for this portion. Remember, when setting the timing, begin low and advance the timing until borderline knocking is detected, as opposed to running the engine in knock and backing the timing down until the knock goes away.

## Initial Startup

Firing a newly built engine for the first time and hearing it roar to life can be an awe-inspiring experience. Don't get caught up in the moment. Stay focused and pay attention to all of the gauges.

Learn to watch the oil pressure; you want to hold the RPM steady at a low speed, but certainly above idle, to allow the camshaft to break in without wiping out a lobe. This is especially critical with flat-tappet camshafts with high valvespring loads.

If during these first critical minutes the running engine starts to slow down for no apparent reason, resist the temptation to feed it more throttle to maintain the speed. If the engine is losing a bearing and trying to tighten up, you may find yourself

---

### Lambda

Lambda, our symbol for which is "λ", is derived from a letter of the Greek alphabet, and is used to signify the ratio of an excess or deficiency of air to the amount of air required by the stoichiometric ratio. For example, if an engine has a 3% excess of air, the lambda reading is expressed as a Lambda of 1.03. Conversely, a 3% deficiency of air or rich condition would be signified by a Lambda of .97. A perfect stoichiometric ratio of air to fuel (14.7:1) would be represented by a Lambda (λ) reading of 1.0 (lambda = 1).

Lambda Sensors are wide-range $O_2$ sensors used to determine air-fuel mixtures. Rather than a display that reads 12.47 air/fuel, a lambda sensor would read .848 for the same mixture. It may take a bit of getting used to, but either system will work equally well.

# CHAPTER 6

looking at replacing a connecting rod if you continue to increase the throttle to keep the engine from stalling.

On the other hand, improperly set idle air control motors (IAC) or carburetor idle circuits may cause you to have to play with the throttle to keep the engine running until all of the initial adjustments are made. The watchword here is *care*. Don't lose your focus, and keep a watchful eye (and ear) on the critical sounds and values such as temperatures and of course oil pressure.

Watch the air/fuel ratio to make sure that it is not too rich or too lean. Aim for a ratio of around 12.5:1. If you have $O_2$ sensors, make sure you monitor the side to side variances. If one side is consistently richer or leaner than the other, start looking for the problem. You may find a plugged injector or one that is not firing. You may find a bad spark plug or one that has too much gap, or a gap that has been closed inadvertently. Stop and correct the problem. While most of the unburned fuel from a misfiring cylinder is pumped out of the cylinder, some will remain in the cylinder and eventually work its way into the oil pan. In doing so, aside from diluting the oil, it may wash the oil off the cylinder walls. This creates two problems: first, the cylinder will not seal well because the oil acts as a sealant between the rings and ring lands of the piston; second, the fuel will eventually dilute the oil and break it down so it becomes ineffective as a lubricant. If you are using $O_2$ sensors remember that they do not like to work in the presence of leaded fuel. The lead will coat the sensor and eventually ruin it.

If you see a trend, try to understand it. For example, if the engine tends to run progressively richer from one side as the dyno session progresses during the day, think about what could cause only one side to become rich. Obviously an $O_2$ sensor becoming fouled or not working properly could be the cause, but what else could be causing only one cylinder to run rich? Since we are dealing with a ratio of air to fuel, instead of thinking of rich as a condition where too much fuel is present, also think of it as a condition where not enough air is present. When you think of it in this way, it becomes obvious that a broken intake rocker arm would mean that one cylinder would not be able to deliver fresh air for combustion. In this case, before you make any changes, you might want to swap $O_2$ sensors and see if the problem stays put or follows the sensor.

A worn intake lobe on the camshaft would be the best guess, however, since a broken rocker arm would make a big difference from one run to the next, while a lobe would take some time to wear off, promoting a gradual change in the ratio.

## Oil Problems and Camshaft Wear

As production automotive engines have almost all gone to roller cam followers, the oil formulations have changed also. Today, different performance-engine builders are beginning to experience abnormal wear on a variety of flat-tappet camshafts. The prevailing theory is that some crucial additives have been removed from engine oils that prevented flat-tappet cam and lifter wear in the past. Be sure to adhere closely to your camshaft manufacturer's installation and lubrication recommendations, especially if you are using a camshaft with high valve-seat spring loads: you may have to break in the camshaft itself. Reduce the valvespring load by either removing an inner spring or removing some shims. Run this lowered load *only* at reduced RPM during break-in.

## Catalytic Converters

If your vehicle uses a catalytic convertor, be especially careful of letting the engine run with a non-firing cylinder since the convertor may be ruined with too much raw fuel being dumped into it. The additional heat coming from a catalytic convertor subjected to an over-rich mixture will plug the convertor as well as potentially overheat and start a fire in, on, or around the vehicle.

## Fuel Distribution

Since there may be a fuel distribution problem either from cylinder to cylinder, from side to side, or for the entire engine, check the fuel delivery as close to the injector or carburetor as possible. Don't forget to look for the small in-line filters, which may be partially plugged and often go unnoticed.

## Valve Lash

Look at the valve tips and valve lash. If a valve tip is receding or a clearance is tightening, it may signal trouble. Valve lash that opens up may signal a valve seat that is moving out of the head, a worn pushrod, or worn adjuster screw. A valve gap that tightens up may signal a valve that has tuliped from excess heat or increased seat load, or one that has simply pounded the seat in. Stop and fix the problem before it costs you more money by spreading debris throughout the entire engine. There has never been a time in recorded history where revving the engine or continuing to run the engine has healed these problems; nevertheless, we still have diehards out there trying to be the first one in history to do so.

Continue working your way through the engine break-in by using this method. As the break-in gets more intense, check the timing and air/fuel ratio more frequently while keeping an eye on the EGTs and the knock sensor data.

Do not do the WOT power runs scheduled at the end of the break-in with an engine that has not been at least rough-calibrated! You can be much safer and produce truly meaningful data after the calibration session. Also: If you have lowered the valvespring load for camshaft break-in, remember to change to the recommended valvespring load before any significant engine speed is used.

## Begin Tuning

Once you have completed and passed another round of engine health checks on the engine, we are ready to begin the serious tuning. Start by picking a fairly low RPM like 2,400 and, while holding RPM steady, gradually increase the load. Listen for spark knock and keep an eye on the air/fuel ratio. Back off immediately at the first sign of trouble and add more fuel or take out spark to correct the problem, working to a rich and safe combination. By repeating this procedure and holding the RPM steady, you should be able to make a complete sweep from 10% all the way to 100% throttle opening, while holding the engine at 2,400 RPM. When this is done, move to 2,800 and repeat the process. You will continue increasing by 400-RPM increments until you get to 4,000. By then, you will probably not want to hold the engine at 4,000 constantly while you crank in load. Rather, hold it and add or subtract spark, then add or subtract fuel, and then go back and reset spark.

Above 4,000, you will probably want to do spot checks by picking an RPM and throttle setting and quickly go there and adjust accordingly, then roll out of the throttle to a low-load, high-idle setting and allow the engine to cool.

Once you have established a matrix with values for fuel and spark at regular RPM points with these spot checks, you can begin making some very tentative, short power runs. Make these short runs at WOT, but be ready to abort the run and chop the throttle at the first sign of trouble. Fix the problem by adding or subtracting fuel or spark, then go back and try again. Soon you will be able to make a full pass with some margin and feel pretty safe. Gain some confidence, but don't get stupid. Above all, don't get in a hurry! Now is when the process starts getting sensitive. By using the method we just covered, you will have created an RPM-based surface map of fuel and spark. Many aftermarket ECU systems will allow you to move small areas or this entire surface up and down by a percentage amount.

This method is most convenient at this point, when we want to lean down the engine and start to make some power. Rather than correcting each individual cell, you can lean the whole fuel curve or just a small group of cells with just a few keystrokes.

When you have mapped a good safe fuel and spark calibration, you can start changing header primary and secondary lengths. As you change and find better solutions, remember that you will have to go back and optimize the fuel and spark again. It stands to reason that if you pick up 20 horsepower with the headers, you will be running lean unless you have added extra fuel to match the gain. So, as you work with the combination, remember to go back and readjust after each gain. Typically you would wait to see a 1–2% gain before recalibration. The system will make the coarse adjustments. Your fuel system, carburetor or injector (if you are using a mass air flow system), will compensate for the additional air by adding fuel to a point, but don't rely on it to be perfect.

The next thing many people do is to start moving the camshaft centerline to move the torque curve, or, once the curve is good, to increase the overall torque.

## Part Throttle

Many tuners only want to tune for wide-open throttle (WOT) since that is where the maximum horsepower numbers are made and theoretically the race is won or lost. There are many situations where part throttle is far more important. A street rod rarely if ever sees wide-open throttle, but will spend hours idling or cruising at 15% throttle opening. A good tuner would want to make sure that the engine was very drivable and had good fuel-economy numbers here.

Oval track racers need good part-throttle tuning because they may have to spend 10 minutes circling the track at 20% throttle at 3000 RPM

# CHAPTER 6

# Shaping the Torque Curve

In the beginning, most tuners simply look to increase the torque numbers from the previous configuration. As you gain experience, a nice "fat" torque curve that is steady, without a bunch of dips and hollows, is the goal. A torque curve that rises quickly with a broad peak for a wide range of RPM is desirable. While you may actually give up a small amount of peak torque to achieve this well-shaped curve, it will produce a faster car because the driver will have a very steady throttle response, which allows smooth acceleration at a constant throttle application, as opposed to pedaling on and off the throttle to keep the tires from breaking loose. Remember, you can always get rid of too much torque by either not pushing the pedal down as far or by changing the gear ratio to reduce the final drive ratio (e.g., go from a 4.10 down to a 3.90). On the reverse side, it is virtually impossible for the driver to make up for a lack of torque, or to drive a car smoothly where the torque is rapidly rising and falling as the RPM increases.

Assuming that the air/fuel ratio and spark advance is fairly consistent throughout the range, getting rid of the humps in the torque curve can usually be done in several ways. Start by changing the headers. Add an H pipe if your system does not have one. Shorten and lengthen the primaries until you maximize the torque. Next move to the collectors and lengthen and shorten them to gain the best torque curve. Go back and try the different primary lengths. As the system starts to respond, remember to keep going back to fuel, air, and spark and check them to make sure you are not getting too far away from the base calibration. Remember that you achieved your increased torque by making the engine breathe more air. Therefore, you will have to add fuel to maintain the optimum air/fuel ratio.

Cam selection and cam timing can play a big part here. Advancing or retarding the camshaft has many effects and is obviously the best place to start. Once you establish a good baseline, start advancing or retarding the cam in 2-degree increments to see the effect this has on torque. This technique requires that you are absolutely sure that you have adequate piston-to-valve clearance to prevent contact. If you are unsure, put a solid lifter in the engine and check the clearance again.

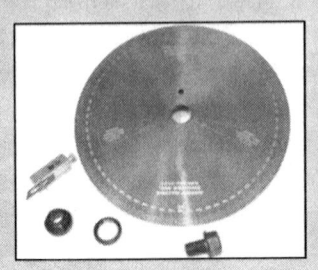

Another technique of camshaft testing is to increase the lift by changing the rocker arm ratio on pushrod engines. This allows you to test the effects of a larger cam without having to buy one. The cam event timing remains basically the same, but the area under the camshaft area curve changes dramatically. Before you run this combination, however, you must check for pushrod clearance, valvespring solid height, and valve-to-piston clearance.

If this change makes a difference, you may want to incorporate a different cam lobe or simply run different rocker arms in the engine. You can simulate either more or less lift and apply it across the board, or only on the exhaust or intake as may be applicable. As your tuning continues, you must constantly check the air/fuel ratio to ensure that you are not headed for disaster. Remember to check for piston-to-valve clearance if you increase rocker ratio, since that will increase the valve lift.

Once you settle on a combination that fits your needs, go back and make sure the combination is driveable. Some dynos will let you get a feel for the driveability by "driving the dyno around." This technique involves applying load while increasing or decreasing the RPM.

You can get a good feel for what the engine will produce in the field by doing this. An engine that stumbles at part throttle will not be fun to drive in the vehicle.

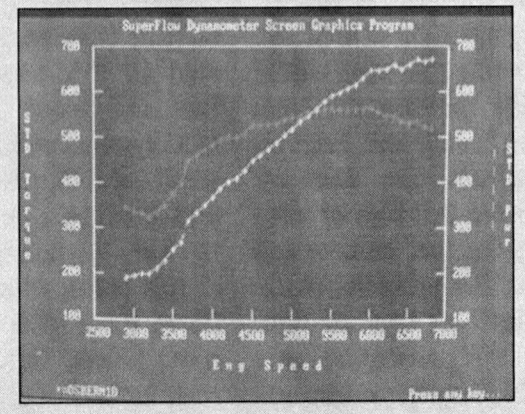

*A good degree wheel is a necessity to measure cam centerline, cam events, and to keep track of where valve-to-piston clearance gets tight.*

*This is what we live for—a nice broad torque curve without any humps and spikes. This will drive like a dream. With a torque curve like this you can focus on the chassis and handling.*

DYNO TESTING AND TUNING

while a wreck is being cleared. Many knowledgeable people feel that a caution lap is the hardest duty a race engine sees because suddenly everything in the engine is going the wrong way. An engine perfectly tuned for wide-open throttle and perfectly outfitted with a good cooling system is suddenly slowed from 180 mph to 60 and forced to run in tight formation. The heat from its previous high-speed running is trapped in the cooling system with no way to escape (the pump is turning slowly, the air flow through the radiator has slowed to a crawl and blocked by the car in front of yours, and because the tuner didn't plan for it, the spark advance is usually too high). With the engine running at less than half speed, this, combined with poor part-throttle fuel distribution, means certain cylinders may be running lean. By now you get the picture. It should be no surprise that engine failures often occur after a caution period.

Prepare for this by spending time tuning at part throttle. Find areas and create areas where you can operate without running lean and risking detonation. Fix the part-throttle fuel distribution. Often you will see a note for the driver, taped to the dash, with some gear selections and RPM ranges that are safe to operate in while under caution.

By now you should be getting a better appreciation for the team that developed and calibrated your production street vehicle at the manufacturer. It takes months to develop and verify a final calibration. If all a car had to do was run well at wide-open throttle, life would be easy. After all is said and done the production vehicle still has to meet stringent emissions requirements and last for 100,000 miles. Here is a final product that may tow a 30-foot trailer from New York to California for one owner, while an identical vehicle will allow a retired couple to drive from Chicago to Miami on vacation and get good fuel economy.

## Cylinder Head Flow

Once we start tuning, we soon realize that one of the fundamental "corks" of engine performance is the amount of air an engine can flow. Until we can get more air in the engine, we can't burn more fuel. Without additional fuel and air to burn, the power will not increase. While increasing the engine airflow is typically accomplished by either porting the heads, increasing the valve size, or both, it is not always the answer. It is actually possible to have too much flow or to have an imbalance of flow between the intake and exhaust systems. Intake flow velocity also plays an important role in the distribution, mixing, and hence the burning part of the cycle. A smaller more-efficient port with high velocity, properly aimed into the cylinder, will easily out-perform some huge port that might have higher raw flow numbers. On the other hand, the large port is required for a 500 cid Pro Stock engine or a 350 cid small-block designed to turn 9,500 RPM. Balancing the port size and velocity to the engine and its intended usage is the job for the cylinder head specialist.

Testing cylinder heads on the dyno brings several sets of challenges. You must balance compression ratio, the various clearances, and hardware compatibility such as manifold fit and alignment so a proper comparison can be made. If these important considerations are not made, there will be little learned from a test. The results may be easily misunderstood. Compression ratio is an especially important contributor to power.

## Exhaust Tuning

Exhaust-system tuning can be just as important as other types. Always try to make valid comparisons. One of the biggest mistakes people make is to hook the exhaust to the dyno-cell output fan with an airtight connection. This not only affects the tuning length of the system but also introduces artificial scavenging that the engine would never see in the real world. Varying backpressure is also another roadblock to an apples-to-apples comparison.

Changing the lengths of the various exhaust-system components such as the primaries will have an effect on the overall power output but perhaps more importantly on the shape of the power curve. In the end, eliminating the big dip spanning 2,000 RPM in the middle of the power curve may be much more important than gaining the last two horsepower

*Never make a solid connection between the vehicle exhaust and the room exhaust for performance development. When you are doing durability tests on a production engine, it is fine to hook the engine up to mufflers and connect them tightly to the outside exhaust. Caution: Never run an engine without fans and ducting to evacuate the exhaust from the dyno cell to the outside.*

## CHAPTER 6

# Aluminum versus Iron: A Tale of Two Heads

You may find yourself comparing two pairs of cylinder heads—one made from aluminum and one made from iron. If you prepared two identical pairs of cylinder heads made from the different materials and tested them, you would find that the aluminum heads produce a lower power output. How can this be? Everybody knows that aluminum heads are better. The truth is that they are better especially in their ability to transfer heat away from the combustion chamber into the coolant. By transferring the heat away from the combustion chamber, however, the pressure is lowered in the cylinder, and in most cases this results in a power loss because less cylinder pressure is available to push down on the piston during the power stroke.

In the real world, most aluminum heads have other performance enhancements above and beyond improved heat transfer and lower weight. Typically aluminum heads have larger valves, improved flow capability and in some cases higher compression ratio by using smaller combustion chambers than their cast-iron counterparts.

If you did compare two pairs of cylinder heads that were identical in every way, except one pair was made from aluminum and the other was made from iron, you would find after careful testing that in most cases the compression ratio in the aluminum heads needed to be raised by 1.5- to 1.75:1 in order to compensate for the loss of heat and make the heads perform equally.

Also don't forget that in the car, if everything is equal from a power standpoint, the aluminum heads will produce better performance because of the lower weight. In a drag car, this translates directly to improved elapsed times if you can stand to lose the weight. If you have to keep the weight the same on your rear-wheel drive car, you can improve your weight distribution by removing weight from the front end and putting it over the rear wheels. On a short-track car, the results are more dramatic. You typically accelerate twice and decelerate or brake twice a lap, which translates into power or time. Also, being able to remove front-end weight has added advantages of lowering the polar moment of inertia for the vehicle, making it easier to turn into the corners.

In short, maximize the value of the aluminum heads by making sure that the dynamic compression ratio is maintained. If you simply change to aluminum cylinder heads with the same static compression ratio as the iron heads you removed, you won't see any improvement short of that associated with the change in overall weight.

# Intake Tuning

Intake manifold testing relies on a clear objective and a coherent test plan. The intake manifold is more than an adaptor to mount the carburetor or throttle body above the cylinder heads. The manifold has a crucial importance to tuning and fuel distribution.

Initially we want to make sure we get equal amounts of fuel and air to each cylinder under all conditions. That goal itself can be a huge challenge with some manifold combinations and designs. While some of the process is somewhat straightforward, the last little bit can be quite difficult. You will find yourself building dams made from wooden popsicle sticks (Starbucks has wonderful sticks and plenty of them!), which are epoxied in the floor of the manifold. These dams serve to direct the flow of the air and fuel either toward or away from different cylinders as the mixtures or temperatures dictate. Try to craft these dams to produce equal cylinder-to-cylinder fuel distribution throughout the usable RPM range. Once you have good distribution, do the fine tuning with staggered jets. Do not try to start with staggered jets unless the temperature differences (EGTs) are less than 150 degrees F.

The popular tuneable features of an intake manifold are plenum volume, runner volume, runner taper, and, to an extent, runner length. Most of the tuners will want to experiment with a variety of spacers to increase the plenum volume. These spacers typically come in a variety of thicknesses and configurations, as well as different materials. We won't go into all of the various claims, but suffice it to say that the major impact of these devices is to change the plenum volume. This volume change may produce power and torque gains. Changing the runner volume requires porting and in some cases can be achieved with spacers, which not only change the port volume but also the runner length.

# TUNING

over the last 100 RPM. Different-style headers such as stepped or even Tri-Y design may yield dramatic improvements in vehicle performance.

When testing headers, be careful to use open exhaust systems. Do not have an airtight connection between the collectors or end of your vehicle exhaust system and the dyno exhaust system. If you do not have an air gap here, the exhaust system will tune as though you had a 20-foot tailpipe (or however long your dyno-room exhaust system happens to be).

Once the fuel distribution is under control and will not create a lean air/fuel mix in one cylinder and burn a piston, then we can focus on power and driveability. To drive the dyno, apply some moderate amount of load (40% might be a good starting point) and bring the speed down to 2000 RPM, then give it some rapid throttle and see how the engine behaves. If driving the dyno results in a series of pops and stutters (often referred to as "shooting ducks" because it sounds like the opening day of duck season), you have more work to do. If it takes off and then sags, you have more work to do. These conditions will typically require work on the fuel-enrichment side of the carburetor tuning. The accelerator pumps, the pump shot, the spray nozzles, and the power valves will need work.

If you have an electronic fuel-injection system, you may want to change the enrichment schedule by adding more fuel. Perhaps you'll want to factor in the coolant temperature by scheduling less fuel as the engine warms up. We will make references to various strategies throughout this book.

*Don't laugh—Tri-Y headers are back and they still work quite nicely. They will make lots of torque, and we all know what torque does.*

## Fuel System Tuning

Fuel systems are perhaps the most complex subsystem of an engine. They can be a topic and area of expertise all to themselves. Since it is impossible to cover all of the combinations and permutations, we will cover the testing in general terms, focusing on the principles and highlighting the important issues. As you pursue your own high-performance goals, take the next step and thoroughly familiarize yourself with your own engine and its components, refining these principles for your needs.

First, get the latest and best available technical information on tuning your particular system, be it a Holley 4150-4 bbl, Carter AVS-4 bbl, or the latest FAST or AEM fuel-injection system. There are full-length books devoted to the details of tuning just these individual components. Look in the bibliography section for some of the recommended titles. While there are specialists out there who sell finished carburetors, the more you know the better off you are, because each change you make to your other components may require changes to your carb. If you know its exact specs and how it works, you can be your own expert instead of paying someone else. Besides cost, knowing your carb thoroughly allows you to make changes trackside rather than running poorly all afternoon and visiting your specialist later.

All internal combustion engines rely on discrete settings of fuel, air, and spark for each point on a graph of manifold pressure vs. RPM. Optimizing these settings is known as "mapping." This graph may also be presented as load vs. RPM, or, Throttle opening vs. RPM. A production engine undergoes months of mapping to achieve a calibration that fits a broad range of uses and applications used by the general retail consumer, while at the same time meeting all of the mandated EPA emissions and fuel-economy requirements.

Racers do not require this broad range of mapping, but they should not stop too short either. A good example might be a fuel-injected blown street/strip car. Properly calibrated, these combinations can be very docile and have good street manners while having a tremendous power potential.

*There are a variety of electronic injectors in a full range of styles and flow ratings. Calculate your individual requirement and then add 15% to determine your flow rating in lbs/hour to size your injectors.*

**DYNO TESTING AND TUNING**

# CHAPTER 7

# TESTING TIPS ON HOW TO USE A DYNO

## Testing for Spark and Fuel on a Dynamometer

For reliable data on how particular parts will help your engine's performance, you need to be sure the engine is running properly during the dyno run. Spark and fuel tests will help you determine whether ignition and combustion are optimal. This test can be done on an engine dyno or a chassis dyno, but not on inertia-only chassis dynamometers. It is necessary to be able to control the load on the engine via the chassis dyno or the load control on the engine dyno.

The best settings provide the best engine performance, but are directly related to the fuel selected for use. It is a given that poor fuel will not stand very much ignition timing while very good fuel is somewhat more tolerant of spark adjustments.

Fuel and spark tests require that the dynamometer has been properly calibrated per the manufacturer's instructions.

### Testing Terminology for Spark and Fuel Test

The correct terminology for the spark adjustment is MBT (minimum spark advance for best torque).

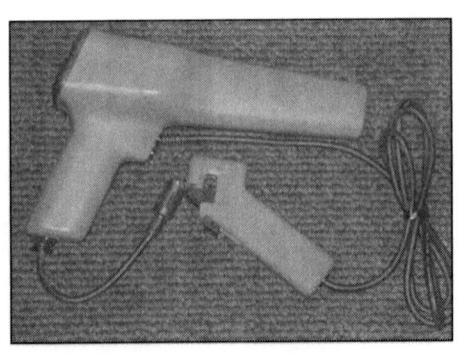

Terms for the fuel adjustments include LBT (leanest mixture for best torque) and RBT (richest mixture for best rorque).

The correct reference for the air and fuel ratio is A/F (Air–Fuel ratio), although there are some who refer to the fuel–air ratio, which is the reciprocal of the air–fuel ratio.

Fuel consumption relative to power produced is denoted BSFC (brake specific fuel consumption), while air consumption relative to power produced is BSAC (brake specific air consumption).

Throttle positions used in the testing described are WOT (wide-open throttle) or PT (part throttle).

## Description of Testing Procedure

At the peak power RPM reference, the back pressure on the exhaust should not exceed 8–10 inches of $H_2O$ (.29 psi–.36 psi) for performance applications. See elsewhere in this book for comments about exhaust systems and backpressure.

For a quick reference, a guy drag-

*The timing lights in the photos are the very best to establish a reliable timing point on engines. They are both MSD products. They are not overly expensive and provide reliable output. The chrome one is powered by an external battery (requires 12VDC) and the red one is self-powered with its own battery pack.*

DYNO TESTING AND TUNING

ging hard on a cigarette is applying about 3 to 4 inches of water. Remember that just one pound per square inch (1 psi) is equal to 27.69 inches of water ("$H_2O$).

In order for it to be adjusted correctly for either spark or fuel adjustments and other testing, the engine must be properly run-in and be verified for correct ring seal. Cranking compression, cylinder leakage, or blow-by can test the correct ring seal. Some tuners prefer a combination of all three methods to provide an engine condition baseline that is recorded.

## MBT (Minimum Spark Advance for Best Torque)

MBT testing is done at steady state (fixed RPM). For impatient testers, some testing can be done at transient rates, but not to exceed 100 rpm/sec as the faster acceleration rates will skew the results to apply too much timing.

Testing for MBT using an engine dynamometer is a simple process, but can be time consuming if done at various engine RPM points to establish a complete spark curve. The dynamometer is placed in auto control to target the peak torque RPM point. The most common method of testing for MBT is done at WOT and at the engine's peak torque point. The timing is advanced 2 degrees at a time until the final 2 degrees does not increase the torque. At that point, the timing is retarded 1 degree and that is referred to as MBT.

Another method for MBT testing is again referenced to peak torque, and the timing is advanced until there is a loss of 1% in torque reading. Then the timing is retarded until there is a loss of 1% in torque reading. Halfway between the two points is MBT. Sometimes the maximum advance point is referred to as MBT,

*Yeah buddy! The crew chief on this circle track car is elated as he signals the driver that they have gone over the target 400 Hp mark at the rear wheels. The engine is on safe enough tune-up that they can probably make the season without too much grief. Dyno testing and tuning is far less expensive than track testing. Rob Kelly photo.*

+4 degrees. For a performance application, establish the MBT point very carefully with known good fuel and appropriate caution.

If a tester wishes to vary the timing and verify the engine's sensitivity to spark advance, then the procedure is the same as above, but retarding the timing is factored for a point of 3% and 5% or more torque loss, so that those points are known.

It should be easy to adjust the timing from the operations console of the dynamometer. Although many

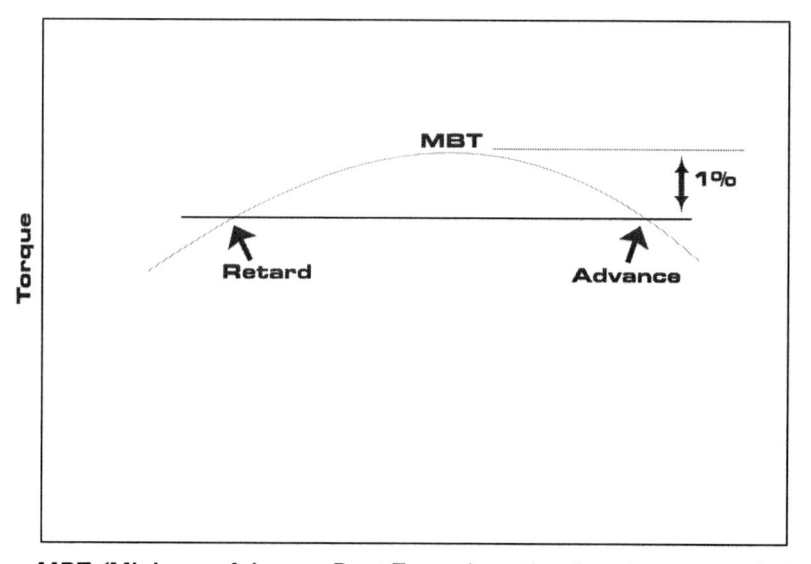

*Finding MBT (Minimum Advance Best Torque) on the dyno is easy to do but is time consuming. The engine is held at a steady RPM point and the timing is advanced until there is a 1% loss in torque. The timing is retarded until there is a 1% loss in torque. Halfway between the two timing references is MBT.*

# CHAPTER 7

*The testing on either an engine dyno or a chassis dyno to find RBT is much like finding MBT. The engine must be loaded and the air/fuel ratio is varied to find the point that is the best compromise. It is slow testing that pays great dividends in the best tune-up combination. No, it is not so simple as tossing fuel at it until it loses power, but it is close.*

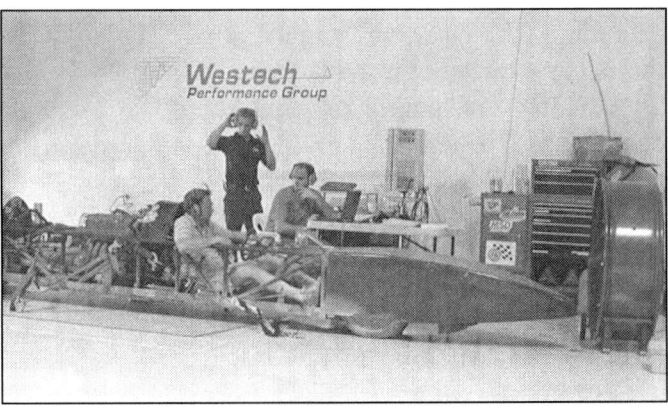

*Almost anything can be done on the dyno. The tune-up for this streamliner (minus body panels) was successful enough that it went to Bonneville (looks as if it was already at El Mirage) and set a record for its class. If you look closely, you might recognize the guy with the electronic screwdriver doing the tuning. It is Ben Strader, author of CarTech's* Building and Tuning Electronic Fuel Injection. *Photo courtesy of Westech Performance Group.*

types exist, the most popular method is to use an electronic spark control such as the MSD pn 8680 for batch timing control or the MSD pn 7553 dyno tuning programmer. The 7553 provides individual cylinder timing that can be the guideline for making mechanical changes in the reluctor on magnetic-triggered systems.

Some electronically controlled engines can be adjusted by communicating with the ECU via an external controller.

### LBT (Leanest Mixture for Best Torque)

Testing for LBT requires some method of changing the A/F for the engine being tested. The task is more cumbersome for carbureted engines. Carbureted engines can be adjusted by changing the main jets or the air bleeds, fuel pressure, or all the above.

EFI engines are the easiest to change if the tuner has access to an EFI controller where the original fuel map can be adjusted.

The testing for LBT should also be done at various RPM data points, but is often expedited in some performance applications to target peak torque and peak-power RPM points only.

Varying the A/F on the lean side to the target of the torque falling off by 1% (approximately) will allow you to find the LBT. Go too far and there are other parts in the engine that become fuel to be burned, such as pistons, head gaskets, cylinder heads, and even the oil in the pan.

### RBT (Richest Mixture for Best Torque)

The verification of RBT is done in the same fashion, but is not normally applied to naturally aspirated, gasoline-fueled engines. RBT is commonly applied to supercharged or turbocharged gasoline engines, or to naturally aspirated and supercharged engines using methanol, ethanol, or other fuels.

The reference to RBT and the testing process to establish the point is not well known in some groups. This particularly applies to the "leaner is meaner" crowd, and normally they have sacrificed an abundance of aluminum parts to prove their points.

### Test Results for Timing and Mixture

Engines produce horsepower as a result of burning fuel. In a performance application burning gasoline, it is better to adjust to 3%–5% rich than 1% lean. It is tricky balancing between maximum performance vs. minimum fuel used vs. engine component damage. Putting it into perspective, fuel is far less expensive than pistons or other components, and the attendant machine work and labor to repair a poor choice in tune-up configuration.

Spark-induced detonation must be avoided, but maximum power might be on the fringe and the very edge of spark induced detonation (light audible knock point).

# TESTING TIPS ON HOW TO USE A DYNO

*At the racetrack, cutting the engine clean and coasting to a stop will allow you to take a look at the plugs. This racer is a very successful guy in the Quick 16 category, and he accomplishes that by paying attention to the details. His engine was dyno tested before it went into the racecar. Checking plugs is just good sense.*

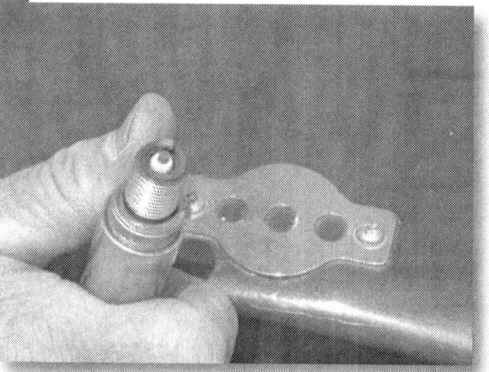

*This is just about a perfect appearance for a spark plug. It still has an end on it and it is showing that the combustion chamber is happy with the amount of fuel and spark. Checking plugs and regular leak down testing will keep you from having problems. Reading spark plugs is not magic.*

The span between LBT and RBT for gasoline (even racing gasoline) is narrower than the span between LBT and RBT for methanol or ethanol. E85 (85% ethanol and 15% gasoline) is likewise more forgiving on the LBT/RBT span.

Methanol is very prone to pre-ignite, so it is normal to adjust the mixture much closer to the RBT side without resulting in power loss. Methanol is also a very forgiving racing fuel for many reasons, thus its popularity for the last 80 to 100 years.

The working relationship between ignition timing and fuel mixture affect an engine's efficiency and how close it is running to "stoichiometric" or "stoich."

This term is derived from the Greek words *stoikheione* (element) and *metron* (measure). In dyno technology, stoichiometric is defined as the mixture of air and gasoline in the correct proportion to achieve perfect combustion. Complete combustion means that no fuel or oxygen remain after the timed combustion event.

Maximum power A/F ratio for typical gasoline varies with the amount of carbon and hydrogen atoms, but the ratio is generally close to 12.5:1 while the stoichiometric (chemically correct) ratio might be closer to 14.7:1. It all depends on the carbon and hydrogen content. A typical gasoline might be described with the chemical formula $C_8H_{18}$ (isooctane); however, there are hundreds and hundreds of "gasoline" compounds. The stoichiometric ratio on these "gasolines" might range from 14.1 to 15.2, as it all depends on the compounds of carbon and hydrogen. The term gasoline is not descriptive enough when you want to know the details.

Maximum power A/F ratio references for methanol ($CH_3OH$) will be close to 5 to 5.5:1 while the stoichiometry will be closer to 6.5:1.

*These photos were taken on the "Great White Dyno" at the Bonneville Salt Flats. As you can see in the first frame, the car has just left the starting line and is tossing up a little bit of damp salt. The next frame has the car heading off into the distance where the arrows are pointing at the entry to the first timing trap, which is two miles away. The last frame shows that the car is still not to the first timing trap still highlighted with the arrows. All this happened fairly quickly because the car went about 198 MPH. This was taken in the middle of the week, so they were running 'er safe. Photos courtesy of Larry Ledwick.*

DYNO TESTING AND TUNING

# CHAPTER 7

*Being around for the next round often depends on having the correct tune-up and, even though it takes a little time to keep checking the plugs at the end of the strip, it is worth the trouble. This particular guy also likes to wave at other racers and let them know that he is still in the hunt for the win.*

motorcycles and snowmobiles also fall into these categories. You had better start rich if you are going to stay around very long. And you had best have a conservative tune-up in place unless you have loads of parts to abuse before you become a believer.

There is certainly much to be said for dynamometer testing, but consider that most testing is done at WOT and some racetrack conditions will sometimes require the driver to use less than wide-open. What was the condition of air and fuel ratio at part throttle? If it was lean and the driver has to leave the throttle there for very long, uh-oh...there goes another head gasket or piston or both.

Ethanol ($C_2H_5OH$) will be close to 8.9:1 at stoichiometric while maximum power will be produced at close to 7:1 or richer. However, these target numbers are not absolutes. The stoichiometric ratio of E85 will typically be about 10:1, while maximum power will probably be at a ratio of 8.5:1 to 9:1 (depending on what the makeup of the 15% "gasoline" portion really is). Nitromethane ($CH_3NO_2$) is chemically correct at 1.7:1, but is regularly run at about 0.7:1 for maximum power production. Good test procedures and good testing methods on dynamometers prove what numbers fit specific circumstances. Take a closer look at the sidebar listing for lambda references (see page 130 of this book) and consider that they are for gasoline as the fuel. If you add any $N_2O$ (nitrous oxide) into the engine, then everything changes yet again, depending on whether it is a "dry" or a "wet" system. Start out those tune-ups with the manufacturer's recommendations and carefully go from there.

There is a very wise old saying at the Bonneville Salt Flats: "If you want to stay at Speed Week past Wednesday, you had better run 'er rich." The Bonneville salt flats are at an elevation of about 4215 feet above sea level and the vehicles are on the throttle for anywhere from two and a quarter miles to 5 and more miles at WOT (wide-open throttle). Traction permitting, the time frame of WOT ranges from 60 seconds to about 90 seconds. It all depends on how fast the vehicle is traveling and how much power is used. Not exactly the place for drag racing-style "stick some more advance in it" or "lean it out" philosophy, unless you brought a whole bunch of spare parts.

Certainly the same can be said for circle racing or sports car racing or any kind of endurance racing. Performance-oriented boats and

*Over-the-road testing for miles-per-gallon fuel consumption is very time-consuming and difficult as well. Filling the tank to the right level, keeping constant speed and other factors make this kind of testing frustrating. However, it is possible to test on a dyno for mileage under much more controlled conditions. Photo courtesy of Kathleen Henry.*

DYNO TESTING AND TUNING

*Yep, you can test just about anything on a dyno. Notice that there are no tie-downs and restraints in place. All that is required on this Go-Ped is to hold the front brake on and let 'er rip. These things are scary to start with, but trying to tune one cruising around in a parking lot or on the street is way scary. Photo courtesy of Westech Performance Group.*

## Testing on Dynamometers for Miles per Gallon Results

The use of an engine or chassis dynamometer to gather various data is commonplace, but some testing can be by special application. Fuel economy testing is one of many special tests that can be done on dynamometers.

Testing for miles per gallon (MPG) is a specialty test, but it can be accomplished easily by knowing some requirements outside the dynamometer test environment. Applying the necessary controls to the engine dynamometer will allow testing for MPG and can be done at various road load duplications. This would include both partial throttle as well as WOT.

### Input Data for Vehicles

One must know (or be able to accurately estimate) the required road load in order to duplicate the requirements for a given vehicle. The road load will include the chassis, rolling and aero losses that would be imposed on the engine to accomplish a given vehicle speed over the road. Over-the-road data would typically include the engine revolutions per minute (RPM) and the vehicle speed in miles per hour (MPH). Sometimes a manifold vacuum or manifold absolute pressure (MAP) reference can be useful.

A typical calculation for aerodynamic power is

$$HP_a = [(C_d A (V^3)) / 146600]$$

Where $Hp_a$ = Horsepower to overcome aerodynamic load, $C_d$ = Coefficient of drag, A = frontal area of vehicle in square feet, V = vehicle velocity in MPH

Rolling resistance calculations are pretty straightforward, using the equation

$$Rr_f = Cr_f \times W$$

Where $Rr_f$ = rolling resistance force in lbs, Crf = coefficient of rolling friction (typical auto tires at normal inflation = .015), W = Vehicle weight in lbs.

Power required to overcome Rolling resistance is dependent upon vehicle speed.

$$HPr_f = [(Rr_f \times V) / 375]$$

Where $HPr_f$ = Horsepower to overcome rolling resistance, $Rr_f$ = rolling resistance force in lbs, V = vehicle velocity in MPH

One must know the specific gravity (SG) for the fuel used. That number can translate to a weight per gallon for the fuel used. Most dynamometer measurements provide a few channels to measure the fuel flow, and that fuel flow is normally presented in pounds per hour (lbs/hr). The brake-specific fuel consumption (BSFC) is typically presented in pounds per horsepower hour (lbs/HP-hr).

### Test Setup on an Engine Dynamometer

For MPG testing, the engine dynamometer must have a constant speed (RPM) control capability. This is also referred to as an auto controlled test. In this test, the engine RPM is set to some target speed and the throttle varied to attain a target power number. This test would be applied for a spark ignition engine.

If the MPG test is to be set up for

# CHAPTER 7

*Testing a high-performance diesel on a chassis dynamometer is as easy as testing a rental car. It is a lot easier to do outside than in a shop if there is not adequate airflow across and through the room. The Ohio college student who owns this truck is studying engineering, and it showed in the performance of his rig. Photo courtesy of Kathleen Henry (kid's mom).*

a diesel engine, then the auto control must be set up for constant torque mode. The diesel engine does not have a throttle control, and instead the engine load controls the fuel rack or injectors. Otherwise, the method of testing is the same once the outside inputs are used to duplicate the road load that the diesel-powered vehicle applies.

### Test Setup for a Chassis Dynamometer

Testing for MPG on a chassis dynamometer is somewhat easier than on the engine dynamometer. The chassis dynamometer must be able to provide a load as the vehicle is set to a speed (requires that the dynamometer have an absorber). For very accurate results, the dynamometer must have the capacity to also add the load to simulate aerodynamic and rolling chassis losses. Of course the chassis dynamometer must also have the capacity to measure the fuel flow during the testing.

### Example for an Engine Dynamometer Application for the MPG Test

Given: Vehicle is mid size, where the vehicle has a $C_d$ of .40 (manufacturer's data) and a frontal area of 22ft$^2$ (manufacturer's data) and over-the-road load inputs for 60 mph include the RPM required is 2200 (on level road with no wind). The vehicle weighs 3000 lbs. The fuel used has a SG of .740.

$$.740 \times 8.34 = 6.172 \text{ lbs/gal}$$

Where 8.34 = pounds per gallon of water

The weight per gallon of fuel changes as the specific gravity (SG) changes.

Estimated road load at 60 mph from the aerodynamic drag power calculation listed above:

$$HP_a = [(.4 \times 22 \times 60^3) / 146600] = 12.97 \text{ hp at 60 mph}$$

Estimated road load at 60 mph from rolling resistance calculation listed above:

$$Hpr_f = [(Rr_f \times V) / 375]$$
$$Hpr_f = [(.015 \times 3000 \times 60) / 375 = 7.2 \text{ hp at 60 mph}$$

Note: The horsepower required increases with vehicle speed.

Total road load at 60 mph is estimated to be

$$12.97 + 7.2 = 20.17 \text{ hp.}$$

Note that this estimate does not include any drivetrain losses, but they could be added if they are known or manufacturer's information is available.

Based on the previous calculations, the dynamometer would be adjusted to apply a load of at least 20.2 hp at 2200 RPM. Assume that the displayed BSFC for the engine example is .42 lbs/hp-hr. Assume that the fuel flow reading is 8.48 lbs/hr.

$$MPG = (F_{wg} / F_c) \times V$$

Where $F_{wg}$ = wt of fuel per gallon in lbs,
$F_c$ = Fuel flow, in lbs/hr,
V = Vehicle velocity that the test represents in MPH (this will be the vehicle speed that the power is set to represent; in this case it is 60 mph)

$$MPG = (6.17 / 8.48) \times 60 =$$

## CHAPTER 8

# ACCURACY AND REPEATABILITY

You often hear of accuracy and repeatability, but they are easier to say than to accomplish at the test site.

As you scanned through the earlier sections of this book, you saw references to the importance of accuracy and repeatability, but we should establish a succinct definition for them as we continue to look at their importance in testing.

**What is accuracy and how can you make sure the test system is accurate?**

Something that is accurate provides correct information in accordance with an accepted standard. The center of the bull's-eye on a target is a known standard. Another way to refer to accuracy is with a paper target that has five bullet holes equally spaced around the center.

Or another example is where a crankshaft has been ground to the *correct* diameter on all the main journals (within +/- .0001 inch). That is accuracy, and, if they are all the same diameter, that also is very repeatable.

**What is repeatability and how can you make sure the test system is repeatable?**

Repeatability is a test that readily duplicates another test under the same conditions. It is probably more critical than accuracy because it will give you a level of confidence in the data collected and helps to make comparisons in your own tests much easier to do. That is not so easy if the

*This target shows a good way to define accuracy. All the rounds passed through the target at an equal distance from the center. However, it is not something that displays repeatability. Dynos need to be accurate, repeatable, and reliable.*

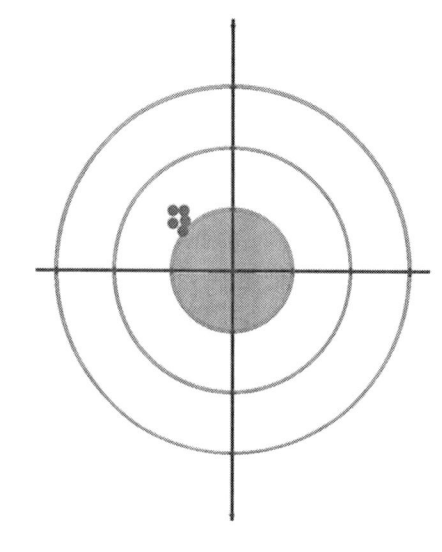

*This target shows good repeatability but the accuracy is not too good. Dynamometer data needs to be repeatable and reliable and accurate for dependable tuning to occur.*

comparisons are made with another dyno or another site. Then accuracy becomes just as important—that is *if* the other site is *accurate* as well as *repeatable*.

Another way to refer to repeatability is five bullet holes on a target that are very close to each other, but not in the center of the bull's-eye. What is called good grouping in

DYNO TESTING AND TUNING

# CHAPTER 8

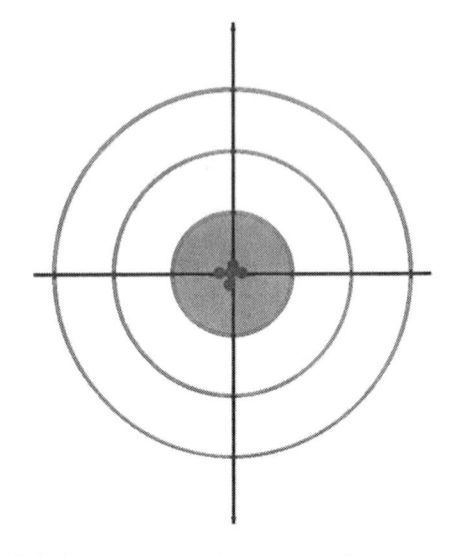

*This target is what you are after as a shooter and a dyno user or operator. The target shows excellent repeatability and accuracy. This would be very reliable data.*

shooting parlance is a very good example of good repeatability.

Another example could be a crankshaft that has been ground to exactly the same sizes on all the main journals, but that doesn't guarantee that the journals are the *correct* diameter. If you were measuring the journals with a micrometer that was not in calibration, you can still have very repeatable results but with inaccurate numbers of measurement.

## Accuracy and the Torque Calibration

In order to insure accuracy with a test system, the first thing to verify is the torque calibration. If you have an accurate weight (75.00 lbs, for example) for reference and hang it on the calibration arm of a known length (2 ft, for example), then the answer displayed on the torque scale should be 2 ft x 75.00 lbs = 150.00. Then you would need to add the effect of the calibration arm by itself (suppose it was 20 lbs). So the real answer would be 150 + 20 = 170 lb-ft of torque indicated. The point here is that the effective weight of the calibration arm is an important piece of the puzzle if accuracy is a goal. Of course the exact weights of the calibration weights are equally important. If the calibration weights are a little off, all of the values the dyno produces will be off. Inexact calibration weights, whether intentional or otherwise, is one of the most common areas for errors.

What if the system has no torque system to calibrate? Well, if that is the case, it makes you wonder whether this dyno is a trustworthy source for data. You may be able to get repeatable results from it, which would allow comparison among tests run on that dyno, but the value of comparisons with tests from other dynos would be questionable. Without calibration, you can't assure a dyno's accuracy.

Beware of any system that you can't verify or anyone who uses "trust me" as an answer to your questions on calibration.

A great way to get off on the right foot and to have a high level of faith and trust in a test facility is for them to just show you the calibration process and verify that the torque system is properly calibrated. The weight used for calibration needs to be verified to be the correct amount. Many people have carried their own weights to a test facility to confirm that the numbers on the torque system were correct. A suggested minimum amount would be something between 50 and 75 pounds. Some facility folks have used cylinder heads, flywheels, or even laboratory-grade weights for the base verification. The lab-grade weights are the preferred choice. The weight can be almost anything that has gone across a certified scale.

However, you must be very wary of the all-too-easy-to-find barbell weights. They might be marked with a weight and, if weighed on a certified scale, perhaps not be the same numbers. Remember that the weight is very important because it will be multiplied by the effective length of the calibration arm. As an example, if the weight difference is only 2 pounds and the calibration arm is 4 feet long, then the shift in accuracy is easily 8 lbs-ft of torque. At 6,000 RPM that would perhaps generate an error of over 9 hp (observed). And if the correction factor was about 6%

*Calibration of any dynamometer is necessary for one to have confidence in the results. All three of the weights in this photo could be used for calibration IF you know what each weighs. The flywheel would have to be weighed on a certified accurate scale to be of any use. The lab weights are much more accurate than barbell weights. The lab weights are typically plugged with lead over small shot in the drilled holes in order to trim the weights to specification. The arrow shows one of the plugs. These are the type of weights that should be used for dynamometer torque calibration.*

86  DYNO TESTING AND TUNING

## ACCURACY AND REPEATABILITY

to 8%, then the power shift is toward 10 hp. Calibration is critical to establishing a program that can be trusted to supply dependable results.

Today's NASCAR cup team engine shops expect to be able to detect with confidence a difference as small as 1 hp to less than 2 hp when comparing engines. The extra details that go into each of those impressive engines are carried out during development and testing procedures. That is down in the few tenths of a percent! You can't get there without good testing procedures, an excellent facility, and precise calibration. Just how close does the required measurement of torque have to be in order to qualify small increments of 1 or 2 hp at 8500 RPM? Well, all this is very basic and if you look at the basic equations for horsepower, torque and RPM, the answer is hopefully obvious. T = (5252 x 1HP) / 8500 = .618 lbs-ft. Putting that tiny amount of torque into context and assuming that the engine is 8 cylinders all working the same, the tiny amount of torque per cylinder is only .077 lb-ft! Now that is getting down to sorting the fly dung from the pepper. Most of us would be tickled to death if we could count on data within +/-1% of the target numbers. This kind of measurement accuracy is phenomenal and is much easier to write and to say than to produce in testing.

What are some good numbers to rely on? We maintain that the comparison of data at two or more separate testing sites should be within +/- 2%. If the dynamometers are properly calibrated and the same rigid standards of testing procedures and operations and test methods are applied, 2% is a good target. However, it is possible to narrow that down a bit if the repeatability at each site was within +/- 1%.

It is imperative that the data for RPM vs. time and speed vs. time (for chassis dynos) be available for evaluation. If tests are not done at the same rate of acceleration, there is no effective way to compare data with any realistic results. It cannot be possible to achieve good and reliable data if the RPM vs. time slope is not smooth. If it is ragged, then the data collected is also very likely to be tainted because of the variations. Software or sales guys might try to tell you differently, but if they do they are full of soup!

A special word of caution for chassis dyno comparisons: The variables in chassis dyno testing are generally much greater than with engine dyno testing. The variability of tie-downs alone causes the tires to distort differing amounts and that by itself will generate variations in data relative to speed and power. Expecting to compare reliable results on chassis dynos to within +/- 2% is really very wishful thinking. Figures of +/- 3% to 4% are much more realistic when you are looking at the power at the drive tires.

*Variability in chassis dyno results can be because of tire inflation and tie-down configuration and many other influences. The photo has the tire patch highlighted so that you can appreciate the distortion at the contact between the tire and the roller. For uniform results, the tire inflation should be the same and the tie-downs should be at the same tension.*

### Additional Calibrations for Accurate Results

Your test plan should include initial calibrations of both the dyno and the critical instruments before you start your test. There are several methods of calibration. Static calibration is the most common method, whereby a transducer, for example, is given a known input, such as the temperature of boiling water at 212 degrees Fahrenheit, and the corresponding transducer output at the dyno console is compared to the real value of 212 degrees F.

### Barometric Pressure

The barometric pressure can be compared to a mercury column barometer nearby, or you can call a local airport and ask for the station pressure. You may have to recalibrate your instruments to match the known inputs. Make the calibration procedure part of every test plan to ensure you are not wasting time and money by taking worthless data. Plan to follow a written recalibration schedule. It is too easy to forget the calibrations when you are in the middle of a long testing program—like waiting too long to fill your gas tank on a trip; when you realize you are almost out of gas you may end up walking.

When you don't keep up on the calibrations by keeping readings accurate, you will produce bad data. With a dyno test, you may have to go back and rerun a portion of the tests, or worse yet, have your car actually

*The calibration of the number used for local barometric pressure should be based on station pressure (pressure at site, uncorrected) by relying on a good-quality mercury barometer. The temperature affects the expansion of the mercury and a slight correction must be made for that and for gravity.*

slow down when you use the new part or fuel and spark calibration.

## Dynamic Calibration

Dynamic calibration is, as the name implies, done in a moving or dynamic condition. For example, you may want to check your tachometer reading. Typically we use a portable digital optical tachometer. By placing a piece of reflective tape on the vibration damper and aiming the hand-held tachometer at the tape while the engine is running, we can get a good reading and compare it to the dyno reading. By checking the readings at several different RPMs throughout the speed range, you can see if the dyno tachometer is accurate throughout the range. Having the dyno tachometer read accurately is at the very core of good data, since virtually all readings are referenced to the speed range of the engine as a baseline. Tip: If you use a rev limiter, while you run your engine on the dyno, bring your rev limiter to the test and check to make sure that the limiter really shuts the engine off at the selected point.

## Air Flow Meters

Calibrating the air flow meters is best done on a flow bench. For that reason, many dyno shops have the capability of moving their flow bench physically near their dyno. This allows them to turn the dyno on and register air flow while the flow meter is running on the flow bench. Compare the reading on the flow bench with the dyno console reading. Once the comparison is made between what the flow bench reads and what the dyno reads, the flow meter reading on the dyno can be recalibrated to match the known flow from the flow bench. This is only good for fairly low air flow numbers, since a complete engine flows much more air than a typical flow bench can handle. If you are not able to move your flow bench close to your dyno, you may have to make a long auxiliary cord to extend the range of the flow turbine so it can reach the flow bench. Prior to installing the flow meter, carefully inspect the meter for damage, such as broken or missing blades, missing or bent honeycomb air straighteners, or other conditions that might affect the accuracy.

## Transducer Placement

Transducer placement is just as important as calibration. Putting a sensor in the wrong location will produce inaccurate results and drive the wrong decisions. For example, something as simple as the placement of the inlet air temperature sensor can greatly affect your results. Proper placement for this sensor is in the center of the inlet air stream, just as it enters the carburetor or throttle body. If you place it at the periphery of the air stream in a much warmer place, it will record an artificially high number. Because the air temperature value recorded will be used to determine the correction factor to recalculate engine output, the artificially high air temp will show more power than was actually achieved. Armed with this faulty data, you might be compelled to choose a less effective part or tuning specification. Some unscrupulous dyno shops will use the inverse relationship to convince a customer that their engine is down on power and therefore in need of a rebuild or additional tuning. This might involve casually leaving a wet shop towel on the temp sensor during a run to create an artificially cool inlet air temp, which would translate to an artificially low horsepower calculation.

If you place the exhaust thermocouples at different distances from the cylinder head, the temperatures will vary greatly. As an experiment, drill a series of four holes in an individual header pipe starting two inches away from the header flange and every two inches thereafter. Then place four thermocouples from one side of the engine into these four holes. Fire the engine up and make a run. Look at the difference in the readings from the same cylinder at different distances away from the head. This will convince you to take great care in thermocouple placement. You should try to place pressure transducers at key points in the system to enable you to take pressure drops. For example, if you place a pressure transducer just before an oil cooler and one just after an oil cooler, you will be able to measure the pressure drop across the cooler. Engineers often refer to this pressure drop as the *Delta P* or the differential pressure.

## Baseline

Setting a baseline is quite often the most crucial part of a test. Unless you carefully monitor all of the test conditions to ensure that you are making each run under exactly the same conditions as the previous run, you will have data that varies substantially. While you can average any set of data produced, accuracy begins with using only data that varies less than 1–2%. Most testing is done using the ABA method (see Chapter 4). The basis of each comparison begins with a baseline formed from an average of at least three runs that are very close. The part is then changed or a new adjustment is made and the runs are then repeated using the same set of conditions. When all three of the second set of runs are within 1–2%, then they are averaged and the two sets of averaged data are compared. Learn to look at data in percentages. People may tend to dismiss 2 horsepower, but if it results from a tuning session of a 100-horsepower engine it is just as impressive as finding 20 horsepower on a 1,000-horsepower Pro Mod engine. Two percent is two percent! Any top NHRA or NASCAR team would pay dearly for a two-percent improvement. These teams quite often will work for an entire year at enormous cost and labor just to see a 2% gain in power.

This process of comparisons continues throughout the test session. As the test session progresses, good operators will go back and reconfigure the engine to the original specification and rerun the very first test series to reconfirm that the engine produces the same average corrected data that it did when the session started. This process is called closing the loop or reestablishing the baseline for the engine. While this may seem redundant at first, it actually saves time and effort in the long run.

Suppose the engine had suffered some damage during the second test that caused it to lose 4% power and subsequently lose 1% for every three runs after that? Chances are that you would have written off the second test part or calibration as inferior to the first one, and then written off each succeeding test as worse yet, since a 1% loss would not have been alarming. In fact, the engine may have been slowly wearing off a cam intake lobe. By repeating the baseline at the end of the session, you would have noticed the flaw and might have been forced to find out why the engine could not repeat its earlier performance.

## Break-in

The break-in phase for a dyno engine is critical to the overall test accuracy. Think of the break-in as conditioning for the engine where every mating surface is carefully lapped to a fine fit. As the break-in continues, the internal engine friction drops and the cylinder sealing increases. If the engine is not broken in properly, it may continue to break in and improve its performance during your testing. If this is the case, the test results will get better as the engine ages, up to a point where the engine is properly aged and settles out. Once an engine is properly broken in, it will perform steadily at the same power level. Over a good period during its life cycle it will produce relatively stable test results. Eventually the engine will wear out and rapidly begin to lose its capability.

At the top racing levels where established teams compete weekly, the difference in engine power between the contenders is quite often less than one percentage point of the full-scale output. It is therefore critical to carefully analyze all facets of dyno testing and data analysis for accuracy and repeatability. Simple errors here could spell a long, expensive trip down a path that was wrong to begin with.

## Engine Condition

Nothing will hamper repeatability more quickly than an engine that is worn out or wearing out. Something like a cam lobe in the process of wearing off may cause you to lose a day while you chase it. Once you find it, the problem seems obvious, but while you are looking, it may be elusive. For that reason, always watch the brake specific values as you test. Brake specific fuel consumption (BSFC) or brake specific air consumption (BSAC) is really an efficiency check. If it suddenly falls for no apparent reason, or if it gradually trends down during a series of runs, look for the answer. Don't test any more until you find the answer; you may be wasting valuable time and a precious engine. The standard cylinder leakage and compression tests may highlight potential problems. Blowby will measure the dynamic sealing capability. Oil-filter debris will reveal some of the potential trouble spots.

# CHAPTER 8

As we pointed out in Chapter 4, performing health checks on the engine at regular intervals will help to ensure that you are taking meaningful data. If, for whatever reason, your engine suffers damage or premature wear, its output will most likely suffer. Catching this change in engine condition may save you from an expensive engine failure or save you from choosing the less powerful part for the upcoming race. A bearing may have been overloaded, or a piston may have scuffed during a particular test. If you catch these failures early, disaster can be averted. If you get lazy or caught up in the rush of testing, you will most likely miss the telltale signs of imminent disaster. Then, suddenly, big trouble will occur.

Quite often, test engines incorporate prototype parts that are not as robust as their final versions. Experimental cylinder heads that started life as a production head, or last season's race head, often have been opened up until the head porter hit water. This hole or void is filled with epoxy if it is in an intake port, and the heads are run briefly to get a quick evaluation. If the quick test is promising, the heads may be repaired by welding, and additional testing undertaken. If the overall testing is successful, then the casting may be changed and a new head or port created. When using highly modified components, it is critical to make sure they are performing properly. In this case a pinhole water leak could adversely affect the test. A leaking port could fill a cylinder with coolant while the engine was briefly stopped. When the engine was re-fired, the trapped water could cause the engine to either bend a rod or break a piston and possibly damage a cylinder wall.

*This is the aftermath of floating the valves or a broken valve spring. The valve hits the piston, bends, and then the head breaks off. This will also happen if you don't have enough clearance to begin with.*

Admittedly, some failures are sudden and dramatic as well as devastating, such as losing the head of a valve. This valve failure typically takes out a head, piston, bore wall, rod, and then the engine pumps debris from the damaged cylinder to all of the rest of the cylinders—all in the time it takes to turn off the ignition and let the engine coast to a stop. A good dyno operator should be ready to stop the test at the first sign of trouble. Sometimes an engine, just like a baby, will give you a small clue. You have to be attuned to the faintest tiny clue and react accordingly.

## Oil Temperature

Perhaps the most dramatic effects of power gain or loss from one run to another occur due to changes in the engine oil temperature. Go to great lengths to ensure that you establish a set of conditions for fluid temperatures that can be easily achieved and are somewhat representative of actual running conditions.

*An oil cooler is important if you will be running hard for extended periods. Without cool oil, the oil gets thin and then pistons scuff and bearings seize. Be sure to test with the one you use in the car.*

Once you choose a test temperature, it pays to be very precise about starting each test precisely at that temperature. A degree or two can make a difference in the engine's output.

If you are just starting out in dyno testing and tuning, do yourself a favor. Run four identical tests in rapid succession, not letting the oil cool between runs. Look at the data spread and you will see how the increasing oil temperature drastically affects the overall results.

While running an engine test with an oil temperature of 125F saves a great deal of warm-up time, it does not adequately represent what the engine typically sees unless it is in a drag car being raced in cold temperatures. Conversely, running oil temperature in excess of 225F may replicate what you see during an endurance race, but you will spend a long time trying to warm the oil up on the dyno prior to making each dyno run.

Wearing out a $70,000 race engine by using it as an oil heater really doesn't make sense! Use of external oil and coolant pre-heaters has

## ACCURACY AND REPEATABILITY

become quite widespread. Note: When using an oil heater, put it on a timer, so when you forget to turn it off after the test, you don't fry the oil in the pan and catch the room on fire!

Each test may bring about a new set of compromises. The rule you must follow is to make comparisons only with similar sets of conditions. Sometimes good comparisons can be made between runs where the oil temperature is 200 degrees F. Adding another 25 to 50 degrees F to bring the test conditions up to 225 degrees F or 250 degrees F will not change the difference (Delta) in performance, just the numbers themselves. For example, an engine tested with two different sets of headers will show a 17-hp gain with the oil at 200 degrees F (600 hp vs. 617 hp) as well as at 225 degrees F. (602 hp vs. 619 hp). What do we learn here? First, the second set of headers makes better peak power. Second, the engine makes more horsepower at higher oil temperature. Third, the time spent warming the oil from 200 to 225F was wasted. Having said that, always validate any final combination at vehicle conditions for a final check.

*This pad gets glued to the bottom of the oil pan and serves to pre-heat the oil prior to a test. It makes no sense to wear out a valuable race engine while heating oil. Just remember to unplug it before you go home at night.*

### Water Temperature

While water or coolant temperature is not as critical as oil temperature, it is significant and somewhat co-dependent on oil temperature. You would never want to run a test with cold coolant unless you were simulating what a car at the drag strip might see after having the water changed between runs. Be sure to run the same type of cooling system on the dyno that is run in the vehicle. If a pressurized system is used in the vehicle, try to exactly replicate the entire cooling system for the dyno. When mounting the various cooling-system components, heights are critical as well as placement of the parts. Don't just use the parts supplied by the dyno facility. As stressed throughout this book, use the parts you plan to use on your car. Remember, you are testing, and finding out what doesn't work is sometimes as valuable as finding out what does work!

Equalized coolant distribution within the cylinder head is critical. Not unlike fuel distribution, proper coolant distribution is crucial to equalizing the power potential of each cylinder. A cylinder that operates warmer than its adjacent cylinders will be more prone to detonate than its neighbors. Conversely, a cylinder that runs cooler than its adjacent cylinders has room left when its partners have given up. The goal should be to make everything equal so the cylinders all contribute equally until they have reached their maximum output. Again, fuel, air, spark, and cooling all directly affect this capability. You may have to use various internal dams and diverters in the cooling system, as well as modify the water transfer holes in the head gasket to ensure coolant flow where it is most effective.

### Weather Conditions

Whenever you test, you are constantly making comparisons between runs. Corrected numbers play a big part in the process by allowing us the capability of comparing data taken on two days with totally different weather. Accuracy of barometer and temperature readings plays a huge part in determining the

*Being able to get the oil hot quickly and keep it hot during a test is difficult sometimes. This cart employs some serious heater elements as well as a circulating pump and lines. It circulates hot oil through the pan. This allows testing at very high oil temperatures.*

*If you plan on doing any endurance running, you will need a cooling tower in order to scrub off the heat created during extended periods of running at high loads.*

DYNO TESTING AND TUNING

CHAPTER 8

overall accuracy of these correction factors.

As a test session wears on, the weather conditions are typically changing. The ambient temperature as well as the humidity and barometric pressure routinely change as the day progresses. When a storm approaches, there will be a drastic pressure drop compared to an average day. The relative humidity is another very important variable. The percent relative humidity (RH%) is a measure of how many tiny water droplets are suspended in the air. When the air becomes saturated, the excess vapor bonds together and falls to the ground as rain. The water molecules suspended in the air displace oxygen molecules, and therefore humid air prevents an engine from making as much power as it can produce breathing dry air, which contains the maximum amount of oxygen per volume.

It is extremely important to stay ahead of the weather-correction factor when testing, since it so greatly affects the outcome of your individual tests by influencing evaluations or comparisons. Take barometer and vapor pressure readings quite often if the day is changing or if the weather is humid. If the weather becomes too extreme (a zero-degree F day or a day where the carb air temp is 140 degrees F), consider suspending testing for the day since you will probably not be able to make meaningful and accurate test comparisons and conclusions. Better to wait until you have a consistent day where the swing in temperature and barometric pressure is not as great. While the correction factors theoretically cover all contingencies, they have been found to be lacking in actual practice. Unless the engine has to leave tonight, find something else to do. It is fine to break in an engine during these times, but try to avoid any serious rating or comparative runs and any critical tuning procedures.

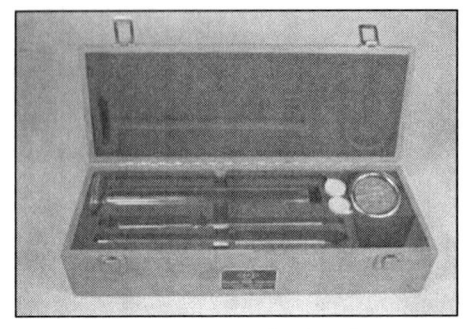

*Some tuners use an air density meter like this one from Kinsler Fuel Injection to keep track of changing weather conditions. If you use one at the track, use it during your testing on the dyno so you can correlate between the track and the dyno.*

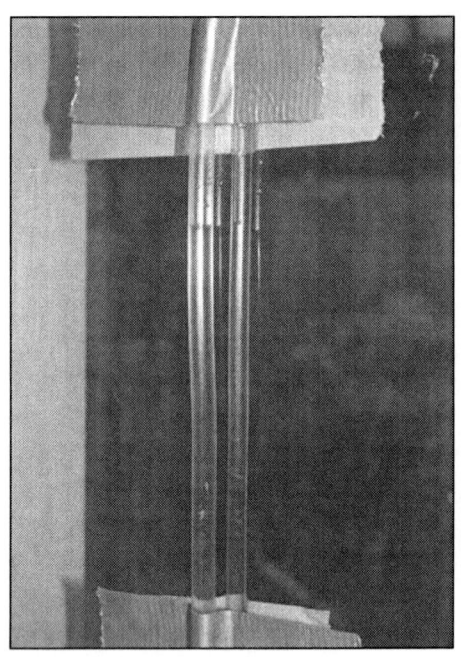

*An 8-ft. length of clear plastic tubing serves as a water column manometer to track the pressure differential between the dyno cell and the outside room. This gives the operator a quick accurate visual indication that the room fans are running and how well they are working.*

*Many tuners use an altimeter to track the barometric pressure at the track or in the dyno. Often the ones found at surplus stores are inaccurate. Have them calibrated at an FAA-approved instrument service center.*

## Room Depression

Almost all test cells are run at a lower pressure than the rest of the building they are in. This slightly negative pressure is important because it prevents harmful gases like deadly carbon monoxide, an odorless and colorless gas, from escaping to where people are located. This slightly negative room pressure will not affect your results if you are careful to calibrate your dyno barometer and make sure that it properly records the pressure in the room during the runs. By using corrected data, you ensure that subtle variations are all properly weighed and factored into the final valuation. The horsepower that the engine makes is corrected and serves as a fair and accurate measure of what the engine would produce on a so-called perfect day.

Suffice it to say that perfect conditions very rarely occur; the rest of the time, we correct up or down from the perfect day. If your dyno does not show the correction factor,

DYNO TESTING AND TUNING

## To Pressurize or Not to Pressurize?

Any performance engine that runs for more than a few seconds typically uses a closed-loop pressurized cooling system. The lone exception might be a boat running in fresh water. The pressure in a cooling system is important for several reasons. First, the pressure raises the boiling point of the coolant being used. The laws of heat transfer tell us that running coolant at a higher temperature is better because on any given day, the engine with the higher temperature will have better heat transfer because of the greater difference (Delta T) between the ambient air and the coolant. However, coolant can become too hot with a radiator that is incorrectly sized or run at too high a pressure. At this point, you run the risk of overheating and damaging the engine. Additionally you run the risk of overheating the incoming engine air charge, which would upset your air/fuel ratio, or boiling the coolant and losing it out of the pressure-relief radiator cap. The downside here is a slippery mix of coolant being sprayed onto the pavement and tires.

In some cases, coolant can actually be too cold. Temperature becomes a big factor in marine applications. Lake or river water is much cooler than the normal operating temperature of almost any engine. Marine cooling systems are quite different from car systems—the block must be kept full and warm while the heated wastewater is used to cool the exhaust manifolds. Then, the wastewater is literally dumped into the stream of exhaust gases passing out through the exhaust system, with which it returns to the atmosphere. Because of the corrosive nature of salt water, many marine engines uses either a water-conditioning treatment or a completely separate pressurized cooling system with an outside-water-to-engine-coolant heat exchanger. This allows the engine block and heads to have a pressurized cooling system and to employ coolant free of any harmful corrosive effects or particulate matter. Only the exhaust system sees the salt water in this instance.

Some vehicle racing applications omit a thermostat in order to prevent the flow restriction they produce. Thermostats prevent coolant from circulating through the cooling system until the coolant in the engine reaches the optimum operating temperature.

Whatever testing you undertake, use a fully functioning vehicle-cooling system that closely duplicates the one you plan to use. Heights of the various components, such

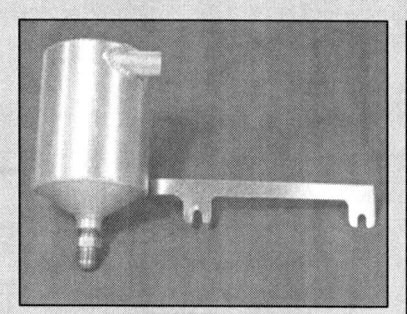

*Use a surge tank to allow the air a place to go when it escapes from the coolant. Without this, the air remains in the coolant and therefore is not as efficient.*

*Marine engines have a unique set of requirements. The cooling system is totally different from any in the automotive world.*

as the radiator and overflow chamber, are especially important. The coolant flow within the engine should be carefully directed and managed to prevent steam pockets, which would prohibit coolant from reaching these areas and create hot spots. If these hot spots endure, they will damage the gaskets or warp the heads. Hot spots can also create detonation by allowing the temperature to rise in a cylinder or combustion chamber until the incoming mixture of gas and air ignites prematurely.

When pressurizing a cooling system, be careful to include a de-aeration system to remove the air from the coolant. Moroso and others offer a small tank to be mounted above the radiator or heat exchanger that separates the air bubbles from the coolant as it circulates through the cooling system. These are called "expansion" or "surge" tanks in some applications. Trying to cool an engine with a mixture of air and coolant does not work too well. The air bubbles sometimes separate from the water and collect inside a dome or pocket in the water jacket of a cylinder head and eventually turn to steam. When the steam forms, it rapidly expands in volume. Once this happens, you have an invisible steam bubble trapped in the cylinder head. With no way to purge or burp itself, the steam pocket may prevent coolant from reaching the heat-affected zone while the heat continues to rise, creating more steam. This goes on until the entire combustion chamber is essentially surrounded by steam, which prevents any cooling from occurring. With the chamber getting hotter and hotter as the engine continues to run,

## To Pressurize or Not to Pressurize? Continued

it does not take too long before pre-ignition or detonation occurs, resulting in engine failure.

Take a look at a series of head gaskets for the same engine family and note the steam and coolant holes. While the bores and bolt holes are all the same, the coolant holes will vary quite a bit from one gasket to another and from one application to another. This variance represents many solutions to the common problem of keeping the coolant flowing so that it effectively cools the block and cylinder head and prevents steam pockets from forming. Quite often in racing engines, external plumbing is used to direct water toward or away from critical areas. For example, by drawing coolant out of cylinder heads at the top and toward the rear you may be able to prevent the rear cylinders from overheating by creating more flow in that area. This removed coolant is routed directly to the water outlet at the front of the engine.

Careful selection of components and rigorous, well-instrumented testing of the cooling system on the dyno can uncover these trouble spots. The equation is quite simple. In an engine, we typically tune around the weakest cylinder, or in this case the cylinder most likely to knock. When we reach knock, we stop and back off. Your development goal should always be to have all of the cylinders develop the same power and have the same knock limitation. You would never create a wagon team consisting of seven horses and a pony; always balance your cooling capability to allow all of the cylinders to be properly cooled, so they all become knock-limited at approximately the same time.

---

simply divide the corrected numbers by the uncorrected numbers. You might see a value of 1.030 for example, which would indicate a 3% upward correction. This would mean that if you were testing on a perfect day, the engine would actually produce 3% more power than your uncorrected or actual test value. Occasionally you may hit that cool dry day in October where you will actually make more horsepower than you would under the so-called perfect conditions. In this case, the engine that made 490 hp observed and uncorrected might correct down to 482 hp. This negative correction might only happen one or two days per year in Michigan, but it might happen 12 days a year in Arizona.

### Fuel Flow

When we are measuring the performance of an engine, it is important always to measure fuel flow. We want to know how efficient the engine is and how close it is running to stoichiometric, which, as introduced earlier, is defined as the mixture of air and gasoline in the correct proportion to achieve perfect combustion. Again, perfect or complete combustion, referred to as "stoichiometric" or simply "stoich," means that no fuel and no oxygen is left over after combustion. Become familiar with fuel-flow rates and the overall fuel-demand curve of your engine to ensure that you always have more fuel available than the engine will need.

Fuel-flow meters should be calibrated dynamically since they must have fuel flowing through them to record a value. There are several ways to achieve this calibration. The preferred method is by attaching a variable-orifice device with a pressure gauge to the end of the fuel line and flowing fuel into a bucket or can placed on a scale. By timing how long it takes to flow a given weight of fuel, you can determine fuel flow in lbs. of fuel per hour. Make sure your fuel-flow capability exceeds your engine's maximum fuel needs by at least 15%. You must always check and calibrate fuel-flow ratings at your fuel system's operating pressure, since this will affect the amount of flow that can be achieved.

It is important to have both pressure and flow in your system, especially if you are using fuel injection. Pressure not only forces the fuel through the system, but it also determines the droplet size coming from the injectors. Generally, the finer these droplets are, the better burn we get. Always calibrate your fuel system in lbs./hr. at a given pressure.

We always speak in terms of "weights" of fuel and air because that is how they are chemically combined. This goes back to chemistry and refers to the atomic weights involved in the chemical equation.

If you are unsure what power your engine combination might make, consider using one of the readily available PC-based engine simulator programs discussed earlier to get an estimate. If you are careful, give the program all of the information it asks for, and provide good data, the results

ACCURACY AND REPEATABILITY

# Fuel-Flow Testing

This simple test will help to establish you as a serious tester or operator but more importantly will prevent you from wasting time and possibly damaging your engine. It stands to reason that if we knew the horsepower of our engine we would not be testing it, so here we have to make an educated guess. We need to determine the fuel-flow requirement necessary to support the maximum power capability of the engine. Size your fuel system to be capable of delivering at least 15% more fuel than is required at the peak power expected. Let's look at how we derive the fuel-flow requirement. First we need to come up with an estimated maximum horsepower number for our combination. This number can come from a number of sources.

Performance calculations can be as simple as multiplying the engine displacement by a horsepower-per-cubic-inch factor to arrive at horsepower, or as complex as using some of the high-end programs like Engine Expert or Dynomation, which allow the user to simulate and predict the performance very accurately prior to ever buying a part or turning a wrench. Once the peak horsepower is established, divide the horsepower by 2 and you will arrive at the pounds per hour required to have enough fuel delivery to run a high-performance engine on most racing gasoline. The tricky part of this number is that the flow is at a rated pressure.

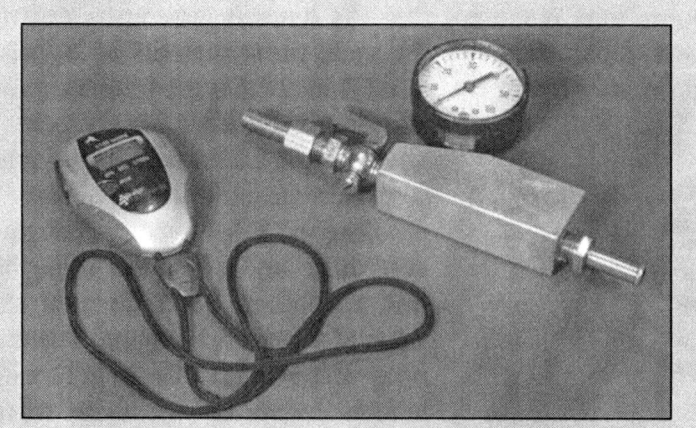

*By timing how long it takes to flow as little as 2 gallons of fuel or a safe substitute at rated pressure, you will be able to verify that your pump is capable of supplying adequate fuel flow to achieve the expected power.*

To better understand this principle, think of it this way: If you were given a garden hose and told to stand on the ground and fill a bucket atop a 15-foot step ladder with water, you would have to increase the pressure by using a nozzle to get the water high enough to fill the bucket; when you passed the water through the nozzle to increase the pressure for this, you would decrease the flow. Like our example, all fuel systems rely on pressure as well as flow. One without the other is useless. If either pressure or flow gets out of range by becoming too high or too low, the fuel system will fail by not delivering the correct amount of fuel to the engine. Therefore, it is absolutely imperative that your fuel system be able to deliver enough fuel at the required rated pressure of your fuel system to allow you to reach your engine's maximum potential.

By using the device shown in the photo, attached to your fuel line, carefully flow a non-flammable fluid with the same density as the fuel you plan to use into a measured five-gallon jug and time how long it takes to pump two gallons of fluid while maintaining the pressure your fuel system requires. Prior to running the test, turn on the fuel pump and adjust the valve shown in the picture until the pressure matches exactly that of your fuel system. Then go back and empty your container and, this time using a stop-watch and a scale, time how long it takes to flow two gallons of fuel-substitute into your container. If, for example, your system fills two gallons in 120 seconds, that would be a fuel flow of one gallon per minute, which would let you theoretically support 800 horsepower on gasoline with an 11% safety margin. Note: when you test your fuel system, always use low pressure to blow the test fluid out of the lines before reassembling them so the residual flow test fluid does not contaminate your fuel. Obviously, never use water as a test fluid! Mineral spirits is a suitable fuel substitute with a fairly safe flashpoint that some people use for flow testing. If you use a rough figure of 7.4 lbs per gallon for gasoline, one gallon per minute equates to 444 lbs per hour. With a brake-specific fuel consumption of .5 lbs/horsepower hour, you could support 888 horsepower, or 11% more than our 800-horsepower target.

DYNO TESTING AND TUNING

will be extremely accurate. Having the wrong air/fuel ratio can be quite harmful to an engine. Too much fuel will mean that the engine runs extremely rich and some of the excess unburned fuel will go out of the exhaust, while the rest will go past the rings and wash the oil off the cylinder walls. In addition to lubricating the rings and piston skirt, the oil acts as a sealing agent, filling the gaps between the rings and piston as well as the gap between the rings and the cylinder walls. When the oil is washed away by excess fuel, the rings and piston skirts rub on unlubricated cylinder walls. Very quickly temperatures rise, and the rings and piston skirts try to weld themselves to the cylinder walls. If the fuel flow is not capable of supporting the engine power potential, the engine may lean out and the ensuing heat may burn a piston or torch a head gasket.

Having too little fuel will cause the engine to run lean, and the combustion temperatures will get hot, possibly causing damage such as detonation or knock.

## Exhaust Gas Temperature (EGT)

Exhaust gas temperatures (EGTs) are critical and something that we like to monitor during a run to make sure we are not going to melt a piston. If the exhaust thermocouples are not well-placed and accurate, we can be in big trouble. There are two types of thermocouples: grounded, and non-grounded. The non-grounded type relies on a special fitting that tightly holds the thermocouple between two non-conductive lava rock washers carefully crafted to prevent the thermocouple from touching the fitting and grounding out and not reading. The grounded-type thermocouples are much easier to use. The accuracy between the two types is quite comparable.

The most common failure in thermocouples occurs when the temperature in one cylinder drops or rises by more than 200 degrees with no change in components or adjustments from the previous run. The first thing to do is to swap the thermocouples with an adjacent one to see if the low temperature stays in the same cylinder, which would indicate that the cylinder is in fact differing from the adjacent ones. If the temperature follows the thermocouple, it suggests that you have a bad thermocouple or connection. No matter what the problem, stop and fix it immediately before making any WOT power runs.

The response time of a thermocouple is directly dependent on the wire thickness. In order to get decent life from a thermocouple, make sure the wire size is sufficient to enable it to stick out in a 1,600–1,800-degrees F. breeze found in an exhaust pipe and not melt or get blown away. This relatively sturdy wire has one drawback, however: the response time is much too long to register rapid thermal changes. Years ago, in an attempt to

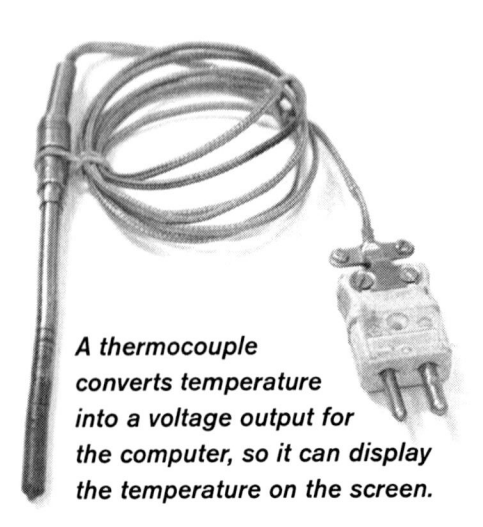

*A thermocouple converts temperature into a voltage output for the computer, so it can display the temperature on the screen.*

capture random misfires, a group of engineers looked at the possibility of using thermocouple wires so thin they could capture individual cylinder firings. Going on the theory that the temperature in the exhaust pipe momentarily decreased when the cylinder misfired, a thermocouple was selected that could respond quickly. The test was a success, and the misfires were captured on tape and the results were graphed. The downside of the test was that the thermocouples did not last much longer than a few runs down the drag strip, but those few runs were enough to capture the random misfires and allow the engineers to correct the problem.

## Repeatability and the Calibration Engine

The sign of a good dyno operation is its capability of exactly repeating a test, even if a year has elapsed between runs. To ensure they can build on their development data year after year, many teams have calibration or reference engines that serve no function other than to establish that the dyno is generating exactly the same measurements as in prior tests. Think of it as the ultimate overall systems check for a dyno room.

Having a calibration engine may seem extreme until you have chased a problem for a few weeks, changing everything under the sun trying to find a solution. Don't discount the value of a reference engine. There is no greater comfort than to put a calibration engine on the dyno when you have had a problem and have it come to life and produce results identical to the last time it was run. At that point, you know the problem is in the test engine and not the dyno or the room. This reference allows you to eliminate half of the potential problems from your troubleshooting.

The most perplexing problems are not the obvious ones. Most of us can find the simple problems. The subtle problems, where the engine is off by only a few percentage points, can cause sleepless nights and untold dollars to isolate and correct. In one case, the calibration engine was off by the same percentage as the test engine. Ultimately the problem was diagnosed as plugged air filters leading to the dyno room. Without a calibration engine, this team could have picked at their test engine indefinitely without isolating a fault, because it lay elsewhere.

The key components to repeatability in testing are typically a good written work plan anchored by common sense and executed in minute detail. Become almost robotic in your test procedures and practices. Don't get in a hurry despite the pressure to get some data. Mentally rehearse the test prior to ever firing the engine.

## Electrical Grounds

More money and time have been spent chasing what ultimately turned out to be poor electrical grounds than possibly anything else. When a starter won't spin, almost everybody can find a faulty ground very quickly. After all, we are looking for a cable capable of carrying 600 amps. Sparks, smoke, and heat will help us locate the faulty item. Even the least skilled among us will eventually find this particular problem.

Let's take a situation where a digital control system is used. The current passing through some of the circuits is measured in milliamps. A mildly corroded terminal, far from view, with no sparks and no accompanying heat or smoke, will be incredibly difficult to find. These problems become increasingly vexing in their initial stages when they are often intermittent. This faulty connection, however, will affect the entire power range, or in some cases only a small fraction of the range.

Disassembling the connection and carefully cleaning both halves will cure the problem. The bad news is the number of these connections. Take time to solder all connections and maintain all bolted connections by taking them apart and cleaning both sides of the connection. Use special woven ground straps. In the short term, a solid core wire will carry the same amp rating as a woven strap. The strap has 100 times more surface area to act as a ground, making it more effective for small currents and less reactive to electro-magnetic radiation or EMR. Take care to be gentle with plastic connectors.

Current practice in production vehicles is to use elaborate sealed connectors containing dielectric grease to shield the terminals from the corrosive effects of the atmosphere. If you choose to use these connectors, remember that the designed service life of these connectors is typically less than four connect/disconnect cycles. If your application requires that you disconnect and reconnect the terminal with each engine change, for example, you might want to rethink your choice of connectors.

## How Do We Separate a Dyno Problem From an Engine Problem?

Let's say we have an engine that gradually loses power during a day-long test session. Where is the problem? Before you get too crazy, begin with the basics: fuel, air, and spark. Once you have determined that you have plenty of fuel and air and a nice fat spark, make sure that all of the grounds are good. Check cylinder leakage, valve lash, and compression. If they all check out, run a blowby test and check your calibrations and recalculate your correction factor data inputs to ensure that you are using the right correction factor.

Assuming everything checks out well, cut the oil filter and look at the oil and any debris inside the filter. If all of that looks good, check the fuel quality. We usually do this by switching drums to a known good drum from another cell. When switching fuel, make sure that you are using equivalent fuel so as not to damage the engine.

If everything checks out up to this point, try switching engines. Keep on hand a healthy engine of around the same horsepower and similar design. This engine should have no other purpose than to sit on the shelf ready to perform on a minute's notice in cases like this. A quick warm-up and three power runs should provide a quick answer. It may seem premature to try another engine at this point, but think of it as eliminating half the problems. By making the original corrected horsepower, you have qualified the fuel, the electrical input power, the dynamometer cell, your calibrations, and your instruments.

## How's Your Engine's Health?

We call them health checks, but blowby, cylinder leakage, and compression tests are three of the quickest tests to determine an engine's cylinder

CHAPTER 8

health. Spend some money on a compression gauge and cylinder leakage gauge and learn how to use them. You may want to mount a blowby meter in your vehicle to read during testing. Get in the habit of checking compression pressures and doing a leak-down test after at least every 10 runs or after two

## Cylinder-Sealing Testing

An engine's overall efficiency is determined in part by how well the gases are sealed within the cylinder. Cylinder leakage or "leak-down testing," as it has come to be known, is a very effective test to determine the amount of air leakage in a pressurized cylinder while it is being held statically at TDC. Further, the test will help pinpoint where the leakage is occurring. Whether the leakage is past an intake or exhaust valve past the rings, or even through a blown head gasket, the hiss and flow rate of leaking air tells the tale. The beauty of a leak-down test is that the apparatus is relatively inexpensive, and the test takes very little time to run and is non-destructive. All that is needed is a cylinder leakage gauge and a source of compressed air (100 psi). There are two different types of leak-down gauges. The original one, made by Sun, employed one gauge. Most gauges today employ two separate gauges. There is an array of leak-down gauges available, ranging from under $75 to over $400. Try to find a good one that will render consistent results while withstanding frequent usage, and stick with the same one. Good race-worthy engines typically leak in the 2%–4% range. Use a leak check calibrator to have a dynamic calibration on your tester. Once an engine gets higher leakage (10% range) you won't learn a whole lot if you are trying to establish a race-worthy tune-up.

Cylinder leakage is very important. The variance between cylinders is also critical. If you have eight cylinders ranging from 3%–6%, you have a good engine. If one cylinder turns up with 10%, you will want to check that problem and fix it before proceeding. In some cases, it may simply be a small piece of carbon lodged between

*This meter made by Dwyer allows you to measure the amount of blowby flowing out of your engine at speed and under full load. Many racers also run these in the vehicle during test sessions. Think of blowby as a dynamic leakdown reading.*

a valve and the valve seat. If you lightly tap the valve tip or simply run the engine for a few minutes at a high idle, the problem may disappear. The piston rings rotate as the engine runs as a normal course. Occasionally, when you leak-test a cylinder, it may have higher leakage because the ring end gaps have lined up one above the other, creating an abnormal leak path. Before you panic and disassemble the engine, run it briefly, and if everything else looks good, retest. Obviously, if the cylinder still has high leakage and the borescope shows a deep scratch in the bore, no amount of running will cure this problem.

Make frequent checks and follow the clues to a logical conclusion. Find the root cause of the problem and fix it. Nothing spells "rookie" more than someone who continues to rev the engine when it is obviously hurt. The need to blow out the carbon deposits has caused many fine engines to have a shortened life.

### Blowby

Blowby, as the name implies, is the flow of hot combustion gases past the piston rings into the crankcase. By flowing or "blowing" past the rings and into the crankcase without pushing on the piston, the high-pressure mixture doesn't contribute to the power potential of the engine. Think of a blowby test as a dynamic leakdown test. Perhaps the ultimate measure of dynamic cylinder sealing is to use a blowby meter on the engine. The conscientious race engine development teams routinely use blowby meters both on the dyno and in the car

98  DYNO TESTING AND TUNING

ACCURACY AND REPEATABILITY

## Cylinder-Sealing Testing *continued*

to allow them to monitor the dynamic sealing of an engine continuously.

A flowmeter measures the flow in SCFM (standard cubic feet per minute) of blowby gas coming out of the engine crankcase. Ultimately we would like to see this number as close to zero as possible. Unlike either leak-down or compression testing, the blowby test takes place while the engine is running. The key to an accurate blowby test is carefully sealing every exit from engine, such as breathers, dipstick hole, and PCV valve, so all of the leakage coming past the piston rings must pass through the meter. Dry sump engines or engines using a crankcase vacuum system must hook the oil tank breather to the blowby meter. Care must also be taken when running a dry sump engine not to suck the crank seals inside out.

Potential leak sources like the valve covers and their gaskets must be sealed with great care. Test your sealed engine with a regulator, and pressurize the crankcase to 3–5 psi while listening for leaks. Be careful not to use too much pressure, because you may unknowingly blow out or "flip" the front or rear main seal, causing you to have to replace the seal. The sealed engine should be able to hold this pressure for several minutes. An excellent blowby number for a 350 cid V-8 engine is 1–2 SCFM measured at WOT and 5000 RPM. Obviously larger-displacement engines have higher blowby numbers. Get in the habit of testing your blowby at regular intervals during your dyno testing program. Continue to use the blowby meter mounted in the car at the track to monitor the engine sealing condition. Most racers will take a reading in high gear (when driving is not so busy) at WOT.

### Ring Float

During the development process, blowby is also used to monitor ring float. As the RPM and power rise in an engine, the ability of the rings to seal the gap between the piston and the cylinder wall becomes increasingly poor. A sudden rapid increase in the blowby will often signal ring flutter. Engine builders and manufacturers spend a great deal of time and effort investigating the causes and cures of ring float or flutter. If you encounter ring flutter, you must fix it if you have any hope of making power and controlling the engine-sealing process.

Varying the rings' construction, design, material, tension, and mass affects their propensity to float. Many racers simply apply vacuum to the oil pan with a vacuum pump to solve the problem. While this method may cure

*These sturdy diecast valve covers have been welded shut except for a blowby meter hose connection point. The secret to getting reliable blowby readings is to have the engine totally sealed. Stamped lightweight valve covers and dipsticks and their tubes tend to leak under pressure.*

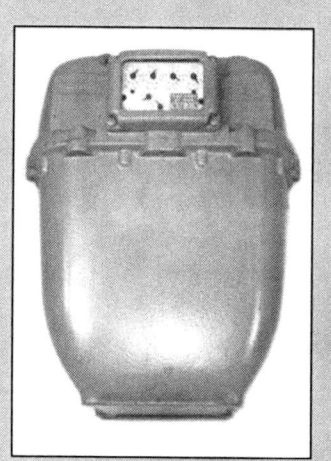

*This is another type of flow meter. It is important to separate the oil droplets from the blowby to keep this type of meter clean inside.*

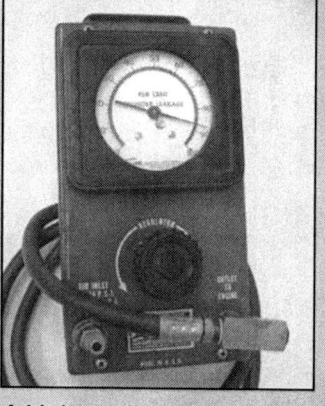

*A high-quality leak tester like this unit will pay big dividends in allowing you to spot incremental cylinder-sealing problems, be they bent valves, worn rings, bad ring lands or anything else. A good race engine measures around 4-6%. A street engine should be less than 15%.*

DYNO TESTING AND TUNING

# Cylinder-Sealing Testing *continued*

the ring float, it costs horsepower. The real solution is to develop a ring combination that seals the cylinder without using a horsepower-robbing pump.

## Crankshaft End Play

Aside from rod and main bearing clearances, a crankshaft must have fore and aft clearance between the thrust bearing surface and crankshaft that allows it to move forward and backward in the block by a few thousandths of an inch. This clearance is known as end play, which allows oil to access and lubricate both sides of the thrust bearing while the engine is running. If the engine is run without proper end play, it will only last a few minutes before ruining the thrust bearing. Mount a dial indicator to measure the damper travel parallel to the crankshaft centerline, then gently pull the crank forward, zero the indicator reading, then push the crankshaft toward the rear of the engine and take another reading. This resultant reading is the crankshaft end play. Always watch this measurement, since it can sometimes signal impending disaster. Take this measurement before you start the engine for the first time just to make sure you have end play and schedule regular end-play inspections along with cylinder leakage and compression checks as you progress through your testing program. If the end play increases or decreases by more than a few thousandths, stop testing and find the cause. You may save a crankshaft and the engine by doing this.

## Compression Test

A compression test is another way of measuring the sealing capability of an engine. The compression tester measures the peak pressure developed in a non-running cylinder by just cranking the engine over with the starter. The test is performed by removing all of the spark plugs and installing a compression gauge in each spark plug hole, one hole at a time. The throttle should be held fully open while testing, and the engine cranked over for roughly five revolutions or until the gauge stops gaining any pressure.

Tip: Many instructions suggest "wiring the throttle open" during a compression test to ensure that it stays open. This practice is fine as long as you remember to remove the wire and close the throttle before restarting the engine!

Be sure to have a battery charger hooked up during this entire exercise, since you will want each cylinder to have the same cranking speed during the test. It helps to have the dyno console turned on while doing this to ensure that the RPM is staying consistent during the test. Always take the reading after the same number of revolutions to ensure equality of the readings. Typically five revolutions will produce a stabilized reading. When evaluating a compression test, you should focus on the difference between the readings from cylinder to cylinder. The overall value is not as important as the variance from cylinder to cylinder. This reading should never vary from cylinder to cylinder by more than 5–10 psi on a good engine. When you change camshafts or camshaft centerline, you may notice a change in the overall compression numbers. Again, the overall number remains less important than the variance from cylinder to cylinder. The overall number becomes important when you are building a number of the same engines, or when you are trying to chart the life cycle of your engine. Obviously as the engine wears, the compression pressure will drop.

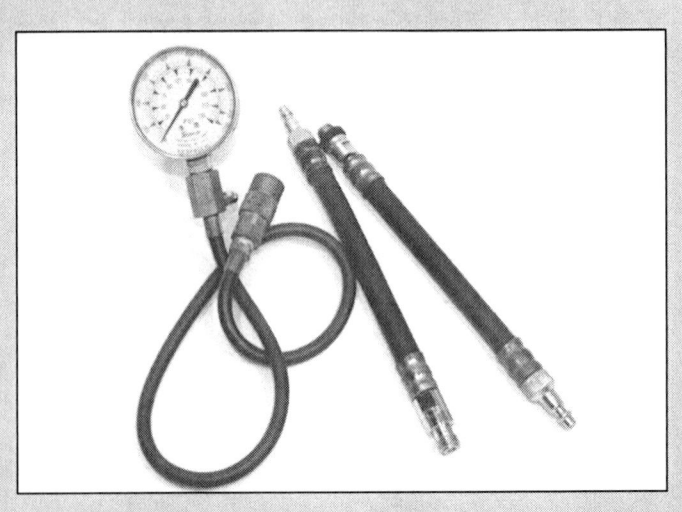

*A high-quality compression gage is recommended to monitor engine cranking compression pressures. Be sure to keep the battery fresh to ensure the same cranking speed as you progress from cylinder to cylinder.*

## ACCURACY AND REPEATABILITY

hours of continuous running. Be sure to keep a log of the results so you can monitor the engine's ongoing condition. These results will often prevent you from wasting time and money trying to learn something from an engine that is essentially worn out on one or more cylinders.

### Calibration

Calibration is a must. Before any test session, check the calibration of the dyno torque link or dyno load cell by hanging weights on the checking arm and comparing the weights to the digital reading at the console. For good accuracy, check the values at half of the maximum torque value and again at the expected full-scale torque reading. If the calibration drifts or is incorrect from the beginning, you could be seriously misled and waste valuable time tuning around a suspected deficiency, so check the dyno calibration often.

## Clutch Slippage

Since we will hopefully be increasing the output of our engine during our testing, we should be careful to select a combination of flywheel and clutch or drive plate that will adequately transfer the power from the engine to the dyno. If a clutch slips slightly during a run, you may not immediately realize it from the data. The run may just be down on peak torque. This is especially true if you have been gradually increasing the power during the test session. You may change a cam expecting a modest gain, when in fact the data shows a slight loss over the previous cam. In reality what may have happened is that the cam did in fact produce more torque and subsequently more power. Unfortunately it produced enough torque to slip the clutch, and once the clutch broke loose, its torque capability decreased.

How do you detect this? First, always enter the dyno room immediately after each test to check things over. If you smell clutch dust (smells like brake dust), chances are good that your clutch slipped. Go back and review your data and check the engine speed versus your dyno input speed. They should be the same! If your clutch slips, you should do two things: first, make a note to change the clutch in the car; second, either get a better clutch for the dyno engine or use a coupler called a drive plate.

### Drive Plate

The drive plate is bolted directly to the flywheel and cannot slip, although it can break or shear the splines. Drive plates typically employ a sprung hub like a clutch disc that will allow for some torsional compliance. Without this damping, the loads produced by a V-8 engine firing four times every revolution will eventually fracture driveline parts. A solid coupler may be fine for a quick burst down the track, but for the long haul on a dyno, the driveline parts will break very quickly.

If you run a clutch disc, make a habit of reviewing the run data and checking dyno speed versus engine speed throughout the power run. If there are any differences anywhere, you have clutch slip. It may be very subtle, and since it may only occur at peak torque, it will not be readily obvious. For this reason, most serious dyno shops have gone to a drive-plate arrangement with excess torque capability.

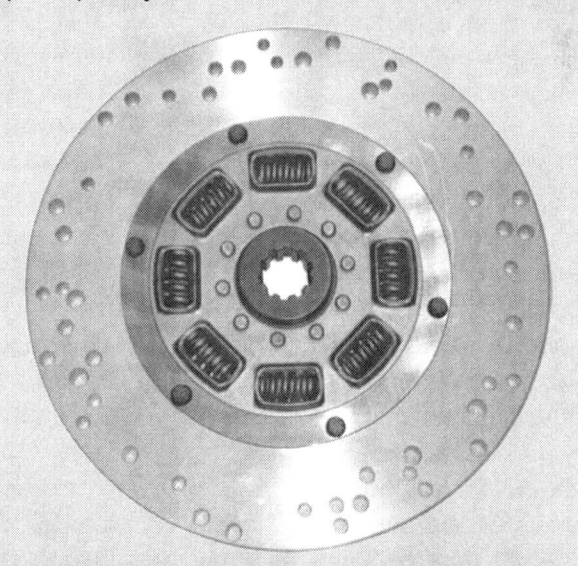

*In order to eliminate clutch slippage, use a drive plate. The sprung hub helps to reduce the engine torsional vibrations, while the securely bolted plate totally eliminates slippage. Photo courtesy Innovation Engineering*

DYNO TESTING AND TUNING

CHAPTER 9

# CORRECTION FACTORS: PROBLEMS AND PROCEDURES

There are many problems that are associated with testing that must be addressed if meaningful data is the goal. Sound testing procedures must be used if dependable results are the intended objective.

To secure accurate and repeatable comparative dynamometer tests, you must follow precise procedures to minimize unmeasured losses. It is very important to measure and record oil temperatures in the engine, transmission, and drive axle(s) of the vehicle. The drive tire temperatures and pressures should also be recorded. Additionally, the bearing temperatures on the chassis dynamometer must be recorded to ensure that potential variables are controlled.

*Correction factors* and arithmetic manipulation are necessary to characterize the data to some standard condition so you can compare it against data gathered under different atmospheric conditions. It is very important to understand where the numbers come from and how the correction factor is applied.

There are many different correction-factor schemes, and the deeper you get into it, the more bizarre it all seems. Just as a simple example of how convoluted the pathway can be, take a look at the following listing:

SAE (Society of Automotive Engineers), USA
JSAE (Japanese Society of Automotive Engineers), Japan
JIS (Japanese Institute for Standardization), Japan
ECE (European Community), Europe
DIN (Deutsche Industries Norm), Germany
ISO (International Standards Organization) International

Each of these bodies promotes its own correction-factor scheme.

## Dynamometer Corrections

Engineers and scientists have used mathematical corrections for various tests for well over a hundred years. Although there are many different ways to correct the numbers to some other condition than that of the test, several have been standardized, making data comparison easier.

Some of the correction methods were specifically targeted to gain position in the marketplace. Others are intended to make it easier to compare data from different tests and different testing conditions. Within reason, the latter is the preferred approach.

### Market Perceptions Concerning Dynamometer Correction Factors

There are many problems in communicating with the marketplace, but one that is particularly troublesome concerns the use of correction factors to generate power-output numbers on engine or chassis dynamometers.

Because we call the power numbers "horsepower," and these figures are a form of currency in the high-performance marketplace, it is important to know how they were or were not corrected. If they were corrected, it is very important to know what arithmetic process was applied.

# CORRECTION FACTORS: PROBLEMS AND PROCEDURES

*The phrase "weight before cooking" is very familiar to anyone who has read a menu in any restaurant. It is a way to draw your attention to conditions before the heat is placed into service on either the grill or in your engine. Just as it does with a steak, heat can have a serious effect on your engine's performance and components.*

*The "weight after cooking" photo is an eye opener for anyone who is concerned with where numbers come from and the results of heat on engine components. Take a close look at the photo and reflect on rich and lean mixtures. It will make you pay more attention to the details the next time you toss something on the grill or fire up your engine.*

## Correction Factors Using WOT (Wide-Open Throttle) Tests and an Explanation of Application

There are no perfect solutions for correcting test numbers to different conditions. However, it is possible to use correction schemes that closely approximate for different atmospheric conditions. The empirically derived schemes are specifically for use when the engine under test is at wide-open throttle (WOT).

The factors for corrections are derived from the most basic equations for compressible gas mass flow rate, which is referred to as the mass flow rate for dry air ($M_{da}$).

$$m_{da} = A \times \sqrt{[(2k/(k-1)) \times 1/R]} \times [P_1 / \sqrt{(T_1)}]$$

The factor $A \times \sqrt{[(2k/(k-1)) \times 1/R]}$ is composed of constants and thus is a constant itself.

Assuming that the pressure ratio of ($P_2 / P_1$) remains constant for wide open throttle (WOT), steady-state speed operation, then for dry atmospheric air,

$$m_{da} = \text{constant} \times P_1 / \sqrt{(T_1)} \text{ or}$$
$$m_{da} \sim P_1 / \sqrt{(T_1)}$$

Therefore, the dry-air mass flow rate is proportional to dry-air intake air pressure and then inversely proportional to the square root of absolute temperature.

The correction factor for dry air mass rate is therefore:

$$CF = (P_s / P_o) \times \sqrt{(T_o / T_s)} \text{ or, } CF = (99.0 / B_{do}) \times \sqrt{(T_o / 298.15)}$$

Where
$m_{da}$ = Dry air mass rate, g/s
$A$ = Critical flow area, $m^2$
$R$ = Gas constant for air, J/kgK
$P$ = Dry air pressure, kPa
$T$ = Absolute temperature, K
$B$ = Barometric pressure, kPa
Subscript Notations
$_1$ = Ambient conditions
$_2$ = Conditions at the critical flow point in the system
$_o$ = Observed conditions
$_s$ = Standard conditions
$_d$ = Dry air pressure = Total pressure–Vapor pressure

This is a metric presentation because that is the way SAE J1349 is written. In English Engineering Units, the correction conditions would be for 29.23"Hg, 77°F, dry air. "Sea Level Standards" would follow the same arithmetic manipulations for a correction to conditions of 29.92"Hg, 60°F, dry air and the reference would become SAE J607 and J606.

Because the indicated power is commonly assumed to be proportional to the amount of oxygen inducted into the engine, it follows that the above calculated correction factor applies to indicated power as well as to the dry air mass rate. The general acceptance of the formulae as listed is due to its very close agreement with experimental results when used in a narrow range of +/- 5% or to as much as +/- 7%. There are, however, some examples that are substantially outside this range in which comparisons were done with surprisingly very good results.

*This engine obviously has two turbos and is about 280 cubic inches in displacement. It has produced reliable numbers on the engine dyno of about 1700 CBHp. It is the engine that powers the fastest Mustang around. These little 4.6L engines are amazing platforms to build from. Dyno development has been an integral part of John Mehovitz's engine program. Photo courtesy of Westech Performance Group.*

DYNO TESTING AND TUNING

# CHAPTER 9

SAE J607 is for WOT testing, and data is corrected to the standard conditions of a barometric pressure of 29.92"Hg, inlet air temperature of 60F, and for dry air (0% humidity). This correction scheme also uses a value for friction power as part of the calculation formula. This is one of the most popular corrections for engine dynamometers and also can be applied to chassis dynamometers. It is one of the most popular and has been somewhat steady and unchanged for many years. By the way, it also gives a larger correction factor than J1349 does by about 4% or so if the tests are accomplished in the same fashion and using the same procedure and fuel.

However, things can be more confusing when you consider that over the years, SAE power corrections have used various barometric pressures as standards.

In the past, SAE has used 29.00 inches of mercury, 29.23 inches of mercury, 29.38 inches of mercury, 29.42 inches of mercury, 29.85 inches of mercury, and 29.92 inches of mercury.

Over that same span of various corrections for barometric pressure, SAE has also used multiple inlet air temperature standards as well. The temperatures used have been 60°F, 68°F, 77°F, 80°F, and 85°F.

As stated earlier, the current SAE J1349 standards are corrected to 29.23"Hg, 77°F, dry air. Note that the current SAE J607 standards are corrected to 29.92"Hg, 60°F, dry air and that the difference between these two methods of correction is about 4%, with SAEJ1349 giving smaller corrected numbers than does SAE J607 if we were comparing the same test data.

The various correction arithmetic is important to know so that you can easily compare tests that were perhaps corrected to different standards.

Using English Engineer's units, the arithmetic for correction factors looks like the following:

$$CF = (29.92"Hg / T_p - V_p) \times \sqrt{(CAT + 460 / 520)}$$

Where $T_p$ = test barometric pressure, inches of mercury;
$V_p$ = vapor pressure, inches of mercury;
CAT = Carburetor Air Temperature, F.

This method of correction factor calculation is for SAE J 606 and J607 and is to be used for testing at wide-open throttle (WOT).

As you attempt to compare data, it is absolutely necessary to know exactly which SAE correction was being applied. If you are looking at old test data and want to compare it to much more recent test data, the different correction schemes can easily consume several percentage points just in the arithmetic.

Can SAE J1349 be compared with SAE J607, SAE J1995, SAE J1312, or SAE J2723? Of course they can, if you have access to the original test values and the corrections used for each. There are hundreds and hundreds of J codes, and they are not that easy to come by. Recent additions to the J code mix are J1995 and J2723, which are part of a move by SAE to create common-ground standards for everyone. They even include a program for having certified witnesses in the process.

If a testing group, a team, or an individual decides on using another "standard" to correct data to, that is perfectly acceptable as long as the method of correction follows some known path. Perhaps some NASCAR Cup team engineer decides that the standard that he wants to correct to is 29.00"Hg, 80°F, at 50% relative humidity (RH %). That's OK, too. But, when comparing data you need to know what the standards are, whether the standards of comparison are yours, the SAE standards, or the sea-level standards. One needs to be very aware of the components that cause shifts in the numbers. There is nothing worse in data analysis than to see some unexplained spike or dip in data on one test and not on another. Sometimes you have to look beyond the "flyers" of data and mentally somewhat "smooth" the data in order to make it fit the trend that occurred before and after the glitch.

As we have mentioned, there are more variables in play on a chassis dyno, making the correction factors applied to chassis dynamometer testing critical for useful comparison.

*The car in the photo produced in excess of 1150 CWHp on the chassis dyno. Its 280 cubic-inch, twin-turbocharged engine made more than 1,700 CBHp on the engine dyno. The difference? Losses in the drive train (transmission, driveshaft, drive axle and tires) and the tires begin to slip on the rollers at elevated power levels. This was an early version of John Mehovitz's Mustang. Photo cortesy of Westech Performance Group.*

## CORRECTION FACTORS: PROBLEMS AND PROCEDURES

The correction factors are used in the following fashion when correcting observed data to a corrected format:

CBHp = (OHp + FHp) x CF − FHp

so that CBHp = Corrected Brake Horsepower, OHp = Observed Horsepower, FHp = Friction Horsepower, CF = Correction Factor.

This correction scheme can only be used if one has numbers for the friction horsepower. Some folks do not use this correction scheme at all, and you need to know, if they did use it, what the input was for the friction power elements.

### Variables Necessary to Control for Maintaining Good Test Procedures

One method that is of great assistance and importance in dynamometer testing is to run the test at least three times without changing anything on the engine while keeping the variables to an absolute minimum. The tests can be averaged to depict the true nature of the results. Good procedures will assist in producing good results.

To get good numbers from your tests, there are minimum acceptable standards and preferred standards for controlling variables. Operate your tests at least within the minimum standards and wherever possible use the preferred standards.

### Minimum Acceptable Standards for Controlling Variables in Dyno Testing

*Oil Temperature:* Oil temperature should be controlled within +/- 3°F.
*Water Temperature:* Water temperature should be controlled within +/- 3°F.

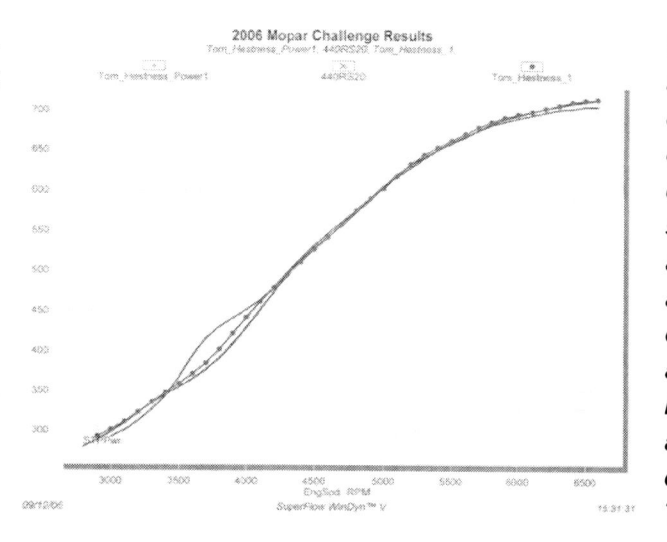

*The graph tells a great story of comparing the same engine on two different dynos and at two separate locations—one at very near sea level and one at much higher elevation. The curves are for corrected brake horsepower. It is amazing how well they compare. Data courtesy Tom Hestness Family.*

*The injected engine in the dyno room was built for drag racing. It produced in excess of 1,000 CBHp and was built to start and run rounds without much maintenance. Dyno testing revealed how to tune the engine to make good power and still be very drivable on the return road and through the pits.*

*Inlet Air Temperature:* CAT should be controlled within +/- 3°F.
*Exhaust Leaks:* Exhaust leaks should be controlled to be at the zero or 0% value.
*Acceleration Rate:* The acceleration rate should be controlled within +/- 5% of the rate. At 300 RPM/sec this is +/-15 RPM/sec.
*Fuel temperature:* Fuel temperature should be controlled within +/- 5°F.
*Fuel source (sample):* The fuel (chemically) used should remain the same type. Most racing gasoline has a limited shelf life, and allowances should be made accordingly.

### Preferred Acceptable Standards for Controlling Variables in Dyno Testing

*Oil Temperature:* Oil temperature should be controlled within +/- 1°F.
*Water Temperature:* Water temperature should be controlled within +/- 1°F.
*Inlet Air Temperature:* CAT should be controlled within +/- 1°F.
*Exhaust Leaks:* Exhaust leaks should be controlled to be at the zero or 0% value.
*Acceleration Rate:* The acceleration rate should be controlled within +/-

# CHAPTER 9

3% of the rate. At 300 RPM/sec this is only +/- 9 RPM/sec, which is tight control.

*Fuel temperature:* Fuel temperature should be controlled within +/- 5°F (this is a critical control issue on diesel applications, too).

## Chassis Dyno Testing

If the testing is being done on a chassis dyno, then the additional variables that follow need to be considered as minimum acceptable standards for vehicles.

*Tire Inflation Pressure:* Tire pressure should be controlled within +/- 2 psi.
*Tire Temperature:* Tire temperature should be controlled within +/- 5°F.
*Transmission Temperature:* Trans temp should be controlled within +/- 3°F.
*Drive Axle Temperature:* Drive axle temp should be controlled within +/- 3°F.
*Dyno Bearing Temperature:* Dyno bearing temp should be controlled within +/- 5°F.
*Fuel Temperature:* Fuel Temp should be controlled to within +/- 5°F (this is a critical control issue on diesel applications, too).
*Fuel Pressure:* Fuel pressure should be controlled within +/- 2 psi (this is critical on rail pressure on EFI vehicles and is *very* critical on $N_2O$ fuel enrichment systems, where the fuel pressure should be within +/- 1 psi).
*Dyno Water Temperature:* Dyno absorber inlet water temperature should be within +/- 5°F (you need to follow the manufacturer's recommendations for the inlet maximum number, but the variation is still to be followed for good results).
*EC Temperature:* The eddy current temperature should be within +/- 10°F. Although this is not as critical as other temperatures, it is a target. Most eddy current absorbers have more than enough capacity, so the exact temperature is not such a big deal to worry about unless the test vehicle is close to the edge of the capacity envelope for the absorber.

*Tie-down Tension:* The tension on tie-down straps should be well monitored and should be within +/- 10 lbs-force. This is difficult to control without equipping the straps with a force gauge or measurement by a tension meter. It is also important that the angle of the tie-downs from the vehicle to the anchor points be the same from one test to another.

*Fuel Source:* The fuel (chemically) used should remain the same type. Most racing gasoline has a limited shelf life.

## What About Supercharged or Turbocharged Engines?

In today's dyno world, the same corrections that are applied for testing naturally aspirated engines are also applied to supercharged and turbocharged engines. That is not necessarily the best package of correction from an engineering point of view, but that is currently how it is done and the way it has been done for at least the last 30-plus years.

The correction scheme for supercharged, turbocharged engines, and naturally aspirated engines should perhaps be based on manifold density. This section and description is presented for your evaluation and consideration. It is not a proposal of changing correction factors; however, it could be the basis for doing so. This section is addressed only to the un-naturally aspirated engine crowd. It is purely for your learning pleasure.

There are many different types of superchargers and they vary in how much friction and pumping power each takes in getting their boost to the engine. Turbochargers are varied in sizing and boost, but exhaust gases passing through their turbine section drive all of them in the same fashion.

*There are a lot of things to consider when testing on a chassis dyno, and they apply to either cars or motorcycles. Proper and uniform tire inflation and tie-down uniformity are important issues. One should also monitor tire temperature as well.*

*The highlighted areas in this photo point out a few things to consider when testing on a chassis dyno. The deflection on the tires is from the heavy load placed on the tie-downs. It is not a tire inflation issue, although that is an item to keep track of. These turbocharged bikes need to be pulled down tightly or the tire slips on the rolls. A larger roll would be of some assistance, but these things can make in excess of 500 CWHp at the tire patch. Also note the color of the exhaust pipe vs some other photos.*

DYNO TESTING AND TUNING

# CORRECTION FACTORS: PROBLEMS AND PROCEDURES

*Boost Pressure and How Things Happen in the Manifold*

Although it is an easy number to measure using a simple pressure gauge, boost alone is not a very good indication of what is happening in the manifold before the engine inducts the flow.

*Measurement Tools and Applications*

The basic need is to measure the average pressure in the manifold/port accurately. This is difficult because the normal pressure variations move around a lot. As an example, if you are using a Roots-type supercharger, the pressure would vary because of the pulses from the blower itself. The pulses caused by the valves likewise affect the measurement. This is why the manifold pressure number or boost needs to be an average value.

Average internal manifold temperature is another important input. The temperature measurement can be simple or complex, just as long as we have some representation of the temperature average during boosted conditions.

*Gauge and Absolute Pressures*

By definition, gauge pressure is the direct reading on a gauge that indicates the pressure between ambient and the gauge connection inside the device, such as a manifold. A good example of a gauge pressure reading is the inflation pressure in your tires. If you inflated a spare tire to 30 psi in Denver (5280 feet above sea level) and took the tire in your trunk to a point near sea level, the same gauge would indicate something close to 27.05-psi inflation pressure. An easy reference to gauge pressure is the abbreviation "psig."

On the other hand, something called absolute pressure is a very good way to refer to manifold pressure and some other pressure measurements. Absolute pressure would be gauge pressure plus the pressure of the ambient atmosphere where the measurement is being made. Absolute pressure will yield the same figure for the spare tire's pressure in Denver and at sea level. The Denver absolute pressure would be 30 psig + 11.75 psi = 41.75 psi absolute. The inflation pressure of 27.05 at sea level would be psig + 14.7 psi = 41.75 psia.

*A Way to Use the Numbers*

Because of the relationship of temperature and pressure, we can readily evaluate the density that perhaps occurs in the manifold with some simple arithmetic. The following calculations are based upon an absolute-pressure reference for clarity.

$$M\rho = 1.325 [((b_{psig} \times 2.036) + (P_{baro})) / R]$$

Where $M\rho$ = Manifold density, lbs/ft³,
$b_{psig}$ = boost pressure, psig,
$P_{baro}$ = barometer pressure, "Hg, uncorrected
R = temperature in manifold, °F + 460

Example: An engine was measured to have boost of 22 psig and the barometer was 29.0"Hg, and a temperature in the manifold was measured to be 200°F during a dyno run or on the racetrack. What was the manifold density condition?

$$M\rho = 1.325 [((22 \times 2.036) + (29.0)) / 660] = .148 \text{ lbs/ft}^3$$

Now, we drag the thing to Denver, where the barometer was 25.0"Hg. We test the engine and change the blower drive ratio in order to attain 22. psig boost. The temperature was measured to be 200°F. What was the manifold density?

$$M\rho = 1.325 [((22 \times 2.036) + (25)) / 660] = .140 \text{ lbs/ft}^3$$

The target is to attain the same manifold density as the lower-elevation racetrack. What should the pressure gauge read to produce the target of .148 lbs/ft³ of the lower elevation racetrack?

Some simple algebraic manipulation allows a quick reference so that the following can be applied: .148/1.325 = .1117, so assuming the temperature remains close to the same, the manifold pressure gauge should be targeted to read about 23.95 psig. The temperature is certainly a variable, but the target is to have the same manifold density.

Assume the ambient temperature was lower in Denver (perhaps racing at night) and the manifold temperature was measured to be only 175°F.

*This Hayabusa is making some serious power and is putting all the power through the single tire patch. Tie-down procedure on turbocharged bikes is typically by attaching the nylon straps in place and then connecting the air shock with compressed air to extend it and preloading the tire. This photo was taken at almost "full song," and the piece made way over 500 CWHp. These hair dryer-equipped bikes are awesome and they survive!*

# CHAPTER 9

What is the net effect on the manifold density?

Back to the 22 psig boost numbers, but at less manifold temperature, yields the following:

$$M\rho = 1.325\ [((22 \times 2.036) + (25)) / 635] = .1456 lb/ft^3$$

So as you can see, the manifold temperature is an important issue. It is another measurement that should be taken in order to have better data on these special applications. Be aware of the effects and it can improve your test data consistency, and if applied at the racetrack, it will also improve the results on race days.

## A Proposed Method of Testing for the Performance Market

### Getting the Magazines and the Marketplace on the Same Page

Historically, the sea level standard that is referred to as SAE J607 corrects to the conditions of 29.92"Hg, 60°F inlet air, and dry air (0% humidity). Those numbers would typically yield the larger correction and the biggest corrected horsepower numbers. This method is also sometimes referred to as "standard temperature and pressure." The same basic outline of testing applies to J606. However, the corrections are somewhat unrealistic in some ways because of real-world conditions that exist at racetracks.

The current SAE J1349 is the latest in a long line of changing corrections, and the corrected conditions are to 29.23"Hg and 77°F inlet air, and dry air (0% humidity).

These conditions are also somewhat unrealistic, although probably slightly more realistic than the sea-level reference. This comment extends to cover the reference to SAE J1995 and SAE J2723 as well. That even might apply to ISO 1585 if one wanted to be world-friendly.

Consider that all the racetracks in the USA never have the conditions that are listed in any of the normally used corrections, so it is proposed that a new and dependable standard be adopted in the performance aftermarket that would use the following conditions for corrected conditions: Most of the racetracks in the USA are at elevations from a few hundred feet MSL to 5880 feet above sea level (MSL or mean sea level); and, the majority of test facilities have average correction factors in use that range from +5% to +10%. Those at high elevations might be as much as 25% to 28% (relative to sea-level corrections).

### A Testing Standard for Performance Applications Dynamometers (SPAD)

There is a real method in the madness here that should be considered carefully, and it is actually revisiting an SAE standard that was used long ago.
1. Test pressure standard: Barometric pressure of 29.00"Hg
2. Inlet air temperature standard: 80°F.
3. Vapor pressure standard: atmospheric water content of 0% Relative humidity or dry air ($V_P = 0$).

So the correction factor would be the following:

$$SPAD\ CF = [(29.00 / T_p - V_p) \times \sqrt{(CAT + 460 / 540)}]$$

The net result would be targeted to be different from the normal J607 and the normal J1349 (includes J1995 and J2723).

Eventually a bureaucrat may investigate the hot rods and racecars industry for some regulatory purpose, like emissions standards, consumer

*Back in the day before many folks had access to dyno time, testing was done at the racetrack by making pass after pass and making adjustments accordingly.*

*This diesel truck is undergoing some major repairs as a result of a tune-up malfunction. The blown head gasket could have been prevented by dyno tuning. Instead the unit gave up during track testing and competition. These guys worked hard to fix it because the truck was their ride home. Photo courtesy of Kathleen Henry.*

*After a successful engine build and dyno testing and development, the engine is installed in the racecar. Knowing that the engine is a solid platform allows the racer to spend important time on getting the power to the ground. In this case, it worked to the tune of 7.70 second ET at 178 MPH at a track that is located at an elevation of 4,900 feet! Owner/Driver Tom Spitzer is a hard racer, and it shows in his preparation and attention to detail.*

protection, or fuel consumption, etc. Less-corrected power (than current sea level standards) is a good thing here. Remember that it is only a number, and you can shuffle numbers all you want to, but track power is still going to be the thing to relate to for performance folks.

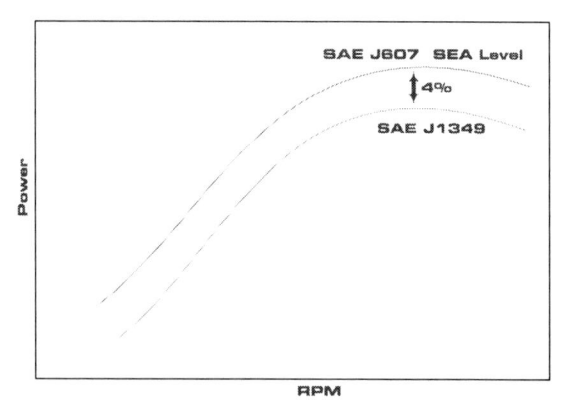

## Test Conditions

The other conditions that the SPAD format would require as standard include:
- Acceleration rate of approximately 300 RPM/sec to 350 RPM/sec +/- (5%) from an engine speed of not less than 2000 RPM to whatever the maximum is for the engine under test. Example: 2,500– 8,500 RPM.
- If a dyno facility does not have the capability of testing in the transient mode, then steady-state testing results less approximately 2% at all data points would be acceptable, but the method of test would require identification.
- Torque calibration using certified standard weights following manufacturer's procedure.
- The test method description details in heading such as steady state or acceleration test used with pertinent engine information.
- The exhaust system (should be non-muffled headers). If mufflers are used, log backpressure for reference with no allocation for power reduction imposed.
- The test cell combustion air between 70 and 100 degrees F and not more than 5 degrees F increase from start to finish of a test.
- The cooling system for the engine would be not less than 170 degrees F, +/- 3 degrees, and not more than 175 degrees F.
- The oil temperature of the engine would be at not less than 190°F +/- 3°F and not more than 195°F.
- The use of various fuels is acceptable as long as they are identified. Manufacturer, octane rating, and specific gravity (SG) should identify gasoline fuels. SG and chemical content should identify methanol fuel. SG and chemical content should identify ethanol or blends such as E85 and others.
- Air cleaners/filters are optional; either way, with or without should be identified with no allowance for power differences.
- A minimum of three separate tests without changes to the engine and an average of the data establishes a test for record that follows SPAD guidelines.
- Corrected to SPAD format and would also use friction power in the equation. In the absence of friction power data, then a standard factor would be used with identification of which method was applied.

*The sketch shows how the Sea Level correction vs SAE (J1349) would be graphically displayed. The difference between the Sea Level (sometimes called STP) correction for 29.92"Hg, 60degF, dry air and SAE J1349 (29.23"Hg, 77degF, dry air) is about 4%. You need to know where the numbers come from and the answer is in the text.*

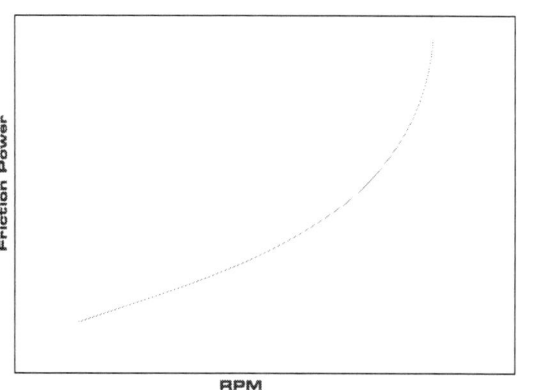

*The effect of friction power vs RPM is shown in this sketch. The curve is exponential in nature. Nothing is for free and friction power varies with crankshaft stroke (longer strokes take more power) as RPM is increased. This curve varies with engine types and diesel engines take more friction power to rotate their internals than do spark ignition engines. Some folks want to pretend that the engine has no internal friction element at all. They also probably believe in the tooth fairy.*

*How can you prepare for a dynamometer session?* Planning, old chum… lots of planning.

*How do you know if you have good data?* "Trust me" is not an option. Verify, verify, and then verify some more.

*Now that you have data, how do you apply it?* Make sure all the data makes sense and then analyze how to apply it to the racing program. You might learn from testing that the oil temperature should be within a certain range before you hit the track. You might also learn that the ambient temperature is the best target to try and get into the engine instead of superheated under-hood air.

# CHAPTER 10

# TROUBLESHOOTING

Problems are almost always a sign of progress. In this chapter we will review some of the common problems encountered in dyno testing and, more importantly, how they are solved. By becoming aware of the potential problems, you should be able to avoid a great many of them and have a template for solving the ones that invariably will occur.

Instead of looking at a problem as a gross waste of time, try to treat it as a learning experience. Before moving on, think about the nature of the problem and its solution. If you understand what went wrong and why, you'll be better able to anticipate and prevent future problems and to respond to those that occur promptly and thoroughly. Sometimes, knowing what doesn't work can be as valuable as knowing what will work. Let's look at how we analyze dyno testing problems and see how we handle them.

We will divide the problems into five areas:
- Room
- Dyno
- Engine
- Vehicle
- Other

Begin solving the problem by mentally reviewing what you know and what you don't know, and then prove to yourself that what you think is true really is true. Sometimes problems can be embarrassing, but nonetheless, if you are to find them, you can't take anything for granted.

> ## Old-School Troubleshooting
>
> Computers have made engines a lot more reliable and responsive. Yet they've also added a layer of complexity that can distract us from basic troubleshooting wisdom. Often when something goes wrong in a dyno test, some old timer from BC (before computers) steps in and asks, "Have you checked fuel, air, and spark?" More often than not the answer to the problem lies in this simple question. It may be a faulty line of code in the software, but until something releases the fuel or fires the coil, the engine is not going to run. When a problem occurs, first qualify or check fuel, air, and spark. While this may seem trite and time worn, it is still a good place to start.

## Room Problems

Let's look at the common problems associated with the room, which typically fall into one of the following areas:
 A lack of air
 A lack of fuel
 A lack of spark

We establish that the room is the problem by starting at the engine and working backwards. If the engine will not run very well and the air in the room smells funny, decide whether it may be because there is no fresh air available to the room.
- Is the problem with the air system?

*Roof air ducts work well to keep incoming rain out of the room. Make sure that the room air filters are clean and full flowing.*

# TROUBLESHOOTING

*This interstitial tank is preferred because it is less susceptible to daily temperature changes. As a vented tank goes from day to day, it breathes. At night, the cool wet air comes in, and in the morning when the tank heats up, it exhales the light ends of the gasoline. You end up over time with water in the tank and skunky gasoline.*

*Be careful with a non-insulated vented tank like this. These tend to inhale water vapor when the sun goes down. Over time, the water accumulates and finds its way into the fuel system of the engine.*

- Are the air doors open to allow fresh air into the room?
- Are the filters in the inlet air system clean and large enough to flow adequate air?
- Did we look at the room depression when we were running?
- Is the room depression sufficient to move air through the room?
- Does the room depression indicate that the inlet is not open or is restricted?
- Do we have a record of when the filters were last changed?
- Did an animal or bird build a nest in the air-supply ducts?
- Did some other blockage get in the ductwork?
- Have you actually crawled up on the roof and looked at the inlet? Perhaps it's time you did.
- Has some of the duct-work caved in and created a restriction?

This can happen if somebody turns on a fan without first opening the inlet air duct door to the room. A high-output exhaust fan can literally suck the ductwork shut.

- Is the fuel system delivering fuel to the dyno room?
- Start by verifying that all shutoff valves in the fuel system are open. Can you carefully open a fitting and get fuel to flow out?
- How much fuel can you flow?
- At what pressure can you deliver the required flow?
- Have you checked to see if your fuel flow exceeds the engine's requirements?

*A high-quality fuel filter is essential. A take-apart filter is preferred to enable the user to analyze the contaminants. A water separator would also be a wise investment.*

- How long can the fuel flow be maintained before it depreciates?
- How many fuel filters are in the system?
- When were all of the fuel filters last changed?
- When was the last load of fuel delivered?
- Do we know that the fuel is good?
- Did you actually check it?
- Have we run another similar engine on this same load of fuel?
- Is the tank low on fuel?
- When was the fuel tank last checked for water?
- Does the tank have a vent?
- Is the vent open?
- Is the 12-volt system working?
- If a battery is used, is the battery healthy?
- Is the 12-volt engine charging system working?
- Are all of the grounds clean and well maintained?
- Is the dyno water supply working properly?
- Is there adequate flow at rated pressure to support your power output?
- Is the water cool and clean?
- Is there enough water, or has most of the water evaporated?
- Is the dyno cooling tower turned on and working well?
- If a pressurized cooling system is used, is the heat exchanger working properly?
- If roof-mounted cooling towers are used, are they working at peak efficiency?
- Do the room exhaust fans work properly?
- Does the room depression gauge indicate that the fans are working correctly?
- On a chassis dyno, are the vehicle fans turned on, aimed

DYNO TESTING AND TUNING   111

correctly and producing adequate flow to cool the radiator as well as carry away heat and exhaust?
- Is the barometer working properly?
- Have you compared the barometer to the local airport "station" pressure?
- Does the mercury column barometer agree with the dyno barometric pressure transducer?
- How accurate is your vapor-pressure reading?
- How often have you checked the vapor-pressure readings?
- How do you take your readings?
- Have you rechecked the charts to see if you made a calculation mistake?

## Dyno Problems

### Calibration

- When did you last calibrate your dyno?
- Have you checked your torque link for accuracy?
- Have you rotated your trunnion bearings?

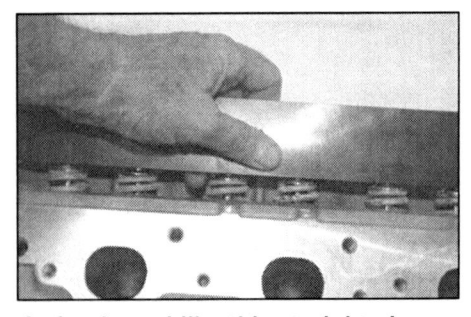

*A simple tool like this straightedge placed on top of the valve stems allows a quick visual check of the relative valve-stem heights. If a valve has sunk, the tip will be higher than the rest. If a valve seat has gotten loose or the valve is bent, the valve tip will be lower.*

- Have you maintained your dyno bearings?
- Have you zeroed your torque reading after each series of runs?
- Have you used a deadweight calibration that is within 5% of your expected peak torque?
- Have you checked the calibration on your low-temperature transducers?
- Have you checked the calibration on the exhaust gas thermocouples?

### Function

- Have you checked the safeties to ensure that they are functioning properly?
- Have you verified throttle actuation?
- Have you verified WOT (wide-open throttle)?
- Does the load control work smoothly?
- Will the dyno hold a steady load for an extended period of time without overheating the water?

## Engine Problems

- Begin by categorizing the problem. Is it a mechanical problem or a performance problem?
- Mechanical problems generally fall into the following areas:
- Failure: Broken valvespring, melted piston, spun bearing.
- Wear: Worn-out cam lobe.
- Clearance: Valve to piston, piston to head, bearing to crank, piston to wall.

## Performance Problems

- Oil pressure (low): Too much clearance, worn pump, worn bearings, broken lifter.
- Oil pressure (high): This is rare, but usually because the oil pump relief valve is set too high or an oil filter has collapsed, rendering the internal filter-relief valve inoperative if the filter has one.

## Engine Health

- Is the engine healthy?
- Have you run an end-play check, a leak-down test, a compression test, and a valve-lash check?
- Did any of the valve clearances tighten up?
- Are there any broken valvesprings?
- Have the valvesprings maintained their seat and open load?
- Are all of the valve tips at the correct height?
- Have you cut an oil filter and inspected it for debris?
- How do the power numbers compare to similar engines, or to the last time you ran this engine?
- Does the engine run smoothly?
- Does it make power throughout the entire range?
- Has the ignition system been qualified on any other engine?
- Is the throttle opening fully?
- Have somebody actuate the throttle while you look down into the carb or into the throttle body:
- Does the throttle position sensor agree with the throttle blade position?
- Are the electronics properly installed?
- Are you able to run a diagnostic check?
- Is the engine running an air cleaner?
- Is it clean?
- Is the cold air door or duct hooked up?

- Is the engine getting cold fresh air?

## Other Problems

Have you looked for the less obvious? Include or reconsider the following fundamental areas:

- Slipping clutch
- Poor weather conditions
- Lack of good spark or fuel delivery at high speed and load
- Engine oil level too high
- Poor current availability at high speed
- Poor fuel delivery
- Poor spark
- Wrong parts installed on the engine
- Backpressure incorrect
- Mislocated or missing timing marks

## Vehicle Problems

- Is the engine installed correctly in the vehicle?
- Has the in-car fuel system been properly tested for flow capability at the engine?
- Are the engine sensors reading accurately?

This will take some diagnostic tools to figure out. The OBDII port in the vehicle (late-model production cars only) will allow you to look at the various outputs and check them against factory values.

- Does the vehicle computer have any torque-limiting features built in that will restrict the engine power output?

Some vehicles are torque limited to enable the transmissions to live past their warranty period. Features such as timing, fuel cutoff, boost pressure, knock control, and limp-in mode all come into play to allow the engine to survive as a daily driver. If the computer senses that the driver is asking for more than the vehicle capabilities, it is programmed to inhibit or forbid the engine from running at those points.

It will usually take an aftermarket computer or controller to overcome these production or OEM roadblocks to performance. If you do bypass or disable these protective features in the production car, remember that your warranty may be voided. More importantly, your vehicle may not function properly, resulting in damage or non-compliance. Seemingly unrelated inputs may in fact be relied upon by the vehicle computer to make command decisions in another part of the system. In short, be cautious here. The damage you incur may be expensive or dangerous.

## Read the Data

Always take time to examine the data while you are taking it. We look for trends that don't look right or that stand out. Check temperatures if something looks funny; cross check against a known value and see if it remains constant. For example, let's say that number-4 cylinder has an EGT that is 200F lower than all of the rest. Two things could be happening, neither of which is good. First, the number-4 thermocouple may be acting up and just reading low, or the cylinder in question may be getting too much fuel and running rich, which would account for the lower temperature. There is also a third possibility; the cylinder in question could be running extremely lean. This condition is often referred to as "cold lean" and indicates a condition where there is not enough fuel to make much heat as opposed to "lean," where the engine makes more heat than the engine can tolerate, resulting in damage.

**This ATI damper shows clear markings that are valuable when timing the engine, but also when checking valve lash and, in a pinch, when checking the cam centerline. When assembling your engine, make sure that the timing marks are correct and clearly visible. Always check to ensure that the outer damper ring has not slipped on the hub.**

# CHAPTER 10

## Graph the Data

Graphical analysis is a great tool. Graph the outputs and look at them before drawing any conclusions. The answer is often waiting there in the graph. Graph one run against another, one variable against another. Get familiar with how things should look. Anomalies can pop out graphically that would often go unnoticed in a string of numbers on a page.

## High Hopes and Misconceptions

Quite often new products are hyped by advertising that is solely intended to sell the product. While not false, the fantastic claims may be only true in a narrow application. In the broad sense, the product may not produce any gain, and in many cases, it may result in a decrease in output. Advertising might call this a substantial negative gain! As we said earlier, a product may in fact work too well. Take the case of a product like a camshaft that actually produces an increase in the torque peak of nearly 50 lbs-ft. When simply tried in the car without a dyno test, the car might actually turn slower lap times at the local short track or higher elapsed times at the drag strip, simply because the car could not handle the extra torque. Only when the car got better traction and an upgraded suspension would it actually perform better. Without using a dyno test to separate the vehicle performance from the engine performance, the owner or driver might incorrectly assume that the new camshaft did not offer any gain.

To read a magazine story or advertisement, or watch a TV tuner show, you might think people who dyno engines routinely find 50 to 100 horsepower in 30 minutes with time in between for two car wax commercials. The truth is much more humbling. While there are instances where those gains have been real, it usually only happens at the low end of the performance arena. If an engine is stock or poorly prepared and the components are not well selected or matched, a sharp dyno shop can actually find 50–100 horsepower. In some of those cases, it is not the dyno shop being a hero, but rather a project starting with an engine that is poorly prepared or in a low state of tune. If a product advertisement boasts about a verified increase of 50 horsepower, the first question you should ask is, "over what?" If you start with an artificially low figure, your product can also be the big pooch on the porch.

Set your expectations realistically. Use an engine simulation program to predict what you should be able to achieve. When used properly with the correct inputs, these programs are amazingly accurate. The days of finding massive gains are gone for all but the beginner. The stock high-performance engines produced by the manufacturers today produce far more power than their same-sized predecessors did during the fabled muscle car era. This increased power density makes our job as tuners and engine developers more difficult and infinitely more rewarding at the same time. Today some production performance cars have cutting-edge technology in an emissions-legal package. All it takes is the proper selection of components, and the engine builder or tuner can produce some very impressive gains.

Another area in which people have a misconception relates to what is involved in a dyno test. Some people actually think that dyno testing produces an engine that will not blow up or have problems. In fact, dyno testing may be the most stressful activity an engine endures during its lifetime. It will be repeatedly run at its maximum load and at its highest RPM for extended periods of time. Unless your test session is short, plan on a possible rebuild to return your engine to its top performance. In the car, the engine might actually have somewhat of a vacation, with perhaps the exception of marine applications.

## Marine Engine Applications

Engines used in boats are run on what some people have called "the big wet dyno." Marine engines are often held at WOT for hours. Here it is not only important to have all of the fuel and spark calibrations correct for the increased cooling capability that is seen in a boat, but also to be acutely aware of waterfront fuel quality. You must be very careful when purchasing fuel at a marina. Due to the seasonal nature of boating in many areas, the fuel you purchase in the spring may be left over from last season. Properly stored, this might not present a problem, but improperly stored, it could produce disastrous results in an engine that was run hard for an extended period. Always try to qualify the fuel purchased in a low volume marina, or from a non-commercial fuel source.

Historically another area of concern for the marine applications has been the vibration damper. A marine application presents a totally different drivetrain resonance profile. A damper designed and tuned for a pickup truck running at 1800 RPM at a 55-mph road load probably will not have the same tuning spectrum as a damper mounted on the same engine in a 40-foot high-performance offshore boat application.

## Over-revving

Another misconception people hold is about over-revving. Many cars today employ rev limiters of one type or another that impede an engine's ability to run beyond a programmed point. By either shutting off the spark gradually or by shutting off the fuel, the limiting device or computer software prohibits the engine from going beyond a certain point in RPM. However, it is possible to over-rev the engine at any time in another manner. This is referred to as a mechanical over-rev. Imagine downshifting normally through the gears while coming to a sharp turn. If you were to jam the transmission into first instead of third, the engine would instantly over-rev when you let the clutch out. While the engine might not have fuel and spark, the mechanical parts would be significantly over-stressed during this misadventure. Imagine breaking a driveshaft or U-joint. The engine will easily over-rev. Nothing can protect a mistaken over-rev, but an ignition shutoff can protect a gradual over-rev. When testing, be sure to calibrate your vehicle's rev limiter, since it is very difficult to safely and accurately check the limits in the vehicle.

## Warnings

Failure to recognize the signals of impending disaster can cripple a

---

## Simple Tests

### Water in the Gasoline

If you suspect water is in the gasoline, a very quick check can be made by carefully taking a sample of fuel from the fuel line leading to the carburetor or injectors and collecting it in a clear container such as a glass jar. Caution: When taking a fuel sample, make sure the engine is cool and there is no spillage or open sparks or flame present. Ground the fuel container to prevent static electricity from igniting the fuel. Allow the fuel to sit in the clear container for 15 minutes and settle. Because fuel is lighter than water, the fuel will rise to the top and you will see a line where the fuel and water meet. In most cases, the fuel and water will have two distinct colors. The remedy is to drain the entire fuel system and properly dispose of the tainted fuel, while taking all necessary precautions to prevent fire and explosions.

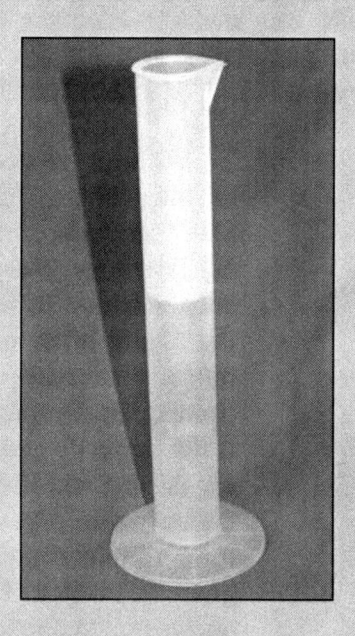

*Sooner or later, you will get water or contaminants in your fuel. Take a sample and let it rest. The two fluids will separate, and usually you can see the two distinct layers indicating water or another contaminant.*

### Water in Oil

While it is relatively easy to spot large amounts of water in oil because it foams the oil when the engine is running, there is a great test to find small concentrations of water in oil. Take a sample of oil and go to the kitchen (preferably when your spouse is away). Put a frying pan on the burner and apply medium heat. As the pan is heating up, take a small stir stick and stir the suspected oil and water mix, then withdraw the stick and flick a drop or two into the hot frying pan. Watch very carefully as the droplets hit the pan. Pure oil will hit the pan and slide out into a flat droplet. If water is present, the bead of water will dance and hop in the pan until it turns to steam. To complete the test, turn off the stove, wash the pan, bury the stir-stick, and deny that anything smells funny in the kitchen.

# CHAPTER 10

dyno test engine. Outside of a sudden mechanical failure such as a broken valve or connecting rod, most engines will give some warning of impending disaster. This warning may be subtle and short, but it is a warning nevertheless. This is where it pays to have a sharp dyno operator. While the operator may not know what the problem is, if they suddenly shut the engine off and say something like, "It sounded funny," it has been proven many times over to trust their instincts. Sometimes, it takes a very thorough disassembly and inspection to find the problem, but when you find the problem, it is well worth the effort. And yes, there are times when it is a false alarm. Often, though, the operator is right. Amazingly, engines will make an increased amount of torque just before they burn a piston. If you see the torque rising suddenly for no apparent reason, back off the throttle immediately.

A sudden change in pitch or a new noise may be the only signal you get. Learn to react quickly. Part of being careful on the dyno is to avoid running combinations without first qualifying them. Don't, for example, just pick up an unknown carburetor and bolt it on a dyno engine without first going through it carefully to make sure it has no obvious problems or deficiencies.

A sudden miss at high speed might signal a pushrod coming out or a valvespring breaking. It may be the electrode falling off a spark plug, or it may simply signal that an ignition system no longer has power to make an adequate spark.

## Electrical Grounds

Without proper grounding, an engine will not function correctly. Many engine-control systems rely on extremely low currents that are very sensitive to improper grounding. Quite often troubleshooting is difficult because the circuit will show up as complete, but because it is not perfectly grounded, the values are skewed and the engine does not control correctly. Learn to spend time maintaining the various grounds, which become oxidized and corroded due to exposure to the elements over time. Never assume that because an engine's starter works that an engine is properly grounded. Starter current of 600 amps can cover a lot of sins when it comes to poor grounding.

Learning to distinguish a dyno problem from an engine problem can save an enormous amount of time.

## Systems Approach to Solving Problems

If we break dyno testing and tuning into systems, it might look like this:

Engine
    Fuel
    Induction
    Ignition
    Oiling
    Cooling
    Valvetrain
    Short block
    Cylinder heads

Dyno
    Absorber
    Instrumentation
    Control system
    Data acquisition
    Drive system

Dyno Room
    Exhaust
    Intake air
    Heat exchanger
    Water supply
    12 Volt power

Vehicle
    Wiring and grounds
    12 Volt power
    Power losses in drivetrain
    Tires
    Systems
        Charging
        Cooling
        Fuel
            Pump, lines, filters
        Exhaust

Learn to go through each item methodically and verify the item to be functional. Learn not to take anything for granted. Use checklists. Keep good records. Above all, use common sense.

*A simple ground strap like this can save a lot of headaches. Be sure to clean both mounting surfaces and the attaching hardware before tightening down securely.*

# CHAPTER 11

# WHAT TO LOOK FOR IN A DYNO FACILITY

Let's look for a suitable dyno facility. We'll begin by looking at our goals; it helps to list your goals ranked in order of importance. Let's begin by asking the questions below to help define our goals.

## Chassis or Engine Dyno?

Perhaps one of the first questions to ask is: do we need a chassis dyno or an engine dyno? The answer depends on whether you want to remove the engine from the vehicle. Is the engine the only component you want to test? If you want to check out the transmission and rear axle, you will have to use a chassis dyno. If you want to eliminate all of the drivetrain and vehicle variables and focus solely on the engine, then you will only want to use an engine dyno. You may want to get a quick number to verify that the engine is installed correctly and all of the vehicle systems are functioning properly. The chassis dyno fits the bill here.

Did you just make some engine improvements that should have resulted in better performance only to have the vehicle actually slow down? Sometimes it helps to be able to separate the engine from the equation. By testing the engine alone, you might find that you did in fact make more power and hence more torque—so much that the vehicle now needs a better suspension or better tires to harness the added power.

*Chassis dynos are perfect when it is impractical to remove the engine from the car, or when you want to test the entire drivetrain.*

## Dyno Rental

Many shops rent their dynos to enable customers to test their own engines. The policies for these rentals are quite variable. Some engine dyno shops will only dyno test engines that they have machined or assembled. As you can imagine, the shop is understandably nervous about

DYNO TESTING AND TUNING

# CHAPTER 11

*Before running, make sure you are fully checked out on all of the controls. Also make sure you know all of the capabilities. There may be additional data that can be gathered by just mounting the appropriate sensor.*

renting a very expensive and potentially dangerous piece of equipment to people who just walk in the door. The renter may just be the world's greatest engine builder, but since the world's greatest engine builder probably has his own dyno, chances are the renter is somewhat less talented.

Most dyno rentals begin with a preliminary visit to a dyno facility to see what is involved and get an understanding of the shop policies and capabilities. The dyno shop is interested to see if the customer has realistic goals and understands the costs, risks, and rewards involved in dynamometer testing. If the prospective customer comes in with the idea that dyno testing involves only making more horsepower without risk, most dyno test operations are reluctant to go any further. Perhaps the most common misconception of dyno testing is that you can spend a day and gain 50 or 60 horsepower. While this is possible if you start with a grossly assembled and poorly tuned engine, and are lucky enough to catch all of the faults before they destroy the engine, 50- to 60-horsepower gains rarely happen. More experienced dyno operators may work all winter to find 10–15 horsepower. However, these same engines power cars that win major championships.

If the preliminary visit to the dyno facility is mutually satisfactory and both parties want to pursue the rental, then the questions start. Money always comes in at the front. Typically, an eight-hour day on the dyno ranges from $600 upward depending on what extras are included. If you are new to the testing game, let the shop guide you through the process. Tell them what you want to test and what results you want to achieve. Most shops have a written document that spells out what each party is expected to provide and who will do the work.

For a variety of reasons, primarily safety, very few shops will let the customer actually operate the dyno. Not unlike an airplane ride, it is usually the best bet initially to let the seasoned operator make the runs while you watch. The operator will review what you are testing and make sure that everything is safe before firing the engine. He will set and engage all of the safety limits to ensure that the engine does not operate outside of the safe zone. You will need to furnish recommended RPM ranges, pressures and temperatures so the operator can properly set the values in the initial data input for the dyno. Fuel is a very important consideration. Shops tend to be divided on whether they furnish the fuel or whether you provide it. There are pros and cons to both policies. In the end, you must make sure that your engine gets the proper fuel, or it will be a long and expensive adventure with a very bad ending.

## Location

Assuming that you have some time constraints, you will want to find a dyno facility that is conveniently located. Driving all night to run on a dyno all day long on the following day, followed by a long drive home, is a mistake waiting to happen. Going to the local dyno facility and getting the engine mounted, then going home to get some rest before a full dyno day, makes a lot more sense. What are the normal hours for the facility? Can you schedule time after work or in the evening or weekends? Many shops close the dyno facility on the weekends to go racing or support customers who are at the track. This leaves the weekdays. You may have to settle for letting the dyno shop run your engine for you if they are willing. Most dyno facilities prefer to have the owner of the engine, or a representative such as the engine builder, in attendance in case something happens or a question needs to be answered.

# WHAT TO LOOK FOR IN A DYNO FACILITY

## Timing and Support

You will need to know how much dyno time you will require. Some testing can be accomplished very quickly while other testing takes time. Going on a chassis dyno and testing a series of timing points can be done very quickly, while comparison testing two sets of heads or camshafts can easily take all day. Murphy's law states, "if it can happen (go wrong), it will." Until you get some time under your belt, testing your engine properly will be a time-consuming process. Once you have tested a few times, it will become easier. Remember, the first time you took your car to the track?

Unless the dyno facility sells parts, they will probably not have the type of valvesprings you need to make the new cam work, and even then they may not have the correct ones. You will need to bring all of the particular spare parts for your engine combination with you.

Unless you have some experience in dyno testing, you will need some help. Any good dyno facility will be more than willing to share their knowledge with you and help you tune your engine. They will probably not share too much in the initial meeting other than to give you some pointers. A good dyno shop has a lot to offer. They are selling their experience. Once you sign on and rent some time, they are usually more than willing to be helpful. Remember, if you make great strides and find some more power, you will tell your friends and the dyno facility will presumably get more business. It is in their best interest to make sure you increase your power and do not hurt your engine. Even though you may be having more fun than you imagined, try really hard to listen and heed their advice. Until you get some experience with dyno testing, it is easy to get caught up in the moment and make a dumb mistake or get greedy and take some chances that you will regret later on. This is called "Dyno Fever."

## Support Equipment

If you have never had your engine on an engine dyno before, you may need some additional equipment, such as a bellhousing and starter, or you may need to modify your vehicle equipment to fit the dyno. In many cases, the dyno facility has the additional equipment you can rent or purchase on site. If you have a rare or unique engine, you may have to make all of the components to adapt your engine to the dyno prior to testing. If it is a rare but well-respected engine, the dyno facility may help you defray some of the cost of making the equipment and either rent or borrow the equipment from you for use by other customers with similar engines. If you are going to test a Hispano-Suiza engine, plan on making everything to adapt the engine to the selected dyno and then plan on taking all of it home after the test.

## Can They Do What I Want?

The data you are trying to collect and the type of test you are trying to run will help determine the facility and type of dyno. If, for example, you are trying to run a 24-hour endurance race with oil-consumption and fuel-economy measurements, you will need a facility with a programmable load and throttle control as well as data logging ability and some sophisticated measuring equipment. Above all, you will need to make sure that their dynos are set up to run endurance tests. An engine produces an incredible amount of heat, a large portion of which is transferred to the water in the dyno cooling system from the coolant in the engine. Also, the water brake converts energy into heat while it controls the load from the engine. Unless the dyno facility uses a total-loss water system, where all of the waste hot water goes down the drain and fresh cool water is supplied by the local water system, there has to be a way to cool the water for the dyno. Obviously, the higher the horsepower number, the more heat the dyno test produces. In a closed-loop cooling system, this heat must be transferred or removed from the water so the water can make laps through the dyno and the engine cooling system to remove more heat.

In this case, it would be wise to bring a tape or data dump from an onboard data acquisition system that gave the RPM profile for the racetrack you want to run in a format that could be loaded or programmed into the dyno computer. Without this programmable control capability, the operator must sit at the console and manually "drive" the throttle and the dyno load control to simulate the race conditions. While this can be done, it is not recommended, especially for 24 hours!

If you have had your engine professionally built, and your engine builder has a dyno, the best bet is to have it dyno tested before it ever leaves their shop. Most engine builders are adamant about testing every engine prior to it leaving, just as a quality check that gives both parties confidence. The owner receives the engine knowing that they got what was promised. They know that they are installing an engine that doesn't leak and will produce a known power level, presuming that all of the vehicle systems are capable of supporting the additional power. The engine builder is confident that the engine left the facility with everything intact. Most race engine shops have a policy that states that once the engine leaves their shop after a successful dyno test the owner is on his or her own. Due to the intended usage, there are virtually no warranties in the racing world!

## Do You Fit In?

Above all, look for a dyno shop where you not only feel comfortable but your project fits in. A particular shop owner may be a great guy, but if he races diesel trucks at Bonneville, he may not be too helpful picking a cam for a Saturday night short-track dirt car. If the shop specializes in Fords, taking a Pontiac project there may not be that rewarding, if for no other reason than that they will be totally unfamiliar with your setup. Beware of the shop who says, "We can work on anything; after all they are just engines." Today each engine has its individual subtleties and unique specifications. If a shop takes on a project that is totally new to them, they will have to spend a fair amount of time becoming educated on the finer points of the engine, which can translate into a significant bill at the end of a project.

Almost inevitably the old saying, "you get what you pay for," comes into play. If there is no reigning expert for your engine, then you will have to become that person. Go slowly and carefully with as much support as you can muster. Books and contacts with other people who have run a similar combination are two ways to ease the learning curve and save you time and money

Once you pick a shop with the right fit, talk to the people you will be working with. If you are working with the owner, he or she may be a great person, but may have to spend time answering other people's questions and taking calls, just like he or she did when you were inquiring about renting the dyno. In a big shop you might never see the owner except for lunch or the sales pitch. Try to meet and get to know the person you will be working directly with. Find a knowledgeable person who is willing to help you and answer your questions. This person will also try to steer you away from disaster if you are willing to listen. Until you have a few hundred runs behind you, remember, this individual has probably made more dyno runs in a week than you will possibly make in your life. They truly have your best interests at heart and want you to be successful and come back again to find more horsepower.

## Listen & Learn

Listen to what these knowledgeable people are really saying, and, more importantly, what they are not saying. They may also have tested your competitor's engine last week. They hopefully will not tell you what the competitor is running; however, if you listen carefully there may be clues. The clues or help they can give you would come in the form of what to run next and what not to try, since they may have already tried it and found it not to work. Note: If they do tell you what your competitor did or the results they achieved, chances are they will be on the phone to your competitor after you leave to tell them what you did. Most shops realize that if they get the reputation for being "leakers" of information, nobody will trust them or will test with them.

Be wary of a shop that wants to base comparisons on one run and one that doesn't see the need to close the loop and repeat the baseline. Yes, comparisons can be made based on one run without backing up the baseline, but in the end, this practice will get you into trouble. If you become a "Dyno Cowboy" and just go in the room and make a series of runs and wildly thrash around changing parts, soon you will become hopelessly lost. Hopefully, if you read and apply what is covered in this book, you will be able to start testing at a meaningful level. Look for the common-sense solution before running wildly in three different directions.

## Be a Good Customer by Having Your Act Together!

Treat going to the dyno like going to a big race. Show up with everything you will need. Have all of the specifications of what you are bringing to test. If you run into problems they can only help you if you know what's in your engine. If your engine was professionally built, bring all of the engine builder's records. If you used a professional engine builder, you should get a build book that lists all of the specifications. Sometimes the engine builder keeps the original so it doesn't get lost, but you certainly should be able to get a copy.

Make sure you show up on time and ready to run. Most dyno shops do not just exist on dyno rentals alone. For many shops, the dyno rental is a side business while the main business is engine building or machining. If you show up a day late, fail to call, or are still assembling the engine as you enter the dyno room, the shop will quickly see you as a disorganized amateur and not worth the time and trouble to have you back again. On the other hand, if you come in early or on time ready to run, you will earn their respect. If your engine fires right up, doesn't do anything dumb, makes decent power, and you listen to advice, they may be impressed and be a lot more willing to help you. In the end, your dyno experience will be very productive and rewarding. At the end of a test session, a dyno shop has often been known to bring out a house carburetor for a couple of free runs, just to let you have a peek at something possibly better than you already have. If you have been a rolling disaster and a royal pain, this will never happen.

Don't be afraid to ask questions, but be respectful of the operator's focus. If the operator is going through the checklist, let them finish before interrupting with a question about weather correction factors. If you do see something amiss, however, speak up and ask about it. It may be something that got missed, or they may simply have a different way of doing things.

Once the testing starts to get intense, the tempo picks up, not unlike a race, and things start to happen fast. The trick is not to get caught up in the confusion and keep a clear head and stay focused on the test plan objectives. If you miss a baseline or forget to make an adjustment at a critical time, it may mean repeating the test. This is where a written test plan and checklist helps. Having these will translate into time and money saved. Picking a shop you can work with or trust to do it your way is critical here if you expect to get good results from your testing program. Spend some time picking the right facility. It will be time well-spent. Make sure that your goals and their capabilities match.

Many dyno shops are somewhat reluctant to rent their dynos to customers whom they don't know. As a customer you are entrusting your valuable engine to them, while on the other hand, they are entrusting their expensive dyno with running your engine. Should your engine fail, they stand to lose a fair amount of equipment and, more importantly, incur some expensive downtime while repairs are being made. For this reason, if they do test your engine, they will want to begin the testing very gently in an effort to avoid a costly mistake either to your engine or to their dyno. This is the time to make them aware of the specifications for your engine, answer their questions truthfully and stand back and let them run the engine. If you can't answer the question, just tell them you don't know. They may want to stop right there and get the answer before proceeding, just to ensure they give your engine the best chance at survival. Most good shops will have all of the questions on a form to be filled out prior to the test session.

## Have Your Engine Data

Some of the questions are:
Bore and Stroke
Cubic inches
Compression ratio
Fuel octane requirement
Type of fuel
Fuel pressure and flow requirement
Heat range of spark plugs
Spark plug gap
Total ignition timing
Firing order
Coolant requirement
Exhaust backpressure
Header size
Crankshaft end play
Operating limits
    Oil pressure
        High and low
    Coolant temperature
    Oil temperature
Ignition system requirements
Oil capacity
    Including filter
Type and brand of oil
Break-in requirements
Valve lash settings

## Support Equipment and Staff

Support equipment at a dyno facility is important. Suppose you need to have a header tube moved and re-welded to clear the dyno or the new oil pan you are trying. It would be helpful to have a qualified welder on staff available to step in and make a quick repair or modification. If you needed a manifold trimmed, it would be nice if the shop had a mill and an operator standing by. Does the dyno facility sell parts, or is there a local auto parts store nearby for routine parts? Additional equipment and capability, while not necessary, certainly makes your testing more productive. Oil heaters to pre-warm your oil or keep it at a given temperature cut the warm-up time in half. Automatic drain and fill for the cooling system allows the hoses to be removed during a manifold swap without having to deal with hot coolant. The added bonus is that, as soon as you change the parts

# CHAPTER 11

*A well laid-out room is a key to look for at any dyno facility. This room at Impastato Racing Engines has all of the necessary components well laid out and within easy reach.*

and hook up the hoses, your engine can be filled with warm coolant and you can test almost immediately with a warm engine. These features mean a lot if you are trying to save time and maximize your testing dollars. Look for extra equipment like mercury column barometers, master pressure gauges to calibrate all the gauges and sensors, blowby meters, and leak checkers (you should already own one of these to use at the track). Ask about their calibration procedures and records.

How convenient are the hours of operation? Is the dyno available during the evening or on weekends? If you are renting a dyno, chances are that you are not a full-time engine builder and you need to have access to a dyno after hours. Most dyno shops that are in the rental business will adjust their hours to meet the customer's needs. Always inquire about overtime policies and the cost. If your test session is running long and you need another hour to reach a good stopping point, can you accomplish this or will the shop be forced to close on time? What additional costs are involved with overtime?

What's it worth to test? If you are building a winner for the Daytona 500, your team may spend an entire year building and testing engine combinations to get the right blend of power and fuel economy with good durability. On the other hand, the chassis dyno is the most cost-effective way to get a baseline horsepower and torque number. The ease of simply taking the car to the dyno shop, tying it down and pulling the trigger is hard to argue against. The numbers produced are real and can be easily correlated to real-world performance. Additionally, the output reflects the combined output of the engine as well as the entire drivetrain. Put more simply, you are able to see the effect of a new torque convertor or of a different ratio transmission. What is this worth? While it may cost more than a trip to the drag strip, if the drag strip is covered with snow or rain and closed until spring, it becomes a bargain.

## Costs

Typical minimal rentals for a chassis dyno cost around $100 for three runs, while a whole day with lots of parts changing becomes more expensive. Rates differ according to what is provided and what is being supplied in addition to your testing.

If you plan on changing internal engine parts or external parts like headers or exhaust systems, you might want to consider an engine dyno. Someone once said that "testing on an engine dyno is like working on a car without fenders." The ease and hence speed with which you can reach and work on all of the engine parts makes testing much easier. However, if you are just getting started, it seems ridiculous to remove the engine to test a few carburetor modifications. The engine dyno and the chassis dyno each have their own unique advantages. You have to look at your budget and your timeline and then make your decision based on how well each method suits your needs and goals.

A typical engine dyno session is usually charged in a minimum 8-hour segment while a chassis dyno session goes in increments as small as one hour. From there, depending on how much more testing you do, the hourly rate is usually adjustable. A chassis dyno is much less costly, and typically time can be bought for as few as three runs.

While most shops don't feel comfortable letting you run their dyno to test your engine, most are perfectly OK with having you work on your engine, and many in fact would rather have you do the work. The exception here is when they build your engine. At that point, they want to take full responsibility for every detail until the engine changes hands and becomes yours. You will be invited to observe the dyno test (if you are not invited or offered to view the test, find a different shop), and once the engine has passed all of the previously agreed-upon testing, you own it, assuming you have paid the bill.

## Policies

If you have an engine tested, ask about the records or run sheets for each run. Policies differ from shop to shop. Most shops like to keep a copy of all runs, so if you have a question or want a copy in the future, it will be available. Some shops give you all of the originals and it is up to you to keep track of the records.

Some shops allow cameras, and others do not. Always ask about the policy prior to showing up with your camera and planning to take pictures. Some engine builders include a video of the engine running on the dyno with each engine as a service to the customers who are not able to attend the testing phase of their engine.

If you plan to work on your own engine, come prepared. Ask about the shop's policy on tools. Most shops have specific policies about whose tools get used during a test. Regardless, you will have to bring any special wrenches and other tools required to work on your particular engine. You must also bring your own parts to test.

Fuel creates another new set of questions. Some dyno shops sell fuel, which makes it very convenient, provided they have the fuel you require. Other shops would prefer that you be responsible for furnishing your own fuel, which relieves them of any liability for providing faulty fuel. Check with the dyno shop and plan accordingly. If the shop does not supply fuel, inquire where fuel is available that will suit your needs. As a side note, be very careful about transporting fuel on the public highway. Make sure you are fully aware of the safety procedures as well as the state and federal laws regarding fuel transport. Remember, 55 gallons of race fuel could be deadly in a crash, or it could be viewed as a terrorist threat if you were headed into a tunnel or parked near something vulnerable.

## Additional Parts

Loaner parts are another dimension to dyno testing. The first place where this is important is in the parts necessary to hook up your engine to the dyno. The following external parts are usually necessary and sometimes available at the dyno facility:

Flywheel
Drive plate or clutch and pressure plate
Engine mounts
Starter
Bellhousing
Oil tank, filter, and lines for dry sump applications
Accessory drive pulleys and belts
Deep wet-sump oil pans

Parts that you should supply, but sometimes are provided, include:

Fuel pump, lines and filter
Headers
Exhaust pipes
Mufflers, if required for your vehicle
Coil and control box
Distributor

## Gasoline Safety

Gasoline should never be stored inside the dyno cell. In the case of float cans, they should be low volume and located in a safe area away from any source of sparks or heat and shielded from potential flying debris. All fuel lines should be heavy-duty high-pressure hose intended for and compatible with the fuel you are using. The fuel lines should be properly shielded from anything that might cut, burn, or pierce them and routed away from hot areas like the exhaust. These lines should also be prevented from becoming chafed or worn by rubbing on anything like a pulley or belt, as well as protected from being stepped on or driven over by carts. Try to make all lines as short as possible and always use high-pressure hose with crimped line fittings to prevent hoses from blowing off and spraying high-pressure fuel all over the room. If the hose does have to pass through a hostile area, it can be run through a piece of protective heavy-gauge steel pipe that can serve as a protective shield. These same rules should be applied to oil lines running from dry sumps, filters, and coolers. A high-pressure oil line spraying on a hot exhaust header can quickly create a huge fire. Avoid plastic fuel filters and clear plastic fuel line.

Before the engine is ready to run, the fuel pump(s) should be turned on to pressurize the entire fuel system. The system should then be

# CHAPTER 11

purged of air and inspected for fuel leaks. Before any serious testing begins, make sure to test the fuel volume capability of the system. This is a simple test almost everybody misses, until they either ruin an engine that leaned out due to fuel starvation, or until they fail to deliver rated horsepower because there was not enough fuel to support the additional power. It is a simple fact that in order to make more power, your engine will require proportionally more fuel.

The fuel supply to the test cell should have at least one manual shutoff valve inside the room between the dyno and the fuel supply, as well as a heat-activated shutoff valve that prevents the flow of fuel when exposed to heat. Prior to any testing, the manual valve(s) must be turned on. It is highly recommended for cells to have an outside fuel shut off, so fuel can be shut off without having to re-enter the room in case it is on fire! Make it a point to identify these shutoffs when using a new facility, so you are familiar with their location and operating procedures in case you have to use them in a hurry.

## Cool Clean Air

Clean, room-temperature air in abundant quantities is an absolute necessity to not only supply the combustion process but also cool the engine and transport the exhaust fumes from the test cell. It seems so rudimentary to discuss this, but

## Fuel Storage and Quality

Gasoline's potency is measured in many ways. The most well-known is by an octane rating. The octane rating basically measures the gasoline's sensitivity to knock. As a gasoline increases its ability to prevent or resist knock, it is assigned a higher octane rating. We typically use higher-octane fuels in a high-performance engine in order to have an added safety factor; quite often we have increased the odds that it will knock by raising the compression ratio, or increasing the timing or operating the engine at higher combustion temperatures. Gasoline octane is typically rated by two methods: research and motor. The research method is accomplished in a laboratory, while the motor method involves actually running the fuel in a special variable-compression-ratio engine so that knock can be induced gradually as the compression ratio is increased. Pump gasoline octane is typically advertised with the average of the two ratings. Often you will encounter the phrase "R+M divided by two." This is simply the formula for determining the average octane rating using two methods.

When delivered fresh from the refinery, gasoline has the advertised values for its octane rating. If stored properly in a full factory-sealed steel drum out of the sunlight and in a cool environment, gasoline will remain potent and will last indefinitely. Stored improperly in a partially full, vented container, the "light ends" of the hydrocarbon molecule will drift away into the atmosphere and the resultant gasoline will not meet the octane requirements you need, at least not for very long. Short of testing a sample of this gasoline in a special variable-compression-ratio rating engine, or by fractional distillation in a specially equipped laboratory, there is virtually no way of truly confirming its properties. While the fuel may have the right color and smell potent, the true test of its capability comes from the results of an octane test. Using your $50,000 racing engine to "prove" somebody's fuel is a losing proposition.

If you have to store fuel, it should be stored in properly grounded, airtight steel drums in a cool, dark location that is not in a high-traffic area. Before storing any amount of fuel, be sure to check with the local fire authority regarding regulations defining just how much fuel you can store and how it must be contained. Again, it is highly recommended that you use only known fresh fuel coming from a sealed drum or a well-known distributor. Once you have removed fuel from a sealed drum, carefully replace the screw-on cap and store in a well-protected, cool area out of the sunlight. If the fuel is allowed to stay in a vented tank for any amount of time, it will quickly lose its light ends and become unusable in virtually anything but a lawnmower. Never return leftover fuel to a sealed drum. Never store fuel in plastic jugs for a long term. Be especially careful of static electricity when transferring fuel from one container to another. Learn how to make and use a proper electrical ground for fuel containers during both storage and transfer. Remember, one stray spark could end your fun forever.

DYNO TESTING AND TUNING

many tests have been wasted because somebody forgot to open the dyno room air vents and allow cool outside air to enter the test cell prior to starting a test. Once the vents are opened, the fans must be turned on prior to starting the engine to ensure an adequate supply of clean cool fresh air at the correct pressure.

To be safe and effective, test cells are typically run at a slightly negative pressure compared to the area outside of the cell. This negative pressure, sometimes called room depression, helps prevent harmful gases like deadly carbon monoxide from entering the console area or work area outside the test cell. Most test cells use a water manometer made from a transparent hose hung in the dyno room window to allow the operator to visually verify that the room has the correct depression prior to any testing.

Like fuel, enough air to support combustion is mandatory. Unlike fuel, additional air is required to cool the engine and transport heat and spent exhaust gas out of the test cell. To provide a room with adequate air, the cell air must be capable of being changed a minimum of 10 to 12 times per minute. For a test cell that measures 12 feet by 15 feet by 12 feet high, we calculate a cubic volume of 2160 cubic feet (12 x 12 x 15 = 2160). So that means that we should have a room-ventilation system capable of delivering 21,600 CFM (cubic feet per minute) (2160 x 10 = 21,600) at a static pressure of at least 1 inch of water. This air flow should ensure that you will change the air in your test cell sufficiently to avoid contaminating the incoming air charge as well as meeting the cooling requirements for the air-handling system. Some high-end test cells are capable of heating, cooling, and controlling the humidity of the incoming air to simulate virtually every weather condition imaginable.

By monitoring your room depression using the water manometer, you will be able to spot the obvious, such as fans not running, closed vents, or plugged air filters. Plugged filters can be very deceiving since they gradually plug up and the power loss occurs over a long time period. Power drops off so gradually that it often goes unnoticed until the engine is blamed and retuned or rebuilt in an attempt to regain the lost power.

Both fresh-air inlet and exhaust-outlet doors or vents to the cell must be opened prior to firing the engine to allow cool fresh inlet air to enter and to allow hot exhaust gases to escape. Some cells have an indicator light at the console to indicate the opened or closed status of the vents.

Some dyno cells bring in outside air through a large-diameter flex

*Air inlet hoses act as a duct to enable the engine to breathe fresh incoming air. Be careful to ensure that you are not tuning around an additional inlet tube. A few carefully monitored runs with and without the tubes in place should confirm this.*

hose connected directly to the carburetor or throttle body. In theory, if this hose is connected with no leakage, it becomes an extension of the inlet tract and becomes an important element in the tuning equation. Be very careful when using this type of setup. Some users report no measurable difference, while others have very strong feelings and recommend against using it. At the end of the day, unless you plan to carry this setup in your vehicle, it might be a good idea to test the engine as it is in the vehicle. While we are on that subject, remember also that the dyno does not replicate under-hood temperatures or air currents. A 180-mph breeze from a hood scoop will drastically affect your in-car tuning. *Never* go directly from the dyno to the track and try to run an engine without first carefully sneaking up on the speed to make sure you will not encounter anything abnormal. Having on-board data acquisition to monitor the engine during the initial track session will pay big dividends here. Be sure to have individual cylinder temperatures available.

## 12-Volt Power

Whether you choose to use a battery or a regulated 12-volt supply, make sure that you have adequate power to run all of the accessories such as electric fuel pumps, ignition, engine-control module, and water pumps. If you have a high current draw from an ignition or fuel system, it is best always to run a functional charging system to ensure full power to the ignition and fuel systems at all times. Again, the rule: Always run the system you will use in the vehicle. This method will allow you to find any inadequacies prior to looking dumb and going slow in front of family and friends at the track. Sometimes low or threshold voltage failures are hard to diagnose. The engine may start and run, but the spark may be so weak that the engine lacks power, or misfires at high RPM.

You should know that a fully charged 12-volt battery will actually measure about 13.2 volts with a voltmeter. So if it only measures 12 volts, it is down on energy.

## Pumps and Dyno Water Supply

These systems must be turned on to ensure that water is available to fill the engine-cooling system, and provide hydraulic braking for the dyno. Many cells use a closed-loop water system, in which the water is stored in a huge water tank and circulated through the dyno cell, where it cools the engine as well as provides the hydraulic operating fluid for the dyno. Some dyno operations that run frequently, or those that run endurance tests, will pump their hot exhaust water through a hydronic heater unit and actually use it to heat their buildings during the winter months.

Some water-brake dynos in areas where water is in abundant supply and not subject to sudden pressure drops use a total-loss system. In this system, water is fed into the dyno, and after it is used to cool the engine, it is sent down the drain as hot water.

## Dyno Water Cooling Tower

If you use a closed-loop dyno water system, which most operations do to save water, you should have a way to cool the dyno water, since a running engine will heat it very quickly. Before beginning a test session, you should make note of the dyno inlet temperature to ensure your incoming water will be sufficiently cool to prevent what is referred to as "flashing" inside of the absorber. Flashing occurs when the water in the absorber undergoes a phase change from liquid to steam. This phase change is accompanied by a release of energy that will pit the dyno's rotor and stators. This erosion, called impingement, will literally eat holes in the rotor if left unchecked. At this point, the incoming water is converted to steam and hence the absorber loses control, so not only are you slowly ruining your dyno, but you have also lost load control of your engine.

## Mount Up!

The big day comes and you show up at the dyno. The facility will usually have some agreements for you to sign before the fun begins. You should get the engine unloaded and on the dyno as soon as possible, since the meter is running. Sometimes a dyno shop will let you mount up the night or afternoon prior to the actual test, if you do the work. If this is the case, consider it a real bonus, since you will get at least a couple of hours of extra testing in.

When you reserve a dyno day or session, make sure that you understand what motor mounts, flywheel, clutch, bellhousing, and pilot bearing configuration the dyno accepts. Nothing is more frustrating than trying to find the right bellhousing on a Saturday while the meter is running on your test session. Sometimes the dyno facility has the specific setup for your particular engine, and will make the parts available for your session.

Once the engine is mounted on the dyno, most operators review a written checklist. Having a checklist helps ensure critical details like verifying timing and making sure that you have colder heat-range spark plugs installed in the engine. Make sure you have the correct amount of oil in the engine and all of the various drain plugs are tight. Check to make sure that the throttle on the dyno produces wide open at the throttle on the engine. Make sure that all of the various sensors and transducers are properly located and calibrated and reading correctly. There is a generic checklist in the appendix that should serve as a starting template for any serious tuner getting ready to go on the dyno for their first time. Modify this list for your own specific needs and unique needs of your engine.

## What to Look for in a Dynamometer Facility

A great reputation for dealing with customers fairly is very high on the list of priorities that should be considered when choosing a dyno facility. A safe testing environment is also very high on the list of preferred items in a test facility.

Don't forget security. If you have to leave any of your parts or your complete vehicle overnight, is the place secure? Have they had any thefts of things from vehicles in the parking lot? Better to find out before problems crop up. Even checking with the local police department for information on crime history in specific areas is a quick way to determine what security worries there might be.

CHAPTER 12

# HOW TO READ A DYNO SHEET

Reading a dyno sheet is fairly easy if you fully understand the terms and conditions of the test. However there are some tricks to know in order to make some meaningful use of the data on a dyno sheet. A graphic reference is always of assistance, for example, and can supply you with some very important information that otherwise would not be so readily apparent.

One valuable suggestion is to request of the dyno facility at least one graph of either speed (MPH) vs. time (seconds) or engine speed (RPM) vs. time (seconds). Those graphs can tell you a great deal at the very first glance. If the RPM vs. time graph is not a smooth slope, then the data on the test is probably not very reliable either. Variation in that slope of acceleration should not be more than a few percentage points. This item is covered in detail in the section on specifications for good dyno testing parameters.

A dyno sheet printout is what gets into the most hands for analysis or even just plain old bragging rights. Although the individual dyno manufacturers do not follow anything such as a standard format for presentation of the data, most at least use the same terms so that some common understanding is somewhat easier to accomplish.

You must consider that when software people configure the output formatting produced by a piece of equipment, it is generally coming from people who have absolutely no idea of why anyone would want to know the details that gearheads want. Normally, they will try to make their jobs easier and not be too concerned about yours. Sometimes you just have to adapt and in time perhaps you can help to influence what is seen and what format is used with various test equipment.

## Type of Test

This becomes an important issue and is a piece of information that some dynamometer systems do not list automatically on the dyno sheet. An acceleration test...at what rate? A steady-state test, or a simulated track test with gear changes? You need to

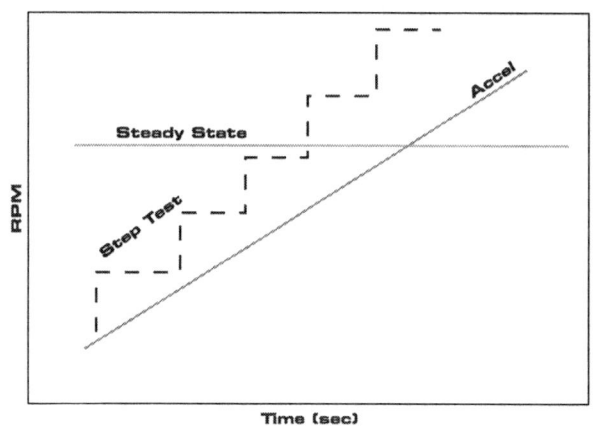

*Comparing RPM vs time shows that an acceleration test is at a uniform slope. Conversely, step testing or simple steady-state testing is also shown. There is not a simple way to compare the results of these tests unless the tests were the same type (such as accel or steady state) and only then when at the same conditions or rates of change. On chassis dynos, the comparison is typically done at speed vs time.*

DYNO TESTING AND TUNING

# CHAPTER 12

know before you put heart and soul into analysis with poor assumptions as your guide. If it is not clearly stated or provided in the information on the dyno sheet, then you need to look at the data so that you can plot RPM vs. time (seconds) or speed (MPH) vs. time (seconds) on a chassis dyno.

***Barometric pressure*** column or listing refers to the local barometric pressure or the station pressure at the time of the test or at the data point. Mercury barometers are preferred for a local reference. Aneroid barometers should not be used. A point to be aware of here is that the station pressure is the uncorrected pressure that is at the location of the dynamometer. It is corrected for temperature and location on the planet only. The temperature correction is necessary because the mercury is very sensitive to temperature, and the gravity correction is for the location on the planet. This barometric pressure reading will not be the same as used by the local TV weather announcer. If you are using a digital gauge reference for barometric pressure, neither the temperature or gravity corrections is necessary, but you must make sure that the barometer is reading local pressure.

***Vapor pressure*** column or listing refers to the amount of atmospheric pressure that water was adding to the local barometric pressure. The vapor pressure is typically listed in inches of mercury ("Hg). Another reference is RH%, which is relative humidity. The RH% is typically expressed in percent. This vapor pressure reading normally comes from a sensor that provides the data to the system. When the vapor pressure is high, it indicates that the amount of atmospheric oxygen is being displaced by atmospheric water. When the vapor pressure is low, it is more favorable for making more power. Simply put, dry air is denser than air that contains more water. Remember this when track tuning.

***RPM*** column refers to the engine revolutions per minute and might have been collected from either a sensor on the engine ignition system or a counter on the shaft of the dynamometer or from a calculation if a gear ratio was in service during testing as on a chassis dyno. On a chassis dyno, sometimes the process is back-calculated from entry of a gear ratio. You need to know how the data was collected.

***Torque*** column refers to the twisting force that the engine or the drive

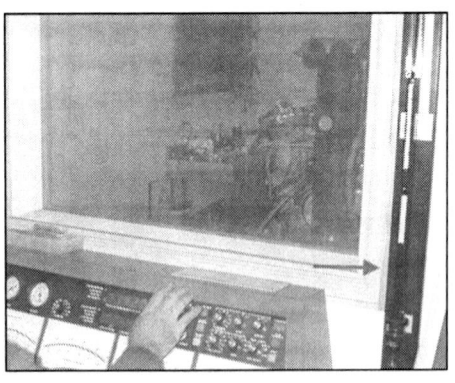

*The arrow in the photo is pointing to an important tool in responsible dyno testing. It is a vertical mercury barometer. The barometer gives the atmospheric pressure at the test site, which is called station pressure. Beware of the TV weatherman, because he speaks with corrected-to-sea-level numbers. The tuner needs to know about these things.*

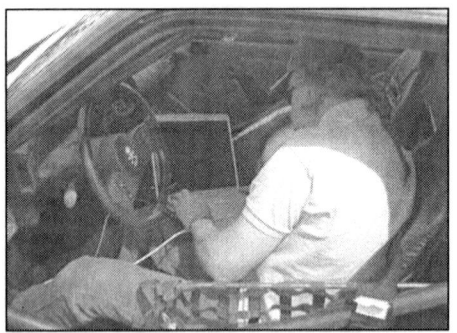

*This racer is doing the "electronic screwdriver" thing in the staging lanes. As atmospheric conditions change, having good dyno data allows the tuner to input appropriate changes in the software-driven electronic map of fuel and spark and other inputs. This turbocharged Mustang has gone 8.54 at 168MPH, and they are still sorting how to put the power down on what the driver calls "snow tires" (drag radials).*

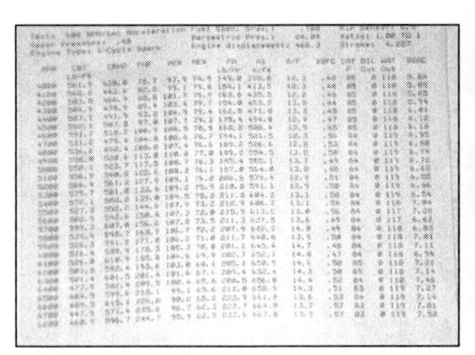

*Most modern dynos provide data in printed form for the operator and tuner to reference. It is important to know what these columns mean and how the numbers are generated in order to apply the data properly to the engine. This applies to engine or chassis applications. These dyno data are from a record-holding Super Stock Pontiac.*

128    DYNO TESTING AND TUNING

# HOW TO READ A DYNO SHEET

*This fuel system is used to measure the fuel flow on a methanol fuel-injection engine while on the dyno. The fuel curve is an important tuning tool, and fuel injection is sometimes tricky to deal with. Burning fuel is how the engine produces power, and getting good control of those numbers is critical in tuning on the dyno.*

wheels exerted. This is typically an observed condition if listed as the single word torque and is typically in lbs-ft units. The torque value is typically measured with a strain gauge, but on some chassis dynos might be a calculated number. You need to know which one was used. If the system does not have a strain gauge or a load cell, then it cannot be calibrated.

**Horsepower** column refers to the power that is calculated from the basic formula and on engine dynos is easy to verify. With some chassis dynos, the horsepower reference might be from some other calculation or measurement. You need to know which one was used. On a chassis dynamometer, the horsepower reference should only be at the drive wheel tire patch. There is not a good way to estimate accurately the power at the flywheel of the engine on a chassis dyno—guesstimates perhaps, but not accurate estimates; too many variables exist in the drivetrain.

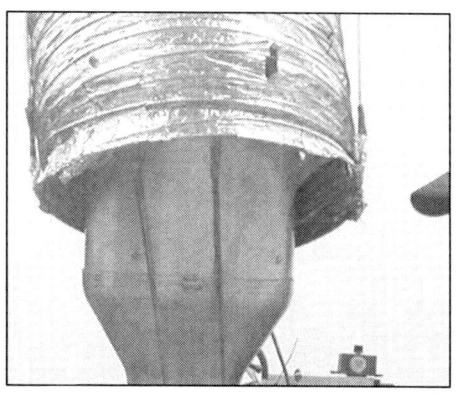

*This airflow transducer (turbine type) provides important airflow information to the dyno operator. The engine is a self-driven air pump and the more that you know about its airflow, the easier it is to apply the data to make more effective use of that airflow. Many dyno manufacturers have various methods of measuring the air flow. Some folks don't go to the extra effort of fixturing an engine to measure the inlet air, but it is worthwhile.*

**Fuel Flow** column refers to the amount of fuel used at each data point and is typically displayed or printed in pounds per hour (lbs/hr). There might be more than one channel of fuel-flow data available, and that is convenient for connecting to a carburetor in order to evaluate the primary and secondary fuel flows on an individual basis. This data can make it much easier to balance the fuel use on a four-barrel carburetor or on two four-barrel carburetors. If used for an engine with either electronic fuel injection (EFI) or mechanical fuel injection, the data can help in sorting out the system.

**Air Flow** column refers to the amount of atmospheric air used at each data point and is typically displayed or printed in either cubic feet per minute (CFM) or standard cubic feet per minute (SCFM). SCFM is the reference to what the airflow would be if the conditions were 29.92"Hg, 60°F, dry air. This data might also be displayed and printed as actual cubic feet per minute (ACFM). Of course it is important to know what sensor and arithmetic created the number that you are looking at. There might be more than one channel of airflow data available for multiple carburetors or for systems that have high airflow demand. The airflow can be used for helping supply data to evaluate the engine as an air pump by looking at VE%, BSAC, and A/F ratio. It is typical that an engine will use approximately 1.25 CFM/Hp at peak torque and the same engine will use about 1.4 CFM/Hp at peak power. These numbers are very good guidelines.

**BSFC** column refers to brake specific fuel consumption and is typically shown or printed at each data point. The units are normally in pounds per horsepower hour (lbs/Hp-hr). This reference is essentially how efficiently liquid fuel was turned into horsepower. A common target for gasoline fuel is approximately .5 lbs/HP-hr. Do not get trapped into thinking that the BSFC number is either rich or lean. That is not the correct analysis. The BSFC number is either efficient or less than efficient relative to targets set for the type of fuel used and the power output of the engine.

**BSAC** column refers to brake specific air consumption and is commonly displayed or printed at each data point. The units are normally in pounds of air per horsepower-hour and indicate the use of air and how efficiently the engine made power with what air it consumed.

# CHAPTER 12

*A/F* column refers to air-to-fuel ratio. The printed record is normally the result of how much air divided by how much fuel was used at each data point. The A/F ratio is dependant upon which fuel is used, the rate of acceleration used, and the response of the sensors involved in collection of the data. The steady-state numbers will be different from those collected during an acceleration test. One must be cautious here in that the numbers displayed or printed should be looked upon as a trend and not as absolutes. If an $O_2$ sensor was used, the number is as a result of combustion and is not a measure of how much fuel was supplied or how much air was supplied. You need to know which one was used.

*Lambda* ($\lambda$) is a reading that comes from a sensor mounted in the exhaust gas stream. In dynamometry, the lambda is a Greek-derived symbolic reference, and it is very convenient to use for a reference to air and fuel mixture. Targeting the lambda value of 1.00 would be very close to a chemically correct ratio for the fuel being used and for gasoline the general A/F reference is 14.7 while lambda is equal to 1.00. For lambda numbers less than 1.00, the mixture is deemed rich, and for numbers greater than 1.00 the mixture is considered lean. However, this number all depends on what the carbon and hydrogen content of the fuel happens to be.

Don't get fixated on the numbers, but watch the trends. See the sidebar reference chart to lambda.

*VE%* is a column of data showing volumetric efficiency. The normal way that VE% is calculated is from the swept volume of the engine vs. the amount of volumetric airflow the engine has consumed. The maximum VE% will normally occur at the torque peak or very close to it. Depending on how the airflow is measured, the volumetric efficiency can go a bit over 100%. However, suspect the process, arithmetic, or calibration of sensors if the VE% is over 110% to 115%, unless the engine is abnormally aspirated (blown). If the VE% is high and the BSAC is also high, the air and fuel might be getting tossed out in the exhaust stream, and this data could be telling you to spread the LCA on the camshaft in order to better capture the flow.

*Manifold pressure* or manpress is a column that is typically scaled for reading the pressure inside the intake manifold. The sensor typically reads negative (vacuum) in inches of mercury ("Hg), and the positive side for blown applications is normally scaled to read in boost pressure in pounds per square inch (psi). The boosted readings can also be scaled in either bar or mm of Hg (1 bar is equal to 14.504 psi or 750mmHg).

### Lambda to Air/Fuel Ratio Chart

| Lambda | Gasoline | Diesel | Methanol |
|---|---|---|---|
| 0.75 | 11.0:1 | 10.9:1 | 4.8:1 |
| 0.80 | 11.8:1 | 11.6:1 | 5.1:1 |
| 0.85 | 12.5:1 | 12.3:1 | 5.4:1 |
| 0.90 | 13.2:1 | 13.7:1 | 5.8:1 |
| 0.95 | 14.0:1 | 13.8:1 | 6.1:1 |
| 1:00 | 14.7:1 | 14.5:1 | 6.4:1 |
| 1.05 | 15.4:1 | 15.2:1 | 6.7:1 |
| 1.10 | 16.2:1 | 16.0:1 | 7.0:1 |
| 1.15 | 16.9:1 | 16.7:1 | 7.4:1 |
| 1.20 | 17.6:1 | 17.4:1 | 7.7:1 |
| 1.25 | 18.4:1 | 18.1:1 | 8.0:1 |

*Manifold temperature* or mantemp is a column allowing calculations for manifold air density or to see what the temperature was during a test. Careful placement of the temperature sensor (generally thermocouples are used) to keep liquid fuel from contacting the sensor provides better reference data.

*Friction power* is a column of data that can either be from motoring the engine under test or it could be from a table in the data-acquisition software. The table would be like a look-up chart and it would have a friction power value vs. RPM of the engine. Friction power is literally the horsepower that it takes to spin all the engine parts up to a particular RPM. The friction power curve is not linear, and it is not the same for spark-ignition engines as it is for diesel engines. The friction power data is needed in order to get to the proper corrected power answer.

*CBT* or corrected brake torque is the brake torque (an observed number) that is corrected by some scheme to a corrected condition of something other than the conditions were at the time of testing. This data might also be displayed and printed in a CWT (corrected wheel torque) format for chassis dynos.

*CBHp* or corrected brake horsepower is the brake horsepower (observed number) that is corrected by some scheme to conditions other than those existing at the time and place of testing.

*CHP* or corrected horsepower data might also be displayed and printed in a horsepower format for chassis dynos. It is the power at the tire

# HOW TO READ A DYNO SHEET

*These IMCA circle track racers are elated after their chassis dyno test session. The car produced more than 400 CWhp at the rear wheels and prepared them to go to the race track to work on getting the chassis to use the power available. This dyno session was held during a dyno shop's open house where the operators shared where numbers come from and helped with tuning. Photo by Rob Kelly.*

patch that is corrected to conditions other than those during the test. It is important to know which correction scheme was applied.

*CT* or corrected torque is typically used for a chassis dynamometer listing. Corrected wheel torque (CWT) is another method of listing. It is the torque at the tire patch that is corrected to conditions other than those of the test. It is very important to know which correction scheme was applied. If the chassis dynamometer was not equipped with a strain gauge for measuring torque, then this value might have been back-calculated from the horsepower number. Follow the numbers if you want to know how the corrected data was calculated.

*ME%* is a column of data representing mechanical efficiency. It is typically calculated by dividing the brake horsepower (BHP) by the indicated horsepower (IHP). The IHP is equal to the observed horsepower OHP plus the friction horsepower (FHP). Stated mathematically, the expression for mechanical efficiency becomes ME% = BHP / IHP. The mechanical efficiency can also be described by the calculation of BMEP / IMEP. By the way, this reference does not mean very much to performance-oriented people, but could help in the evaluation of an engine program that was working on fuel use.

*IMEP* or indicated mean effective pressure is sometimes displayed or printed and is typically data provided for analysis. The number is either collected from an in-cylinder pressure measurement or might be from a calculation. The units are given in pounds per square inch (psi). You need to know where this number came from if it is displayed.

*BMEP* (brake mean effective pressure) is sometimes displayed or printed and can be another way to evaluate the engine's output. The units are given in pounds per square inch (psi). The BMEP can be calculated by dividing 150.8 times the torque value by the displacement in cubic inches, which yields the BMEP in psi. Stated mathematically, it is BMEP = 150.8 x (torque / engine displacement).

*T/in³* or torque per cubic inch is sometimes a reference that is found on engine dyno sheets and is essentially a way to rate the efficiency of the engine under test. The torque is the observed torque number divided by the total displacement of the engine in cubic inches. A good guideline for well-tuned racing engines here is a range between approximately 1.3 lb-ft/in³ and 1.5 lb-ft/in³.

*Oil Temp* or Oil temperature is a column of data that might also be expanded into oil temperature into the engine and oil temperature out of the engine. It is important to know where the temperature sensors were located in the oil system.

Failure to run the engine in the "correct zone" of temperature can easily swing the power results +/- 2% to 3%.

*$H_2O$ temp* or water temperature is a column that might be expanded into water temperature into the engine and water temperature out of the engine. It is very important to know where the temperature sensors were located in the water-cooling system.

*$H_2O$ press* or water pressure is a column that typically would refer to the pressure directly measured in the cooling system. It is very important to know where the pressure sensor or sensors are mounted in the cooling system. This is not to be confused with the pressure rating on a radiator cap. A pressurized system is often an advantage over non-pressurized because of localized boiling on the coolant side of the combustion chamber.

*IAT* or inlet air temperature is a column of data that is also referred to as CAT or carburetor air temperature. It is important to know where the air temperature sensor was located during the test. In a well-controlled test, this number should not vary much during the test.

*EGT* or exhaust temperatures or exhaust gas temperatures (EGT). The normal application on engine and chassis dynos is to use the type K

DYNO TESTING AND TUNING

thermocouple, which uses chromel and alumel metals in direct contact with the exhaust gases. Some types use a closed tip inside a stainless steel tube. It is also important to know what type and size was used. It is very important to know where all the sensors (thermocouples) were located during the test. Note that most EGTs are slow to react (compared to other sensors).

The EGT numbers are typically a good way to look at intake manifold distribution problems. *Normal* differences in temperatures will range from 50F to 100F. If the temperatures are something like 200F in variation, something is perhaps not correct. *Normal* EGT (for gasoline) temperatures will run about 1,200°F–1,300°F. The reference of 1,200°F–1,300°F will also hold true for methanol or ethanol mixtures. It is strongly suggested that you do not try to use the EGT as an indication of either a rich or lean mixture. Unless you know what the A/F ratio was at the peak temperature referenced, which should occur at stoichimetric (chemically correct mixture), assumptions about the exhaust temperatures can lead you astray.

*Oil press* or oil pressure is typically shown in psi. It is important to know where the pressure sensor was located in the oiling system during a test. An oil-pressure reading should indicate the pressure in the oiling system that is just prior to lubricating the engine bearings. As an example, if the pressure is measured before the oil filter instead of after the oil filter, the pressure reading might not indicate proper lubricant available for use.

*Blow-by* is a column that is very important to refer to for verification of ring and system sealing. It is typical that a performance engine will have more blow-by at idle and low engine RPM than when under load. The readout units are typically in CFM. These sensors can be either electronic or mechanical and are typically scaled from zero to 10 or less CFM. It is interesting to note that the CFM of blow-by is typically acceptable in a ratio to power produced. The numbers on a well-sealed engine are normally in the vicinity of approximately less than one or two CFM at maximum horsepower (on a well-sealed engine). In order for sensors of this type to operate correctly, it is necessary to seal off all breathers except the connection that the sensor is measuring.

*Crankcase pressure* or pan pressure is a column that indicates the pressure in the pan of the engine. Typical display of units is in inches of mercury ("Hg), although it might also be in other units. It is not uncommon, in well-sealed racing engines using a dry sump, to display a pressure of a negative 25 inches of mercury (-25 Hg) if the engine uses special seals on the crankshaft. Wet-sump engines (without a vacuum pump) are typically around -10 to -15" Hg, depending on the crankshaft seal type and installation direction. Sometimes the pan-pressure reading in an engine without a vacuum pump is another way to check on the piston ring efficiency. See Blow-by listing above for further information.

## Some Rapid and Effective Analysis of Dyno Data

***Using graphs and looking at numerical data to develop a test philosophy***

One of the easiest ways to look at a dyno run is with graphics. Although graphics can be misleading, you can get a quick sense of what was going on by careful examination of the power run if you know a few things to start with. Keep in mind that modern dynos collect all sorts of data, and you can normally get several sheets of data per dyno run to evaluate after the testing is done.

In fact, most modern dynos will allow you to have a computer disc of the tests that you had done on your combinations, and that will give you a lot of latitude to look at the tests in detail after all the noise is over. Think about what was going on and how the data shows the results. Perhaps you see a dip in the power curve, and then the oil pressure shows a drop of 10 psi and then it comes back up to spec. Perhaps there is a problem with the oil-pump pickup in the pan. Is the pan dented? Pump pickup loose? The data will indicate things that are going on, but the data won't tell you why something happens.

## Chassis Dynamometer Guesswork

The loss in the drivetrain is *not* a fixed percentage of power. If the power is increased or decreased, the loss that occurs in the chassis is not a fixed percentage of the changing power. The loss in the drivetrain depends on speeds and temperatures. As an example, the more competitive NASCAR vehicles that work on high-speed tracks have a loss of about 60 hp at 200 mph. It is not the same number as at 100 mph. In drag racing chassis, it is not uncommon to see losses in the chassis of from 90 hp to 200 hp (depending on how much the converter slips and the general inefficiency of the drivetrain). Simply put, anything that heats up in the chassis power path is an absorber of power.

Although we stated earlier that you cannot check the calibration on an inertia-only dynamometer, there are some tricks that can be applied to find out how close to the real numbers an inertia-only dyno might compare.

The torque to turn (rotate) a chassis dyno is a number that we could use for calculations that can be of some benefit in analysis of a rotating system. The bearing friction and the inertia of the roll are all part of the forces to overcome in order to get the roller to turn at different speeds. The aerodynamic drag on the roll is also part of the loading and that varies as a function of atmospheric changes and speed of the rolls. Think of it as having a fish scale attached to a string wrapped around the roll and you are pulling on the fish scale in a line tangential to the roll and at 90 degrees from the shaft centerline. That would give you a force required in calculating friction and it would indicate the inertia of the roll. And you need that kind of input data at several speeds in order to have reliable data; however, the chassis dyno manufacturer should have supplied the inertia data for that particular dynamometer as part of the calibration process. If they didn't do so, then the numbers that you get from that dyno might be repeatable, but there is not an easy way to prove accuracy. This type of analysis of the system could end up being quite a physics-lab exercise, but the calculation would be something akin to: $T = I\alpha$ so that torque would be equal to inertia times the angular acceleration. No need to go through the drill here, but it could be done to see if the inertia value was correct on a given dyno setup.

Do you know how some manufacturers have generated the so-called calibration numbers on their chassis dynos for inertia-only applications? They built a roll set and ran a few test vehicles across them and timed the runs from a start speed to a max speed, and then they back-calculated the inertia value for the rolls based on what they *thought* the vehicle made in horsepower. Which horsepower number did they use? Net? Gross? Assumed driveline losses? Their guesswork and assumptions have generated more than a little bit of disagreement in the marketplace. However, that is only one of the many things that you should be aware of when looking at dyno test data.

In the very serious game of testing, believe it only if you can prove it. And proving it *more than once* is the real proof. Then track verification of performance is the complete proof.

If you are looking at a graph of dyno data for an engine, it is generally easiest to make sure the X-axis (left to right) is displaying engine RPM. If you are looking at dyno graphics from a chassis dyno, then the X-axis should display vehicle speed. There are additional things that you might want to put on the X-axis, but start with the descriptions above.

The Y-axis should be listed as torque and horsepower and initially scaled so that torque and horsepower are using the same values.

If you see a dip in the curve data, what caused that dip? Take a look at the A/F ratio at the same point. If it made a move at the same time, you might have a problem with the fuel-delivery system. Or, it might even be where there was a momentary loss of data from the dyno data-acquisition system.

You see, the shape of the power curve will tell you a lot about the characteristics of the engine being tested. The same goes for a vehicle under test. If the developed curve is smooth on the rise to peak power and is also smooth past peak power, then the indication is that the engine is fairly smooth in power delivery. What is the A/F ratio throughout the test? If it varies much, then you should try adding some fuel in small increments and see what the result turns

*This closeup of a bike rear tire and wheel also shows what is going on with the drive chain. If the chain is too tight, it causes more loss than if it is looser. If it is too loose, the drivetrain will fail prematurely. The tire is a power robber, too.*

*This Mustang was properly dyno tuned, and now it is time to work out the problems with the chassis. The losses that occur in the drivetrain on the chassis dyno are varied and costly. Simply put, the power at the flywheel is diminished until it gets to the final tire patch. Sometimes the losses can be as low as 90 to 100 Hp to way more than that.*

out to be. Remember that burning fuel produces power, and until you supply too much fuel the power won't suffer much. Following the testing tips that were presented in an earlier chapter, you need to establish the fuel and spark that the engine combination wants over the range of RPM and speed. Always tune to the safe side with rich fuel configurations.

How about that A/F ratio thing, and how do you look at it? We have reinforced several times throughout this book that the A/F ratio is an indication of the ratio of air to fuel. There is no magic number that can be depended upon to be the perfect tune-up. The correct A/F ratio is a number that relates the ratio of the air used to the fuel used. If the tune-up is for gasoline, the correct number might be anywhere from 12:1 to 13:1 where it makes maximum power across the range. It all depends on the carbon and hydrogen content of the particular gasoline fuel being used. The point here is that while on the dyno, toss some fuel at the thing and then take some away while following the guidelines for making the testing for RBT and LBT, with the former being the best target. If you have used an onboard A/F ratio device or a lambda sensor, then you need to reference the same number indications that made the best power across the range. If you do that, it will make your racing experiences a lot better and more effective as well. Remember to use the same fuel type that you tested with, or you are not working with the same database of information anymore.

We could write a whole chapter just on fuel, but the guidelines provided by Tim Wusz at RockettBrand in the sidebar below won't steer you wrong. Whether you end up using their stuff or not, at least believe in the logic and apply it accordingly.

*There is a vacuum pump down in the plumbing somewhere. Does it work? In this case it did. Something around 30 Hp in this application. Engine dyno testing both before and after connecting the pump were done. Perhaps a better solution would be to have better ring seal and run the pump, but it is hard to get large-bore engines to seal as well as smaller bores do. Better ring seal influences the power curve considerably.*

## Flame Speed, Octane Number & Horsepower Relationship

Courtesy of: *Rockett Brand Racing Fuel*

**Summary: Faster flame speed is always better for maximizing horsepower.**
There is a lot of misunderstanding about the relationship between flame speed, octane number, and power. There are some connections between these items, but not as many as some people think. We will address each one independently, then try to tie them together as best we can. For the sake of simplicity, the following discussion will be limited to gasoline unless othewise indicated.

**Flame (Burn) Speed:** The speed at which the air fuel mixture in a combustion chamber is consumed becomes critical in a racing engine. At 6,000 RPM, each spark plug fires 50 times per second. That's a lot of combustion processes happening in a very short time in the same combustion chamber. This is why racing gasoline needs to be capable of burning fast. In your daily driver that may not see the top side of 3000 RPM, flame speed is not as critical. In a racing engine, everything is happening much faster, and in a bigger way because the throttle is wide open. The gasoline must burn as completely as possible to make the most possible horsepower. If the gasoline does not get burned in the time allowed, there will be unburned hydrocarbons coming out the exhaust pipe. Besides not making any horsepower for you, the unburned product contribute to air pollution. Flame speed is determined by the hydrocarbon components in the gasoline. It is critical to making max power, but not related to octane quality.

**Octane Number:** The octane number of a gasoline has little to do with how fast it burns or how much power the engine will make. Octane number is the resistance to detonation. If the octane number is high enough to prevent detonation, there is no need to use a higher octane gasoline since the engine will not make any additional power. Octane number is not related to flame (burn) speed either. Variations in octane quality are independent of flame speed. There are some high octane gasolines in the marketplace with fast flame speeds and some with slow flame speeds. It depends on how they are put together. At Rockett, we like fast flame speeds because we know that a properly tuned engine will make more power on this type of gasoline than one that has a slower flame speed.

**Power:** The ultimate goal in the racing gasoline business is to convert chemical energy from the gasoline hydrocarbons into mechanical energy or horsepower. The most efficient way to convert the gasoline into horsepower is to have the correct air-fuel ratio and the correct spark timing. A mixture that is too rich or too lean will not make maximum horsepower. The same is true of spark timing: too much or too little will compromise engine output.

**Summary:** As indicated above, flame speed and octane number both impact the amount of power that an engine will develop, but they are independent of each other. To get maximum power from an engine, one must have a gasoline with adequate flame speed (faster is always better), and adequate octane quality to support the combustion process. Tied in with the optimized air-fuel ratio and the spark timing, we have a winner.

CHAPTER 13

# TUNING WITH DYNAMOMETER DATA

## Dealing With the Weather on Dyno Day or at the Racetrack

Tuning on the dyno is very similar to tuning at the dragstrip. On the dragstrip, you would typically target your tune-up toward producing the fastest speed (MPH) for the vehicle.

*This elaborate weather station setup is almost a necessity for competitive bracket racers. Left to right are laptop, airspeed rig normally mounted outside of trailer, pager that gets updates from the box at far right, which is weather station information. In the Fast 16 competition in Denver (track elevation 5880 ft), the bump spot (number 16 qualifier) is typically 7.50 or quicker. These races are won by as little as .001 seconds, so this approach is just another tool.*

On either the chassis or engine dynamometer you would be tuning to improve the area under the power curve, which will produce the best results.

The beauty of tuning on the dynamometer is that you can make changes just like you would at the racetrack and see what the numbers do as a result of the changes. If you make a change on the dynamometer and it shows to produce less power

*Computer programs are available to help tune at the racetrack and to help make estimation of the ET to dial much easier based on atmospheric changes. It gets pretty spooky on large shots of nitrous, but it can work based on good data.*

and yet at the racetrack the vehicle produces a better 1/4-mile elapsed time (ET), the data is telling you that at the racetrack you have a problem with wheelspin and should look at the chassis set-up much more closely.

One of the first things to get into your head is that the weatherman and the weatherwoman are not racers, and they will give you an incorrect local barometric pressure reading. Their barometric pressure readings are corrected to a sea-level condition. However, your engine breathes the air wherever the race is going on. So if you are listening to the radio or watching TV in your pit, stick to the music.

If you have dyno data on the engine or the complete vehicle, all you will need to do is to take a look at the conditions under which the dyno testing was done. With just a little time you can equate the conditions at the time of dyno testing with whatever the conditions are at the racetrack and you can go to the line with a fairly well-prepared package.

---

DYNO TESTING AND TUNING  135

CHAPTER 13

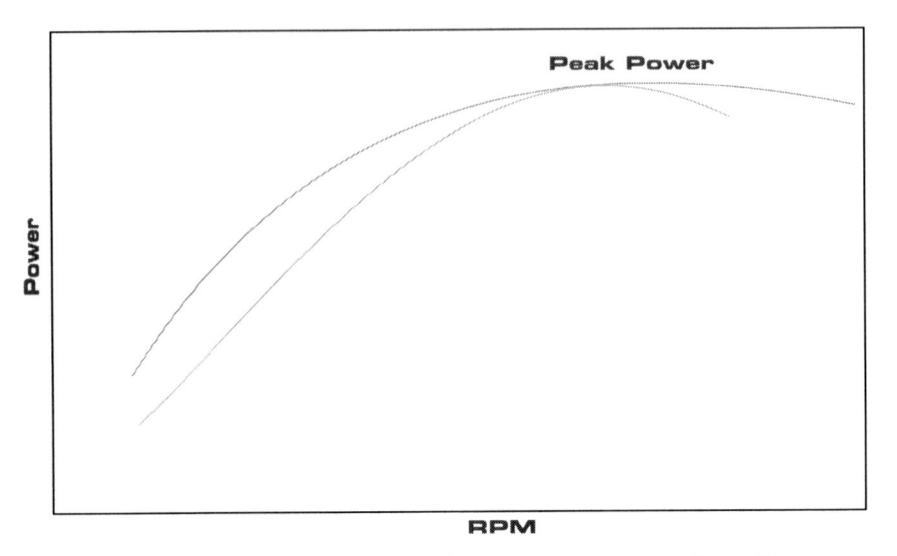

*This sketch graphically demonstrates how two engines can have the same peak power. Although Power vs RPM shows the same peak power for engine A (red curve) and for engine B (blue curve), it is the broader power curve of engine A that will propel a racecar faster and quicker (if the chassis can handle it and get it to the track surface). The greater area under the curve should be the target for any tuner. Note that this only shows power, which is a function of Torque x RPM divided by 5252.*

*This very inexpensive thermometer can help you a great deal in the field or at the racetrack. The outside and the inside temperatures are displayed. It can give you very good indications of what is going on under the hood or in the air scoop. The underhood temperature affects the air going into the engine and the fuel temperature as well.*

## Tuning for the Atmosphere Where the Engine Works: Down and Dirty

After you have applied the dyno testing tips provided in earlier chapters of this book, you can maintain the characteristics of the power curve whenever you go to the racetrack.

If you have an on-board A/F ratio or lambda sensor and you used it during dyno testing, that is the reference that you would want to chase when you go to the racetrack. Because the engine itself is mass sensitive (air-density sensitive), all you need to do is to chase the correct A/F ratio to produce good results. This of course assumes that the fuel used in testing is the same as what you use at the racetrack. With the proper inputs and very little arithmetic the correct metering jet can be used to maintain the proper A/F ratio when atmospheric conditions dictate a change.

Step one is making sure that the power curve is established from reliable dyno data and that the spark adjustment and fuel curve has produced the best power.

Because you have good dyno information from your testing on the dyno sessions, record in your logbook the wet bulb and dry bulb temperatures and the barometric pressure at the time of the dyno tests. Also record the size(s) of the main jet if you were using a carburetor or mechanical injection. Other notes would apply if you were using an EFI setup. These combined data will provide the baseline for what will be referred to as a dyno standard condition.

Step two is to apply the data from the dyno tests to whatever the conditions are wherever the racecar goes. When you go to the field with your racecar you will need an accurate barometer and an accurate sling psychrometer, or a psychrometer that is fan operated. The psychrometer will supply you with wet-bulb and dry-bulb temperatures so that you can use a simple chart for vapor pressure and relative humidity.

This methodology will assist you in tuning for different barometric pressure and temperature and water in the air, but it does not allow for increased pressure in the air scoop of a drag racing car or additional pressure from cowl-fed circle track vehicles.

One of the best-kept secrets for racecar tuning is typically found at RadioShack, Kmart, or Wal-Mart stores and is very inexpensive. It will provide the user with two comparative temperatures. The device is an indoor-outdoor temperature sensor and is battery powered with an LCD display. The unit has long enough wires to the two temperature sensors so that you can have one sensor monitoring ambient air

DYNO TESTING AND TUNING

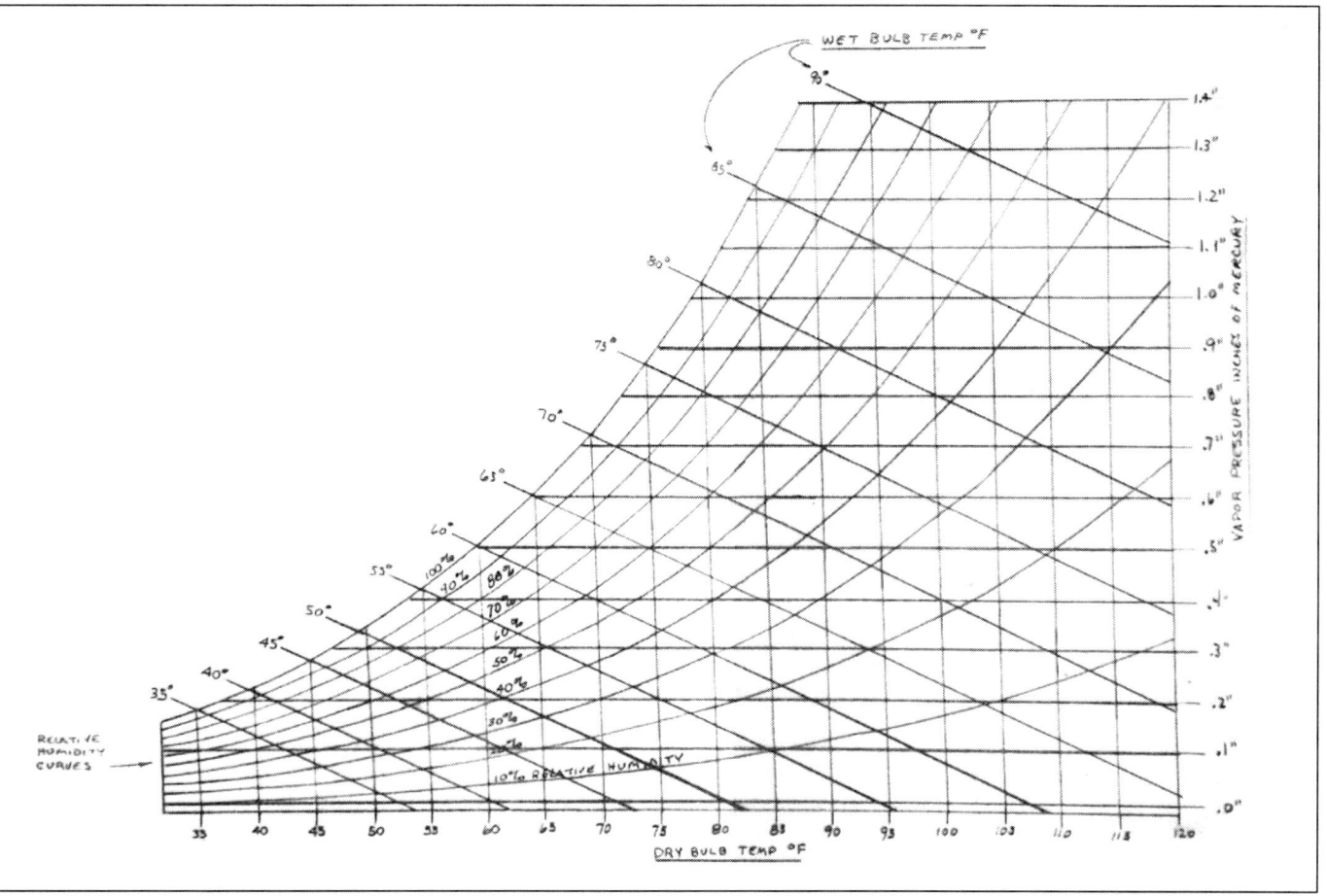

## TUNING WITH DYNAMOMETER DATA

*You won't find this chart (above) very easily other than in this book. It is not a normal reference, but it is handy at the racetrack. The chart makes it easy to directly reference relative humidity numbers to vapor pressure. Vapor pressure is the amount of pressure that atmospheric water is making on the local atmospheric pressure (barometer or station pressure).*

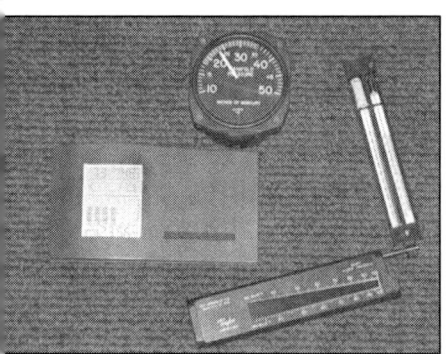

*Left to right are digital barometer with relative humidity sensor, aircraft manifold pressure gauge, and sling psychrometer. These simple devices can provide you with good enough data to make it easier to tune for the racetrack as atmospheric changes occur. Details of how to apply these is covered in the text. The little sock on the one thermometer is soaked with water to provide a "wet bulb" temperature.*

*This is the way that the sling psychrometer is used. The user must apply the same motion so as to keep the psychrometer whirling around at a steady rate of rotation. The psychrometer indicates how much atmospheric water is in the air. Be careful and don't bounce the device into anything while you twirl it.*

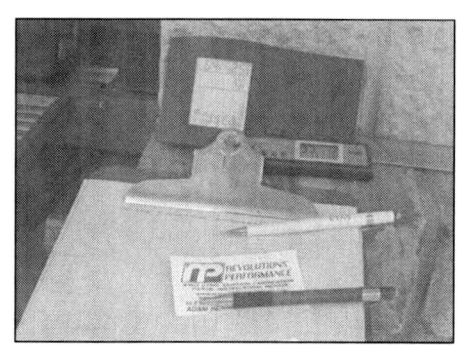

*Always keep a notepad handy when you are testing or at the racetrack.*

DYNO TESTING AND TUNING

and the other sensor monitoring the inlet air at the carburetors or injectors. You want to use the inlet air temperature as the temperature for tuning at the racetrack. The ambient temperature is the target temperature that you would like to achieve if your air inlet is efficient enough. Remember that fresh, cool air is an easy power adder.

## Example of Simple Tuning Arithmetic

During dyno testing, suppose that conditions were barometric pressure reading of 29.75"Hg and dry air temperature was 80°F. And wet-bulb temperature was 68°F. The tests went well and the engine made good power and the tuned A/F ratio was 12.5:1 using a No.78 main jet in the Holley carburetor.

You load the vehicle up and head to the racetrack that is over 150 miles away, and the following weather conditions are prevalent. Trackside barometer is a solid 28.90"Hg and the dry-bulb temperature is 85°F. You check the water in the air with your psychrometer gizmo and the reading is 72°F wet bulb. What jet should you start with? For the sake of clarity, we will assume that the vehicle in this example does not have an air scoop in place that would add pressure to the carburetor inlet. This is a fairly conservative approach because the underhood temperature will be higher than the ambient dry-bulb temperature and thus will allow the mixture presented to the carburetor to be slightly richer than the calculation will show.

This calculation standard is for 29.92"Hg, 60°F, dry air, so at these conditions, the number is 100%

$$Jet = 100 \times \frac{\sqrt{(29.92 / P_b - V_p)}}{\sqrt{T_{air} / 520}}$$

*Ah yes, adjustable air bleeds and precision jets do not a carburetor expert make. However, using the simple arithmetic in the text can help you to tune the thing for different atmospheric conditions at the racetrack. The MaxJets are easy to use and have very small diameter changes a tuner can apply. Yep folks, not everyone has EFI.*

Where $P_b$ = local barometric pressure, "Hg, $V_p$ = local vapor pressure, "Hg, $T_{air}$ = inlet air temperature °F + 460

If the calculated number is greater than 100, the target mixture influenced by the main jet would be leaner. If the number were less than 100, it would indicate the number is richer.

Baseline data calculation:

$$Jet_{base} = 100 \times [\sqrt{(29.92 / 29.75 - .57)} \times \sqrt{540 / 520}\,]$$
$$Jet_{base} = 103.19$$

Trackside data calculation:

$$Jet_{track} = 100 \times [\sqrt{(29.92 / 28.9 - .62)} \times \sqrt{545 / 520}\,]$$
$$Jet_{track} = 105.3$$

The difference (Δ) here is 105.3 - 103.19 = 2.11 so the mixture should be leaner than the baseline jet by 2.11%. Holley jet numbers are supposed to change the fuel flow by about 2% per jet number change. The difference in trackside conditions vs. baseline conditions indicates that you should change the main jet by one number *smaller* than at your dyno testing sessions. So the new jets would be number 77s. That is if they were all the same. Times like these make you want to convert to EFI.

However, there is some general question about how close the tolerance of the jets is to the 2% per number listing. Some very accomplished racers have chosen to use the MaxJets from CompCams because they are available in .001-inch diameter increments. If you were using the MaxJets, then the jet change to lean the mixture would be a reduction of the *area* of the jet by about 2%. That is the reduction of the *area*, not the diameter of the orifice.

*Two adults and a 16-year-old are living the dream as they dyno test a customer's engine. The 16-year-old will be a real firecracker as he gets older because of all this great tuning and building experience. The story here is test, test, test. Take good notes and carefully analyze the results.*

# APPENDIX A

## ARROW
## DYNO BREAK-IN

Engine # _____ Date _____
Customer _____ Oil Type _____ Qts. _____
Engine Description _____ Oil System _____
Operator _____ Room # _____
Fuel _____ @ _____ PSI    Initial Spark Timing _____
Headers _____ Ignition _____
Torque Calibration _____ Lbs.   Spark Plugs _____

| RPM | TORQUE FT.LBS. | MINUTES | TIME ON | TIME OFF | |
|-----|----------------|---------|---------|----------|---|
| 1600 | 100 | 40 | | | |
| 2000 | 120 | 40 | | | |
| 2400 | 160 | 20 | | | |
| 2800 | 200 | 10 | | | |
| 3200 | 260 | 10 | | | |

Three W.O.T. runs @ 200 RPM/Sec.

### Leak & Compress

Leak tester # _____ Compression Gage # _____

| Cyl. Number | 1 | 2 | 3 | 4 | 5 | 6 | 7 | 8 |
|-------------|---|---|---|---|---|---|---|---|
| Leak | | | | | | | | |
| Compress | | | | | | | | |

Comments:

DYNO TESTING AND TUNING

# APPENDIX B

## ARROW
### DYNO LOG

Engine Description _____ Oiling System _____ Cell # _____
Operator _____ Fuel _____ @ _____ psi  Initial Spark _____
Headers _____ Ignition _____ Boost _____
Torque Calibration _____ Lbs  Fuel Calibration _____ Carb/EFI _____

| File # | Run | Date | Time | Torque | HP | Changes/Comments |
|---|---|---|---|---|---|---|
| | | | | | | |
| | | | | | | |
| | | | | | | |
| | | | | | | |
| | | | | | | |
| | | | | | | |
| | | | | | | |
| | | | | | | |
| | | | | | | |
| | | | | | | |
| | | | | | | |
| | | | | | | |
| | | | | | | |
| | | | | | | |
| | | | | | | |
| | | | | | | |
| | | | | | | |
| | | | | | | |
| | | | | | | |
| | | | | | | |

## ARROW
### Pre-Run Dyno Check List

- ❏ Oil fill correct
- ❏ Wide open throttle
- ❏ proper fuel selected and No fuel leaks
- ❏ Coolant filled and checked for leaks
- ❏ Timing set
- ❏ All bolts tight
- ❏ Crankshaft end play checked
- ❏ Battery fully charged
- ❏ Inlet and exhaust air ducts open
- ❏ Proper spark plugs installed

- ❏ Fans and dyno water pumps on
- ❏ Fuel safety valves open
- ❏ Safety shutdown set at correct RPM
- ❏ Vapor pressure & specific gravity input made
- ❏ Termocouples checked
- ❏ Dyno calibrated
- ❏ Safety limits set and engaged
- ❏ Throttle return springs in place
- ❏ Loose wires properly routed and tied down
- ❏ Carb air thermocouple properly located

## Glossary of Dynamometer Testing Terms

**Acceleration** is defined as the rate of change of velocity (physics). Racing use typically refers to acceleration of the vehicle how quickly a vehicle accelerates from a standing start (drag racing) or coming off the corners (circuit or circle racing).

**Accuracy** is defined as a measurement that is referenced to a known standard. Often interchanged with the right or correct measurement.

**B.S.** is an old oil-field term that refers to *basic sediment*. Around dynamometers, it is often used to refer to questionable or unbelievable numbers by an exclamation of "BS!" Sometimes may refer to random lower-bowel expulsions from a bull. Also applies to unrealistic claims of speed or performance. It is quite reliable verbal shorthand that also means "that is somewhat incredulous, friend."

**Control System** is the system that controls the dynamometer. It typically allows the operator to control the RPM and torque of the dynamometer. The control system can be on electrical dynamometers or hydraulic dynamometers.

**Control Valve** typically refers to the control valve that is placed on a water brake power absorber that controls the water flow either into or out of (or both) to the power absorber.

**Conversion Factor** is defined as a number used to convert units to a different reference of units such as converting inches to feet or feet to miles or hours to seconds.

**Correction Factor** is defined as a number that is used to arithmetically correct data to a recognized and defined standard. This issue is very convoluted, and you need to know which correction factor (if any) was applied and what numbers were used and where they came from.

**Data Acquisition System** is the system that collects data from the dynamometer. It can be a very simple system or, more common today, is one that is commanded by an external computer. The most common systems have a data-acquisition electronic board that is in communication with a computer.

**Density Altitude** is an aviation term that refers to the density of the air vs. known altitude conditions for standard atmospheric conditions. The density of the atmosphere is dependent upon temperature, pressure, and atmospheric water. As an example, if the site elevation is physically 3,000 feet above sea level (MSL is mean sea level) and the conditions might indicate that the density altitude is 4,500 feet, then the performance of the engine will suffer accordingly.

**Displacement** is defined as changes of position (physics). Typically used in racing engine parlance as the swept volume of the engine. However, the application needs to be known in order to use the term properly.

**Dynamometer** is a device for measuring force or torque and calculating power.

**ET** is the abbreviation for elapsed time typically given in seconds. Also known to mysteriously improve (when referring to vehicle performance) at some ratio as the distance from the racetrack to the telling point gets further and further. Race results on the Internet have diminished this in some circles.

**EGT** is the abbreviation for exhaust gas temperature.

**Force** is defined as either a push or a pull.

**Horsepower** (unit of power in the English system) is the *rate* of doing work, which is defined as 1 Hp = 550 ft-lbs/sec. By definition of the relationships, Hp = (T x RPM) / 5252, and from algebraic manipulation T = (Hp x 5252) / RPM, and RPM = (Hp x 5252) / T. Note that even with these simple definitions, the horsepower numbers are not necessarily the same in all locations, but they should be. Something about the old saying "figures don't lie, but liars figure," or something like that. You have to watch the arithmetic very carefully in these circumstances.

**Inertia** is the property of matter, which requires a force to be exerted upon it to change either its position or motion. It can also be called the resistance to any change in the motion of a body of matter.

**Legal Ballast** is race-engine builder slang, and typically refers to drivers. Although most ruling bodies allow removable ballast, the legal ballast is generally in reference to drivers. Also sometimes referred to as "the ballast with plane tickets in his pocket." Also referred to as "blameless ballast" and said with tongue in cheek because of personnel dynamics on a race team. It is the responsibility of the crew chief to sort all this kind of stuff out.

**Margin of Error** is a term that is sometimes exchanged with confidence interval and is defined as the variation that occurs when multiple tests are taken. There are three accepted levels: 99%, 95%, and 90%.

**Mass** is a measure of the quantity of matter.

**Matter** is defined as anything that occupies space and has weight.

**MPH** is the standard abbreviation for miles per hour, which is typically a speed reference for vehicles. MPH can also refer to surface speeds of rotating devices such as the roll speed of a chassis dynamometer. Known to increase at some ratio as the distance from the racetrack increases or at least is in some ratio to the number or volume of adult beverages that might have been consumed in telling the story.

**Percentage of Error** is traditionally defined as a theoretical value minus the actual value divided by the actual value times 100.

**Power Absorber** refers to the device that absorbs power in a dynamometer system. The power absorber can be of almost any configuration from a hydraulic or water brake to an electric motor type. The power absorber's function is to place a load on the engine or chassis, and typically the absorber is connected to a system that allows the measurement of torque and speed. As an example of how an absorber works in a system is that of the brakes on your vehicle. The brakes absorb power and turn it into heat and the heat is passed to the ambient air.

**Pressure Altitude** is an aviation term that refers to the readings from an altimeter, which is only a pressure sensitive device. The pressure adjustment for an aircraft altimeter is adjustable within the Kollsman window on the instrument. The pressure altitude is the indicated altitude when the Kollsman adjustment was set to 29.92"Hg. Hint: An aircraft altimeter is not a good tuning-tool reference.

**Probable Error** is a term that can be defined with mathematics and is directly related to the number of samples taken.

**Q.E.D.** is a mathematical term from the Latin that means *Quod Erat Demonstrandum* or literally "which was to be demonstrated." This term can be invoked when showing that something has been demonstrated, proven, or that it has been shown to be proved. However, in the absence of mathematical proofs, this is a term that is just a little on the sarcastic side and is a nice way to indicate an "in your face" solution or answer.

**Relative Air Density** is defined as relating to the ambient conditions vs. known conditions of air density. Also see formulas listings.

**Repeatability** is defined as a test that readily duplicates another test under the same conditions. Often interchanged with consistency or dependable.

**RPM** is the abbreviation for revolutions per minute of any rotating device. Normally used as a reference to engine revolutions per minute.

**Station pressure** is a term that literally means the pressure at the place or station where you are doing the testing. It is normally described in inches of mercury ("Hg) but is also sometimes shown in millimeters of mercury (mmHg) or in millibars (mb). This pressure is typically taken from a mercury barometer at the test site. This is not the same pressure number that the TV weather girl or guy uses, because the numbers that they announce are corrected to sea level. For more detail on this issue see the section on corrections and track tuning.

**Torque** is a twisting force, expressed in pounds-feet (lbs-ft). The units can also be in ounce-inches (oz-in) for small systems. Normal references for metric units are Newton-meters (Nm). 1 Nm = .737561 lbs-ft. Most torque wrenches are not labeled correctly.

**Velocity** is defined as the rate of displacement (physics). In racing parlance, the velocity of a vehicle is also its speed.

**Weak Dog, Woofer, Pooch, and Weak Suck** are all derogatory terms that describe an engine that makes very little power. Sometimes also referred to as a "no hit unit." Skillful use of these terms can also refer to racecars and sometimes drivers as well. Sometimes also a substitute for "that dog won't hunt."

**Weight** is a measure of the attractive force of the earth for a body.

**Work** is defined as force times distance, expressed in foot-pounds (ft-lbs). See torque listing above for clarity of the difference in these terms.

# Reading List Reference Books

*Advanced Engine Technology*, Heinz Heisler, Butterworth-Heinemann, 2001, 2002

*Applied Combustion 2nd Edition*, Eugene Keating, 1993, Marcel Dekker, Inc., CRC Press, ISBN 978-1-5744-640-1.

*Automotive Engine Test Code*, Engineering Standards Department Engineering Staff, sixth edition, 1975, General Motors Corporation.

*Automotive Engine Test Code for Spark Ignition Engines*, General Motors Powertrain Engine Test Code Committee, seventh edition –metric 1994, General Motors Corporation.

*Automotive Engine Test Code*, The Engine Test Code Sub-Committee, fourth edition, 1953, General Motors Corporation.

*Engine Testing Theory and Practice*, M. Plint and A. Martyr, 1995, Butterworth–Heinmann, ISBN 0-7506-1668-7.

*Experimental Methods for Engineers*, J.P. Holman, 1966, McGraw-Hill, ISBN 0-07-029613-8.

*Fluid Mechanics With Engineering Applications*, Robert L. Daugherty and Joseph B. Franzini, 1965, McGraw-Hill, ISBN 0-07-015427-9.

*Internal Combustion Engines and Air Pollution*, Edward F. Obert, 1973, Harper & Row, ISBN 0-352-04560-0.

*Internal Combustion Engines Applied Thermosciences*, Colin R. Ferguson, 1986, John Wiley and Sons, ISBN 0-471-88129-5.

*Internal Combustion Engine Fundamentals*, John B. Heywood, 1988, McGraw-Hill, ISBN 0-07-028637-X.

*Internal Combustion Engines in Theory and Practice*, Volumes I & II, C.F. Taylor, 1966, MIT Press, ISBN 0-262-70015-8.

*Kinematics and Dynamics of Machines*, George H. Martin, 1969, Mcgraw-Hill Inc., ISBN 0-07-040657-X.

*Standard Handbook for Mechanical Engineers*, Theodore Baumeister and Lionel Marks, seventh edition, 1967, McGraw-Hill, ISBN 07-004122-9.

*The Gas and Oil Engine*, Dugald Clerk, eighth edition, 1899, John Wiley and Sons.

*The High Speed Internal Combustion Engine*, Sir Harry R. Ricardo, fourth edition 1953 (reprinted 1960), Blackie and Son.

# CarTech Book References

*Building and Tuning High-Performance Electronic Fuel Injection*, Ben Strader, 2004, CarTech Books, ISBN 978-1-884089-79-4.

*Building Ford Short-Track Power*, Ford Motor Company and Richard Holdener, 2000, CarTech Books, ISBN 1-884089-47-X.

*Engine Management: Advanced Tuning*, Greg Banish, 2007, CarTech Books, ISBN 978-1-932494-42-6.

*High-Performance Chevy Small Block Cams & Valvetrains*, Graham Hansen, 2005, CarTech Books, ISBN 978-1-932494-08-2.

*How to Build Big-Inch Chevy Small Blocks*, Graham Hansen, 2003, CarTech Books, ISBN 978-1-884089-86-2.

*How to Build High Performance Chevy LS1/LS6 V8s*, Will Handzel, 2004, CarTech Books, ISBN 978-1-884089-84-8.

*How to Build High-Performance Ignition Systems*, Todd Ryden, 2008, CarTech Books ISBN 978-1-932494-71-6 .

*How to Build Max-Performance Pontiac V-8s*, Jim Hand, 2004, CarTech Books, ISBN 978-1-884089-67-1.

*5.0L Ford Dyno Tests*, Richard Holdener, 2000, CarTech Books, ISBN 1-884089-45-3.

# SAE Paper References

680178, *The Basic Theory of Hydraulic Dynamometers and Retarders*, Narayan Rao, 1968.

720454, *Transient Engine Testing by Computer Control*, J.F. Cassiday Jr. and J.H. Rillings, 1972.

2002-01-0887, *Listening to the Voice of the Customer: Inertia Dyno Horsepower Versus OEM Rated Net Horsepower*, Rob Smithson and Jeremy Carter, 2002.

933039, *Comparison of Engine Dynamometer Test Procedures*, Michael Clegg, Glen Hall, George Jurick, Robert Kohntopp, Jeffery Sloss, 1993.

# Resources

**AVL North America, Inc.**
(engine and chassis dynos)
47519 Halyard Drive
Plymouth, MI 48170
(734) 414-9600
www.avl.com

**Borghi-Saveri Dynamometers** (water brake and eddy current dynos)
Via Prov. Per Bologna, 28/30
40066 Pieve di Cento
Bologna, ITALY
011-39-051-975-364
www.borghisaveri.it

**CP Engineering**
(data acquisition and control systems and complete dynos)
Sandy's Road
Worcestershire, WR14 1JJ
England
011-44-01-684-584-50
www.cpengineering.com

**DePac**
(instrumentation and control systems for dynos)
201 Mill St.
Rome, NY 13440
(315) 339-1265
www.depac.com

**DSP Technology, Inc**
(engine and test facility instrumentation)
48500 Kato Road
Fremont, CA 94538
(510) 657-7555
www.dspt.com

**DTS - Dynamic Test Systems Inc.** (engine and chassis dynos)
4130 Product Drive
Shingle Springs, CA 95682
(800) 243-3966
www.dtsdyno.com

**Dyno Dynamics**
(engine and chassis dynos)
704 Downs Avenue
Lexington, KY 40515
(866) GET-DYNO
www.dynodynamics.com

**Dyno Resource Corporation**
(dynamometers and equipment consultants)
Steven Walker
Issaquah, WA
(425) 391-6084
www.dynoresource.com

**Dyno-Mite Dynamometers**
(engine and chassis dynos)
Land and Sea Dynamometers
138 Route 111
Hampstead, NH 03841
(603) 329-5645
www.land-and-sea.com

**DynoJet Research**
(chassis dynos – motorcycle and automotive)
2119 Mendenhall Drive
North Las Vegas, NV 89081
(800) 992-3525
www.dynojet.com

**Engine Expert**
(engine-performance simulation software)
Alan Lockheed
PO Box 5142
Golden, CO 80401-0501
(303) 238-2414
alockheed@netzero.net

**Factory Pro Dynamometers**
(motorcycle chassis dynos)
179 Paul Drive
San Rafael, CA 94903
(800) 869-0497
www.factorypro.com

**Froude Hofman Dynamometers**
(engine, chassis, transmission, and brake dynos)

**Go-Power Dynamometers**
(engine dynos, chassis dynos)
45225 Polaris Court
Plymouth, MI 48170
(734) 416-8000
www.froudehofman.com

**Innovation Engineering**
(engine dyno starters and coupling solutions)
Steve McAllister
PO Box 3470
Loganville, GA 30052
(770) 972-2972
www.innovationeng.com

**MaxRace Software**
(engine and performance simulation software)
Larry Meaux
9831 Louisiana Hwy. 343
Abbeville, LA 70510
(318) 893-1541
www.maxrace.com

**Mustang Dynamometer**
(engine and chassis dynos)
2300 Pinnacle Parkway
Twinsburg, OH 44087
(330) 963-5400
www.mustangdyne.com

**MSD Ignitions**
(racing ignition systems and dyno ignition systems)
1490 Henry Brennan Drive
El Paso, TX 79936
(915) 857-5200
www.msdignition.com

**Performance Trends**
(engine and performance-simulation software)
Kevin Gertgen
PO Box 503164
Livonia, MI 48153
(248) 473-9230
www.performancetrends.com

**Power Technology Consultants** (dyno and engine-airflow consultants)
Harold Bettes
www.powertechnolgyconsultants.com

**Quarter Jr – Racing Systems Analysis**
(engine and performance software)
Patrick Hale
12821 N. 18th Place
Phoenix, AZ 85022-5736
www.quarterjr.com

**RockettBrand Racing Fuel**
(racing fuel for dynos and racecars)
Tim Wusz
3703 W. Lake Avenue, suite 75
Glenview, IL 60026
(800) 345-0076
www.rockettbrand.com

**Spintron**
(valvetrain dynos, sold by Trend Performance Products)
23444 Schoenherr Rd.
Warren, MI
586-447-0400

**Stuska Dynamometers**
(engine dynos)
Power Test Dynamometers
(engine and chassis dynos, transmission dynos)
N60W 14630 Kaul Avenue
Menomonee Falls, WI 53052
(262) 252-4301
www.pwrtst.com

**Taylor Dynamometers**
(engine and chassis dynos and towing dynos)
16211 W. Lincoln Avenue
New Berlin, WI 53151
(262) 785-7180
www.taylordyno.com

**Westech Performance Group**
(contract testing for engines and chassis)
11098 Venture Drive, Unit C
Mira Loma, CA
(951) 685-4767
www.westechperformance.com